ELEMENTAL GEOGRAPHIES:

MODERNITY IN THE SHORT FICTION
OF BALDOMERO LILLO & LEOPOLDO LUGONES

BENJAMIN FRASER

Published in 2013

Benjamin Fraser
fraserb2010@gmail.com

© 2013 by Benjamin Fraser

ISBN-13: 978-1491066942
ISBN-10: 1491066946

for my parents

TABLE OF CONTENTS

Acknowledgments — vii

Introduction — 1

EARTH: Into the Mines (Lillo) — 21

    Betwixt and Between: Naturalism/Modernism
    Dialectics, Reconciliation and Contradiction

FIRE: An Explosive Modernity (Lillo/Lugones) — 77

    Lillo's *Sub terra*: Fire and Revolution Underground
    Lugones's *Las fuerzas extrañas*: The Apocalyptic Power of Fire
    Modernity, Materiality, Immateriality

AIR: Planet of Sound (Lugones) — 113

    Lugones as Occult Neuro-Musicologist
    Toward Sonorous Geographies

WATER: A Liquid Modernity (Lugones/Lillo) — 143

    Liquid Modernity/Modernist Liquidity
    Reconciling the 'Barrena'/'Ballena' Dichotomy

Conclusion — 183

Notes

References — 199

ACKNOWLEDGMENTS

This work is greatly indebted to the spirit of inquiry pursued by my father Howard M. Fraser (1943-1998) in the field of Latin American Modernism. He greatly enjoyed the work of Leopoldo Lugones and Baldomero Lillo, and thus I dedicate this book to him. Thanks also to my mother Ruth Fraser whose lively debates centered on Lillo's stories informed and enhanced chapter four. Parts of chapter one were originally published in *A Contracorriente* (2012) and *The Latin Americanist* (2012); part of the chapter on "Air" was originally published in Spanish in *Hispania* (2008); and part of the chapter on "Water" was originally published in *English Language Notes* (2009).

The non-traditional publication of this book owes to a variety of factors whose explanations merit emphasis. I should point out from the outset that I am no stranger to traditional academic publishing—my previous books in chronological order include: *Deaf History and Culture in Spain* (Gallaudet University Press, 2009), *Encounters with Bergson(ism) in Spain: Reconciling Philosophy, Literature, Film and Urban Space* (University of North Carolina Press, 2010), *Henri Lefebvre and the Spanish Urban Experience: Reading the Mobile City* (Bucknell University Press, 2011), *La urbanización decimonónica de Madrid: textos de Mariano José de Larra y Ramón de Mesonero Romanos* (Stockcero,

2011), *Trains, Literature and Culture: Reading/Writing the Rails* (Lexington Books, 2012), *Trains, Culture and Modernity: Riding the Rails* (Lexington Books, 2012), *Capital Inscriptions: Essays on Hispanic Literature, Film and Urban Space in Honor of Malcolm Alan Compitello* (Juan de la Cuesta, 2012), *Understanding Juan Benet: New Perspectives* (University of South Carolina Press, 2013) and *Disability Studies and Spanish Culture: Films, Novels, the Comic and the Public Exhibition* (Liverpool University Press, 2013). In addition I am currently preparing three other scholarly books. I have published some sixty academic articles in the field of Hispanic Studies and beyond, and I currently serve as the Managing Editor of the *Arizona Journal of Hispanic Cultural Studies*, as the Founding and Executive Editor of the *Journal of Urban Cultural Studies*, and as an Associate Editor of *Hispania*.

Rather than a retreat from the ills of traditional scholarly publishing, self-publishing this book has been, for me, an experiment. As the average reader from the humanities is no doubt aware, the nature of book publishing is changing at a rapid pace. This has affected both book publishing in general and the publication of scholarly books in particular. Quite simply put—I have wanted to see for myself what is involved in the process of self-publishing a book. I wanted to see if I could do it, and I wanted to see what would happen to it over the course of my lifetime.

It is necessary, however, to point out that the ills of traditional scholarly publishing have been somewhat of a factor... Over the years I have paid—or rather my sponsoring deparments and deans have paid (well, for the most part)—the fees involved in typesetting and publishing my books. In my experience, some presses have been able to provide high-quality copy-editing, typesetting and production without a fee—but based on the trends I am aware of, this may soon be a thing of the past as subventions become more and more necessary. One of the most recent University Press book series to appear in Hispanic Studies charges authors some 7,000 (Canadian) dollars to publish a book. This is less than ideal, to be sure. Another factor has been not merely the cost but the lack of book series publishing on Hispanic topics. That is, while the book market for History or for Sociology may be different, authors writing books on Hispanic Literature or Cultural Studies have a difficult task before them. Very few university press book series publish in this area;

those that do seldom publish books in Spanish, making English the language of publication—at least at presses in the US. In addition, the junior scholar in Hispanic Studies also faces the additional challenge of a peer-review process that has its quirks, to put it mildly, grounded as it quite often is, in two related problems: 1) the fact that Hispanic Studies faces great internal division over questions relating to its nature, vision and method, and 2) that Hispanic Studies is—despite our numbers—still quite marginalized within the MLA (Modern Language Association)—a situation that I insist needs to be confronted head-on, as I have argued in a small number of previously published and forthcoming co-written articles. But I digress.

As I said before, this book's production process has been an experiment. I assembled the cover art, I adapted my word documents to an InDesign project, and there you have it. Much more time-consuming than it sounds. But the writing of this book was itself also an experiment. That is, it was the work of a summer in which I commuted from my first academic job along I-64—the 'fit' was not ideal—to the University of Virginia's library on a somewhat regular basis. I took this time to digest my father's previous work on Leopoldo Lugones and on Baldomero Lillo, and I read most everything (prose at least) written by the pair of Latin American authors—a pair who seem to have very little in common, at least canonically speaking. I should be up front—while I did submit it to one or two academic presses it was rejected. A third press expressed interest but reminded me that author subventions run between 4-6,000 dollars—a price I was not able to pay at the time (I have other bills pending for publishing...). As most of my scholarship is concentrated on Spain, I thought it best to send out selected chapters as articles. As above in these acknowledgments, these all landed in respected venues. With the sneaking suspicion that I have very little else to say about this research area—an area which in reality was my father's specialty—and rather than either send the entire book out again or publish further segments as articles, I decided to publish it in this non-traditional way.

There are countless people who deserve my thanks—but as this is a book quite different from my others, I want to thank only my parents: a couple who met in graduate school for Hispanic Literature at the University of New Mexico. For me, pursuing Hispanic

Studies (instead of Anthropology or Computer Science) has allowed me not only to stay in touch with the passion for Hispanic culture, literature and the arts which became synonymous with the notion of family, but moreover to stretch the disciplinary boundaries of a field whose contours are so often in debate.

INTRODUCTION

> The modern subjectivity seeks to master both inner and outer nature.
> —Iris M. Zavala
> *Colonialism and Culture: Hispanic Modernisms and the Social Imaginary*

To be modern is to live in a world of constant flux and, particularly, the ongoing contradiction between the material and the immaterial. To wit: Charles Baudelaire famously wrote that "Modernity is the transient, the fleeting, the contingent" ("The Painter of Modern Life," 1863), and Karl Marx and Friedrich Engels that "All that is solid melts into air" (*The Communist Manifesto*, 1848). For these extraordinarily influential nineteenth-century thinkers, as well as numerous others, modernity is thus an awareness of the possibilities and realities of change, of the priority of becoming over being, and of the horizons of knowledge itself. Nevertheless, modernity serves also an acknowledgment of the contradictions upon which all human experience is based: the struggle between and within human societies, the seeming contrast between material and immaterial processes, and the disconnect between individuals and forces that elude their control—forces that threaten to put an end to all that we know and to turn our entire world on its ear.

Many Latin American writers at the turn of the twentieth century—and two in particular—chose to elaborate on the political, social, economic, and cultural aspects of the extensive upheaval represented by modernity through a focus on elemental forces. The short stories written by the Chilean Baldomero Lillo (1867-1923) and the Argentine Leopoldo Lugones (1874-1938) rely on the threatening and ultimately destructive elemental powers of earth, fire, air and water to evoke a sense of a chaotic modern world. By delving into the short fictional works of each, this book seeks to explore how these complex and contradictory, elemental forces were harnessed in the literary imagination of two of the Southern Cone's most important authors, ultimately to point to larger scientific postures and social processes.

Both authors expertly gave a literary inflection to the more philosophical and theoretical issues central to an understanding of our ever-changing and contradictory modernity, each in their own way. Lillo, for example, chronicled the arrival of the particularly modern form of capitalist exploitation to Chile in his stories focusing on the lives of the workers and families comprising its newly created mining class of working poor (chapter one, "Earth"). As his stories document, this sea-change subjected Chileans to the harsh conditions and dangerous consequences of working underground, which included—for example—the fierce explosions of the deadly firedamp gas released through mining activity (chapter two, "Fire"). In addition, the geographical location of Chile's most successful mines—dug many times under the water of the Araucan Gulf—itself presented the curious danger of a mine flood. Despite becoming well known for his mining stories, Lillo also made a concerted effort to depict the power of the sea in his stories, which take-on not merely disasters affecting the mining environment, but also the dependence of the area's residents on the fishing economy, one that was disrupted by the arrival of capitalist mining practices (chapter four, "Water"). Lugones, for his part, dealt with the apocalyptic power of the elements through somewhat more fantastic tales whose contemporary resonance is a matter of more subtlety. Appropriately capturing the particularly modernist anxiety of fundamental change in the texture of modern life, his short fiction prioritizes such fantastic notions as burning copper rain and the flame-like auras visible to sensitives (chapter two, "Fire"), the relationship between sound and the deep structure of the universe (chapter three, "Air"), and the liquid character of the universe as understood from an occult

INTRODUCTION

perspective (chapter four, "Water"). As the chapters of this book assert, drawing attention to current topics in geography, the esoteric content of Lugones's work is far more relevant to contemporary discourse than the casual reader might assume.

It is the friction produced in reading Lillo against Lugones that gives shape to my arguments. A traditional understanding holds that each author's stories are antithetical to those of the other. It is still tempting today to approach Lillo merely as the consummate naturalist (he was indeed greatly affected by reading the works of French naturalist Emile Zola among others), interested in social problems and intent on describing the more brutal aspects of a reality in which the life-experience of individuals is dependent on if not determined by larger social and psychological processes. Similarly, it is all too easy to reduce Lugones to being a mere fantastic author who sought to escape from the real conditions of social experience to a world beyond the quotidian. Yet as the following chapters explore, there were indeed significant modernist aspects to Lillo's work; and Lugones's pseudo-scientific thoughts—and particularly those touching on the power of sound—have proven to be more prescient than critics have previously acknowledged. There is, it seems, something to be gained not only by challenging existing canonical perspectives on both Lillo and Lugones individually but also by integrating discussion of them both. In the variegated union offered by the novel juxtaposition of these two superior writers there is, in fact, a more philosophical reconciliation at stake. Taken as a whole, the short narrative works by this pair of authors can be seen to complete a dialectical circuit by acknowledging the relationship that exists between the material and the immaterial, the tangible and the intangible. Ultimately, my appropriately non-dualistic reading of the Chilean and the Argentine suggests the need for a closer look at the union and disjunction of the strange and contradictory forces at the base of the modern experience.

Furthermore, as suggested by the title of this book, "Elemental Geographies," I believe that a return to the opposed but strangely complementary works of Lillo and Lugones today allows us to gain an appreciation of why contemporary geographers are increasingly emphasizing the dialectical relationship between the material and the immaterial. By pointing to the various shapes taken by this debate throughout each of this book's four chapters—a debate which is central to contemporary geography—I hope also to provide evidence that the mid-to-late nineteenth-century understanding of modernity as a contradictory union is still very much with us today in the larger debates that have shaped new directions in geographical research.

My decision to focus on Leopoldo Lugones and Baldomero Lillo is in part a necessary corrective to what still needs to be seen as a pervasive underappreciation of their short narrative works. Both authors have been paid relatively scant attention within the field of Latin American literature, and discussions of their works have been somewhat formulaic, reducing the complexity of each author's work to a form that is ultimately more easily digested by the machine of contemporary literary criticism in its drive to fit authors within the hard-lines of facile categorizations. Global studies of modernism have been somewhat cursory in their presentation of Lugones, and have proved particularly neglectful of his stories. Certainly, two of the most important canonical authors of Latin American Modernism continue to be—expectedly and perhaps rightly so—the Nicaraguan Rubén Darío and the Cuban José Martí. Nevertheless, studies have by-and-large continued to focus on these authors to the exclusion of others. For example, whereas approximately half of the nineteen essays written by eminent *modernismo* scholars included in Ivan Schulman's *Nuevos asedios al modernismo* (1987) explore the work of Darío and Martí, none takes-on Lugones directly, and, perhaps more importantly, neither do any of the essays in Susan Carvalho's otherwise splendid recent edited volume titled *Modernisms and Modernities* (2006). Where critics go beyond Darío and Martí, it is usually only to include a handful of other authors such as Manuel Gutiérrez Nájera, José Asunción Silva and Julián del Casal—such is the cadre institutionalized in Ivan A. Schulman's seminal *Génesis del modernismo* (1966). The globally titled chapter on "The *Modernista* Short Story" from Aníbal González's recently published *A Companion to Spanish American Modernismo* (2007) mentions only two of Lugones's stories, briefly "Los caballos de Abdera" and then more extensively "Yzur." Lamentably, there is seldom sustained mention of Lugones in these and other studies of Latin American modernism with a broad focus.[1]

Moreover, even where the short stories of Lugones have in-

INTRODUCTION

deed been recognized in book-length studies, treatment of the tales has been somewhat cursory. Naomi Lindstrom's admirable *Twentieth-Century Spanish American Fiction* (1994) does well in highlighting his stories, but—although appropriately given her work's attempt to take on almost an entire century of published works from multiple countries—is content with concisely delivering a broad overview. More often, book-length studies centered on Lugones have tended to focus on the Argentine's poetry—a genre he certainly cultivated quite extensively—but this, at the expense of his stories. Cathy Jrade's otherwise splendid volume *Modernismo, Modernity and the Development of Spanish American Literature* (1998), prioritizes Lugones the poet over Lugones the short story writer, perhaps not surprising as poetry arguably remains the canonical expression of Latin American modernism. Gwen Kirkpatrick's intriguing book *The Dissonant Legacy of Modernismo: Lugones, Herrera and Reissig and the Voices of Spanish American Poetry* (1989) tellingly has a similar focus, as its subtitle indicates. Those works that look at Lugones's short fiction in greater depth, particularly those written in English, have been few and far-between. In this vein, one of the more provocative discussions of Lugones's short fiction in recent decades has been Howard M. Fraser's *In the Presence of Mystery: Modernist Fiction and the Occult* (1992) where the critic engages the occult resonance of a variety of modernist practitioners, including lucid accounts of the stories included in Lugones's *Las fuerzas extrañas* (1906), particularly "Viola Acherontia" and "Yzur."[2] Nevertheless, it is clear that the Argentine's short fiction has consistently been overshadowed by his identification as a poet. In the present effort, pursuing an in-depth discussion of his collection *Las fuerzas extrañas* constitutes an attempt to re-assert the significance of his short-fiction to the debates surrounding our understanding of the modern experience.

Baldomero Lillo, for his part, has seldom been approached in relation to modernity and modernism and has instead been labeled—unfairly I would add—the consummate naturalist. As such, by emphasizing the naturalist aspects of his stories critics have paid attention to him only as a simple spokesman for social equality, whereas his work in fact encourages instead a more sustained discussion of a theoretical and philosophical nature. In articulating Lillo's perhaps indirect but nonetheless significant connection to both modernity and modernism, I hope to breathe life into Evelyn Picón Garfield and Ivan A. Schulman's (1984) insistence that many times "pasan inadvertidos los valores modernistas de obras consideradas naturalistas" (10). This has most certainly been the case with Lillo's work, even and perhaps especially within Chile. In Mario Rodríguez Fernández's *El modernismo en Chile y en Hispanoamérica* (1967), for example—and strangely enough given the work's title—, Lillo is mentioned only once as representative of a determinism at the level of both protagonist and narration that corresponds to a naturalist perspective of the world (118)—an observation applied to not only *Sub terra* but also *Sub sole* as well.

The question of what is meant by modernity is a persistent one, with many critics bemoaning the generalized application of the term.[3] As can be seen in my unorthodox pairing of Lillo and Lugones, this volume is not an attempt to engage the modernist tradition in the strictest sense. Nor does it attempt to synthesize the Latin American modernist tradition with the arguably modernist tradition in Spain including, among others, the so-called 'generation of 98.'[4] Instead, this book's acceptance of a rather generalized notion of modernism as movement and contradiction—imprecise though it may seem to those grounded in more traditional literary criticism— is quite purposeful and leads to a series of quite specific points regarding the current state of interdisciplinary investigations. My goal is not to classify or boil down the work of these two authors along canonical arguments, but rather to engage modernism in a specific way by showing what ties exist between the literary production of Lugones and Lillo and more contemporary investigations in the field of cultural geography. For this purpose, I have drawn upon a helpful if broadly-defined idea of modernism explored by numerous scholars. In her *Colonialism and Culture: Hispanic Modernisms and the Social Imaginary* (1992), for example, Iris M. Zavala writes of modernism in terms of a contrast between the subjective and the objective: "modernism evolved around the question of identity, at the point where the grand story of subjectivity meets the narrative of history and of culture" (41); also "The modern subjectivity seeks to master both inner and outer nature" (41, epigraph to this introduction). Just as Zavala discusses what she calls "the open-ended text of modernity" (1), I want to use modernity and modernism in the reconciliatory

INTRODUCTION

spirit of an opening outward.

This necessarily means directing an implicit challenge toward the assumptions that have traditionally driven criticism of Lillo and Lugones, specifically, a view of the two Southern Cone authors as diametrically opposed, one which is almost itself canonical. In the volume *Manual de literatura hispanoamericana III. Modernismo* (coordinated by Felipe B. Pedraza Jiménez) the text explicitly states the more broadly-accepted notion that

> Leopoldo Lugones [...] abrió las puertas de la generosa veta del relato fantástico y de anticipación científica, que tantos y tan prodigiosos frutos habría de dar en la literatura hispanoamericana posterior. Otra dirección del cuento de principios de siglo, de menor interés que las anteriores [Darío y Lugones], fue la costumbrista, que tuvo en el chileno Baldomero Lillo a su mayor representante. (30)

In my opinion, this contrast between the literary production of the Chilean and the Argentine can itself be seen as a reformulation or manifestation of a split that critics have tackled as inherently modernist. Adam Sharman, for example, writes of "Modernity as Material Reality and as a Philosophico-Aesthetic Concept" (3). Speaking of the "long-standing conflict between the socioeconomic and the aesthetic (romantic antibourgeois) concepts of modernity" (3), he cites a split in "modernity as stage in the history of Western civilization—a product of scientific and technological progress, of the industrial revolution, of the sweeping economic and social changes brought about by capitalism—and modernity as an aesthetic concept" (3). The "two modernities" (3) of which Sharman writes might just as equally apply to the way in which the works of Lillo and Lugones have been received, those of the first as driven by aesthetic categories and discussions of literary presentation and taste and those of the second in terms of the alienation wrought by scientific/technological progress, or alternately still, Lillo as the writer focused on the ills of progress and Lugones as the escapist bourgeois aesthete.

My presentation of Lillo and Lugones is thus implicitly quite critical of what writers such as Octavio Corvalan have advanced as, "una vision unitaria de la literatura hispanoamericana contemporánea" (7). That is, I am concerned neither with the creation or institutionalization of a fixed notion of literary period, nor with the attempt to distill a univocal common essence from a broad range of sources. What this book attempts to do, instead, is to shift debate from an established notion of Latin American modernism in order to show how far we might travel from this center. More than by the need to give my own definitive treatment of Latin American modernism—more than even by a need to merely shed more light on two understudied and notable Southern Cone writers—my choice of Lugones and Lillo has been driven by the same reconciliatory premise which has informed my previously published research (in journals from Hispanism and cultural geography; and also in my interdisciplinary monographs *Encounters with Bergson(ism) in Spain* and *Henri Lefebvre and the Spanish Urban Experience*). The eminent critic Professor Donald L. Shaw[5] was fond of saying that if one wants to read good Latin American literature criticism, one has to write it oneself (see testimony in Carvalho 2006). Driven by that innovative spirit, in the following work I propose a new approach to the contradictory essence of modernity and modernism, appropriately taking a step away from the traditional canon of Latin American Modernism and at the same time, a step away from traditional literary studies. This move is simultaneously a step toward the explicit reconciliation of literature with the key questions of other disciplines.

As each of the following chapters explores, these two Southern Cone authors provide opportunities to dwell on key issues of contemporary geography. Ultimately, this pair of authors sought to articulate a new and newly evolving relationship between humankind and the spaces of a modern world. As this volume sustains, the articulation of this relationship often hinged on the elemental forces of earth, fire, air and water, as Lillo and Lugones evocatively portrayed an immaterial-material social life in transition. As Federico de Onís wrote concisely in his essay "Martí y el modernismo" (*España en América*, 625), "modernismo es esencialmente [...] la busca de modernidad." For both the Chilean and the Argentine, the search for modernity is an attempt to get to the core of an experience that is nevertheless shifting and ultimately ungraspable. Their attentiveness to the elements of earth, fire, air and water was an expression

INTRODUCTION

of this need to attempt to touch the 'essence' of modernity. Before moving on, it is necessary to give a short biographical sketch of each author. Where appropriate, I discuss relevant connections with each writer's short fiction. A concise presentation of the chapters that follow then concludes this introduction.

Baldomero Lillo
(6 Jan. 1867, Lota – 10 Sept. 1923, Santiago, Chile)

Baldomero was one of two children born to José Nazario Lillo and Mercedes Figueroa in the city of Lota at the country's western limits, bordering the sea. He grew up around mining communities in the Chilean south during a time of rapid industrialization, and thus it is not hard to see why many of his stories focus on the harsh realities of mining life. The town of Lota was, during Lillo's youth, home to only 6,000 people, the vast majority of whom were connected with the mines. Chile's coal mines in the south and the salt mines in the north were producing progressively more and more wealth, which was inequitably distributed among the country's newly industrialized working poor. Though he was not employed as a miner himself, Lillo gained an appreciation for the harsh lives of those who were.

His father José had himself traveled north to participate in the California Gold Rush for two years during 1848, and during Lillo's youth was employed by the area's mining Company. Lillo of course became a short story writer, and his brother Samuel became an accomplished poet. Fernando Alegría (1959b), drawing upon published interviews with Samuel, paints the picture of the young Baldomero as a captivating storyteller. His health problems ('whooping cough,' Alegría xi) kept him from much physical activity, and even from regularly attending school, but he managed to acquire work early in the Company's store and became an avid reader—of Pereda, Galdós, Dostoevski, Tolstoy, Maupassant, and of course Emile Zola. Despite the fact that he was not cut out for mining work, Baldomero was able to draw on his own first-hand knowledge of life in the mining communities to craft the fascinating tales for which he was becoming known. Lillo married Natividad Miller, had a number of children and gained notoriety almost despite himself.

Samuel writes that his brother had to be convinced to begin to write his stories down, and that he was forced to read the latter's celebrated "La compuerta número 12" on his behalf at the Ateneo, for Baldomero would not dare (Alegría xv).

Lillo's stories were steeped in the local experiences of the mining families with whom he lived and worked, and it seems he approached his work in Zola-esque fashion as a document of the strong social forces which he knew so well. His first book, *Sub terra*, a collection of mining stories, was first published in 1904—receiving critical acclaim and notably selling out in a short three months. As will be addressed in three of the four chapters of this volume ("Earth," "Fire," "Water"), his stories portray the hardships faced by Chilean miners as they struggle to earn a living wage, and even as they face their own deaths deep underground. The tale titled "El pago," for example, makes the point that compensation for mining work was grossly insufficient, and that work underground even amounted to a permanent servitude—if not, as Lillo's narration itself suggests, a kind of slavery. "El grisú" explores the very real consequences of underground explosions caused by igniting pockets of natural gas or the title's "firedamp." The aforementioned story "La compuerta número 12" stridently takes on the issue of exploitative child labor, although Lillo's criticism of exploitation is by no means limited to children, but rather applies more broadly to all mine workers and even to their non-working families. In "El Chiflón del Diablo," for example, after hearing of her son's death in a particularly dangerous pit, a mother willingly throws herself to her own death in the title's "El Chiflón." The story "Los inválidos" even achieves a masterful denunciation of the crushing power of the mining system by describing its effects not on a human but rather on an old horse extracted from the mine, considered useless and simply left alone to die.

Although the naturalist tenor of Lillo's stories is clearly important—as has been pointed out by more than a few critics—there is also another side to his literary production. Perhaps most significantly, one of his early critical successes is better categorized as fantastic even modernist prose. The story titled "Juan Fariña," which earned a prize and was subsequently published a story in the *Revista Católica* in 1903, describes a devilish newcomer to the mines whose

INTRODUCTION

arrival is followed by unexplained events and whose departure is shrouded in myth. Moreover, in other stories from the collection ("El pago," "Los inválidos," "El Chiflón"), Lillo is curiously attentive to mood and dwells on poetic descriptions of lyrical landscapes and fantastic dreamscapes and visions. An underappreciated if not even forgotten article by one critic has noted that Lillo's stories on water (some of which will be discussed in the final chapter) evoke a notably modernist sensibility (Valenzuela 1956). Yet I suggest that even in *Sub terra*, in his fierce documents of the social ills of a system of underground work, there is reason to look outside the restricting label of naturalism to gain a wider appreciation of Lillo's work.

Although Baldomero Lillo died from tuberculosis in 1923, his stories served as a prescient attempt to call attention to and change the base and exploitative nature of mining work, and were subsequently considered instrumental in effecting social change inside Chile. *Sub terra* resonated profoundly with the social shifts that were taking place in the country shortly after the turn of the twentieth-century. Along with the country's slow but steady industrialization, the progressive harnessing of its material resources, there was also a growing social consciousness, an awareness of the new systemic inequalities that unfolded unevenly over Chilean soil. While the middle class ascended to power (due, in part, of course to the exploitation depicted in Lillo's stories), the lower working class was dynamized into political thought and action parties such as the Liberal Alliance, the Radical Party and the Socialist Party. It is important to note that the seed for such change was certainly sewn before Lillo was born (the Chilean philosopher Francisco Bilbao [1823-1865], for example, had founded the Society for Social Equality and published, among other works, *Sociabilidad Chilena* arguing for a more just Chilean society). Nevertheless, (as discussed in the following chapter on "Earth"), Baldomero's stories provided further impetus for change, according to popular opinion directly contributing to and motivating the many mining reforms instituted in the country shortly after his death.

In terms of quantity, ultimately Lillo's literary production was relatively modest. Apart from *Sub terra* (1904), he later published only *Sub sole* (1907). His other short stories were only posthumously collected in two other volumes titled *Relatos populares* (1942) and *El hallazgo y otros cuentos del mar* (1956), and although he did start the project, he never managed to complete an intriguing novel motivated by the massacre of saltpeter workers in the Chilean North titled "La huelga." Nevertheless, the attention he received within Chile was astounding, and he is commonly listed among the nation's greatest authors. The relatively recent release of a film motivated by the stories in *Sub terra* (directed by Marcelo Ferrari, 2003) testifies to his enduring significance within Chilean culture. Nevertheless, although he is a canonical Chilean author, he is relatively less well-known to scholars working in Latin American Studies more generally. Published books treating Lillo written in English are almost non-existent, and the dissertations and theses that explore his stories can be counted on one hand. While this book is an attempt to correct this critical neglect, it also argues that his stories highlight some of the issues pertinent to the field of cultural geography today. In this context, as I will argue, it is helpful to read them against those of another important early twentieth-century author from the Southern Cone.

Leopoldo Lugones (13 Jun. 1874, Villa de María del Río Seco – 19 Feb. 1938, Buenos Aires, Argentina)

Lugones was born in the Argentine province of Córdoba, the son of Santiago Lugones and Custodia Argüello, "ambos pertenecientes a familias de la alta burguesía provinciana, con casa en la villa y estancia en el campo" (Irazusta 7). The young Lugones was fond of reading "obras de ciencia natural; Saint-Hilaire, Cuvier, Lamarck, Darwin" (ibid., 7), and was seen publicly as an intelligent, outspoken figure. In 1892, he was a key figure of a strike at the Colegio de Monserrat de Córdoba in 1892, whose rector Talasco Castellanos considered him "un alumno indisciplinado debido a su vocación desordenada por la filosofía" (Canedo 20). Around the same time, at 18 years of age, he directed an anticlerical periodical titled *El pensamiento libre* (ibid., 8), and in 1893 he enrolled in the national guard. Moving to Buenos Aires around 1896, a job he had held working for the municipality of Córdoba led to his becoming Jefe del Archivo General

INTRODUCTION

de Correos y Telégrafos (ibid., 8-9). He married Juana González, had a son (Leopoldo Lugones, hijo), and in 1938, recalling the fate of the protagonist of one of his stories (the unnamed narrator of "La lluvia de fuego"), he committed suicide by drinking a fatally poisonous beverage (in this case whisky and cyanide). One critic moves us to understand his tragic end in terms of his characteristically inner-focused energy: "Lugones era un hombre de extraordinario dinamismo pero no de acción. Inquieto, inestable, versátil, impulsivo, pero no extravertido en tensión de arco hacia fuera. La descarga había de ser hacia adentro, como se vio con su muerte voluntaria" (Martínez Estrada 31). Interestingly, too, given his interest in the occultism of figures such as Madame Blavatsky (to be discussed in chapter three), his death took place on a day of great mystical (theosophical) and zodiacal significance (Canal-Feijóo 36).

Over the course of Lugones's life, his views changed drastically from socialism ultimately to fervent nationalism and even fascism. Although he had earlier published articles in the socialist journals of Buenos Aires (*La tribuna*, *La vanguardia*), later in life he supported the military coup of 1930 and made nationalist speeches.[6] Guillermo Ara writes of these "etapas en el desarrollo doctrinario de Lugones":

> el primero que llega hasta 1903, período del entusiasmo socialista. El segundo que llega hasta el fin de la primera guerra mundial, con una relativa confianza en los valores de la democracia y firme adhesión a la causa de los aliados. Antes de 1920 apunta con la quiebra de sus convicciones liberales, la inclinación hacia el militarismo nacionalista que culmina con la revolución del 30. (54)

From being an outspoken critic of the bourgeois State, he shifted over time toward sympathy with a form of fascism, a change that Alfredo Canedo has characterized as a move from freethinker to "ruling class ideologue" (see the latter's chapter "Lugones: ideólogo de la clase dirigente," 89-101).[7] Alfredo Roland, on the other hand, argues that although Darío himself in 1896 presented Lugones as "un poeta socialista" (15), the latter's interest in socialism was from the outset more humanitarian and romantic than it was doctrinal

(18). As a writer, he was a unique almost mythical figure. As Ezequiel Martínez Estrada put it: "Yo sabía, desde que leí *La guerra gaucha*, que Lugones era un ser demoníaco, un 'hecatónquero', un licornio, un hipogrifo o cualquier ente absurdo al que no podía darle mi imaginación una forma semejante a la de los otros seres de carne y hueso que ya conocía"; "él no era un hechicero sino un mago, un espagirista, por ejemplo, que convertía los metales viles en preciosos" (17, 19). Whereas Lillo's stories were almost canonically naturalist, Lugones's writings were seen as "characteristically modernist" (Lindstrom 22). The Argentine was more prolific than the Chilean, penning numerous books of poems, short stories, and longer prose texts. If Lillo's prose emulated the naturalist style of Zola, Lugones tended toward the era's strain of science fiction, squaring with that of Jules Verne and H.G. Wells, and recalling those of E.T.A. Hoffman and Edgar Allan Poe (Alter-Gilbert 16-17).[8] His work, in turn, decisively influenced the more well-known Argentine writer Jorge Luis Borges, who stated in a book-length volume of writings focusing solely on Lugones that "La historia de Leopoldo Lugones es inseparable de la historia del modernismo, aunque su obra, en conjunto, excede los límites de esta escuela" (in *Leopoldo Lugones* 15).

Relative to the more restrained output of Lillo, Lugones's writing was nothing if not prolific His first published work, a book of poems titled *Montañas de oro* (1897) was praised by Rubén Darío himself, and Lugones has since been seen as a quintessential modernist figure drawing, as did other modernists, on symbolism, as is explored in Pierina Lydia Moreau's volume *Leopoldo Lugones y el simbolismo*.[9] Certainly his poetic output has overshadowed his prose compositions. Nevertheless, he authored some four dozen books of poetry and prose, perhaps most notably including *Lunario sentimental* (poetry, 1909), *El payador* (criticism, 1916), and a later collection *Cuentos fatales* (short stories, 1926), as well as what is, in my opinion his most enduring work, the collection of short stories titled *Las fuerzas extrañas* (1906).[10]

This provocatively-titled volume, *Las fuerzas extrañas* (1906), was republished numerous times and perhaps best exemplifies the modernist thrust to go beyond the limits of established rationality toward other forms of knowledge. The "strange forces" encountered

INTRODUCTION

throughout the volume, which for Lugones testify to the elemental basis of the universe itself, are chaotic, dangerous and potentially destructive. Many authors have praised this volume merely for one of its stories titled "La lluvia de fuego." To wit: Julio Irazusta writes "Dijo Alfonso Reyes que 'La lluvia de fuego', sobre la destrucción de Gomorra, es inmortal. No creo que se advierta diferencia apreciable entre unos y otros cuentos, por los que respecta a la composición, el estilo, la hondura de pensamiento" (49); and Rebaudi Basavilbaso, despite including in his book a relatively lengthy chapter devoted to Lugones as "El prosista" (45-74), nevertheless only refers to *Las fuerzas extrañas* in one short paragraph that reads, in its entirety:

> En 1906, Lugones publicó *Las fuerzas extrañas*, una serie de relatos de character fantástico, que se encuentran, por la admirable sencillez del estilo, entre sus mejores páginas. Se destaca, seguramente, la narración titulada *La lluvia de fuego*, cuyo tema es la destrucción de Gomorra. (56)

As the following chapters of this book address (chapters two, three and four), the significance of Lugones's 1906 collection goes far beyond this story alone. In both "La lluvia de fuego" and "El psychon," Lugones posits fire as intimately connected with the secrets of a universe beyond human comprehension ("Fire"); while in both "El psychon" and "El origen del diluvio" as well as other writings, it is liquidity that lies at the base of the modern experience ("Water"). As both a literary modernist and a practicing occultist, Lugones built many of the fantastic tales of his collection on the knowledge gleaned from spiritualist systems such as that of Madame Blavatsky, whose *The Secret Doctrine* (1888) posited an intimate connection between the individual and mystical, universal forces.

But Lugones's stories are not mere fantastic tales or literary explorations of occult premises. A select few resonate quite powerfully with more recent developments in neuroscience. In "La metamúsica" and "La fuerza Omega," pseudo-scientific investigators seek to harness the power of sound, thereby squaring with a more contemporary connection between sound and cognition established by Oliver Sacks, Daniel Levitin and others ("Air"). Moreover, if Lillo's tales are not solely naturalist, neither are Lugones's stories purely fantastic. In addition to resonating with contemporary debates from both neuroscience and geography surrounding the importance of sound, they elsewhere evoke the palpable sense of the chaos of the modern urban experience, as in the story "La lluvia de fuego," where the bourgeois narrator's characteristic detachment recalls early twentieth-century sociologist Georg Simmel's evocation of urban modernity from his seminal essay of 1903 titled, "The Metropolis and Mental Life" ("Fire"). Just as in Lillo's *Sub terra*, where miners are routinely injured or even killed by the harsh social conditions of life on the ground, the protagonists of *Las fuerzas extrañas* are often disfigured or killed by forces beyond their control, and more importantly, even beyond their perception.

Outline of the Present Work

Taken together, Lillo's material forces and Lugones's immaterial forces form a total picture of the chaos and contradiction that underlie the shifting foundation of the modern experience. Although I have already hinted at the organization of this book in the above introduction, I want to more concisely outline each chapter before moving forward.

Earth—Chapter one brings the reader beneath the surface of the earth and into the Chilean mines through the stories of Baldomero Lillo. Lillo's work is approached both from within the paradigm of naturalism, through comparative connections pursued with Zola's mining *Germinal*, and from the perspective of a literary modernism resonating with the work of Latin American writers such as Rubén Darío and others. But more importantly, the discussion focuses on humankind's relationship with the earth, the perceived distance between nature and culture, combining close readings of a number of stories from *Sub terra* (1904) with the Marxian theories of David Harvey, Henri Lefebvre and others, as well as an extra-literary engagement with the historical mining landscape of the South central Lota region in which Lillo lived, worked and wrote. From this perspective, the earth is ultimately an active landscape through which humankind reproduces itself in a certain modern image.

Fire—Chapter two harnesses the power of fire in the stories of both Baldomero Lillo and Leopoldo Lugones to square with

INTRODUCTION

the idea that modernity involves a fundamental upheaval in the forces that form the basis of our shared experience. Intercalating Marxist thoughts on revolution from Lefebvre's *The Explosion*, the discussion picks up deep under the surface of the earth in Lillo's mining stories, where the explosive power of the 'firedamp' gas underground is used to great dramatic effect in the Chilean's stories. The overt political critique launched in Zola's work *Germinal*, although subdued in Lillo's work, nonetheless provides a point of comparison as the stories from *Sub terra* chronicle the disastrous effects of modernity's characteristic social rifts within humankind. Turning to Lugones's more fantastic tales contained in *Las fuerzas extrañas* (1906), fire comes to express an apocalyptic change in the fabric of modernity. These stories allow their author to address less overtly material problems concerning the limits of human knowledge and the alienation in which modern humankind is immersed. Ultimately, reading Lillo against Lugones in this chapter allows a synthesis of material and immaterial approaches to social problems, appropriately squaring with recent disciplinary shifts within the field of geography.

Air—Chapter three hinges solely on the power of sound as evoked through selected stories from Lugones's *Las fuerzas extrañas* (1906). Delving further into this magnificent text allows an assessment of Lugones's deep connections with spiritualism, specifically the Theosophy of Madame Blavatsky, but more importantly with a strain of recent interdisciplinary investigation. Lugones's ruminations on sound, now grounded in awareness of his own declared commitment to occult practice and pseudo-scientific experimentation, resonate powerfully with approaches to sound from neuroscience, musicology, evolutionary biology, and ultimately also cultural geography. As it appears Lugones seemed to understand, recent forays across disciplinary boundaries into the theoretical and material significance of the sonorous concur that we are indeed living on a "Planet of Sound." For the Argentine as for more contemporary thinkers, music specifically must be taken into account as one of the foundations of human experience and not merely as a surface disturbance. Sound today seems to hold a key to understanding humankind's evolving relationship with the environment, not least of all because it is directly implicated in neuroscience's understanding of the connection between sound and thought.

Water—Chapter four is riven through implicitly and explicitly by the distinctly modernist notion that change is the unchanging. Continuing to analyze Lugones's classic work *Las fuerzas extrañas* reveals a number of stories intersecting with this premise and emphasizing the fluid nature of the everyday, sometimes with disastrous consequences. Turning once again to Lillo's work, not only in *Sub terra*, but also in *Sub sole* (1907), *Relatos populares* (1942) and *El hallazgo* (1956) reveals a similar emphasis in the stories that focus on the experience of Chilean men and women whose livelihood depends not on the mines but on the coastal coves and waters. Analysis of the author's stories foregrounding water, the sea, and the practice of coastal fishing and whaling shed light on an aspect of his literary production that has been all too frequently ignored. Nonetheless, bringing the discussion full circle, this chapter not only ties back in to the understanding of Lillo as a writer who made forays into literary modernism that were particularly accentuated in his depiction of the watery environs of Southern Chile, but also returns to the underground environment of the mines to once again portray the destructive power of water beneath the surface of the earth as well. This chapter intercalates the ideas of theorists such as Marx, Henri Lefebvre and others who have argued in their own way, as Zygmunt Bauman has expressly stated, that we are indeed living in a "liquid modernity."

These necessarily interdisciplinary chapters, by bridging key questions of cultural geography with close readings of texts written in Latin America's Southern Cone at the dawn of the twentieth century, themselves constitute a novel response to the limitations of traditional literary criticism. As pointed out throughout the volume, approaching Lillo's works purely in terms of naturalism and Lugones's stories merely in terms of literary modernism can inhibit the relevance of each to contemporary debates. In choosing to juxtapose and synthesize the work of these two notable and underappreciated writers, the following chapters highlight the contradictory elements between and within the output of each author. This contradiction is itself a testament to the contradictory, multivalent and chaotic nature of an ongoing modernity. As this book asserts, read in today's context, both Lillo and Lugones provide the opportunity to assess how contemporary geography has increasingly tapped into

INTRODUCTION

this reservoir of notions of modernity through debates regarding its methodology and new suggested directions for research.

1

EARTH: INTO THE MINES (LILLO)

> For half an hour the shaft continued to gorge itself in this way, with greater or lesser voracity, depending on the level to which the men were descending, but without cease, ever famished, its giant bowels capable of digesting an entire people.
> —Émile Zola, *Germinal* (1885)

> 'Allí abajo no se hace distinción entre el hombre y la bestia. Agotadas las fuerzas la mina nos arroja como la araña arroja fuera de su tela al cuerpo exangüe de la mosca que le sirvió de alimento. ¡Camaradas, este bruto es la imagen de nuestra vida! Como él, nuestro destino será, siempre, trabajar, padecer y morir.'
> —Baldomero Lillo, "Los inválidos" (1904)

One soon forgets that the ground on which he or she treads is not solely 'natural,' but rather necessarily a product of human work. This is true both where humankind has actively worked on the earth and also where the land has been left untouched. Over the course of the twentieth century, human geographers have worked to underscore the dialectical relationship between people and place, to bring it to our attention that the landscape is a human construction, a material expression of our unique immaterial socio-cultural worlds with further constitutive force. As Don Mitchell (2000) notes in his *Cultural Geography: A Critical Introduction*, "Landscape is best seen as both a work (it is the product of human labor and thus encapsulates the dreams, desires, and all the injustices of the people and social systems that make it) and as something that does work (it acts as a social agent in the further development of a place)" (93-94).[1] In 1925, when one of the pioneers of cultural geography, Carl Sauer, published his seminal article "The Morphology of Landscape," landscape was being approached by academics as active, if not already in relation to human cultural production, and not merely as the static backdrop for human history. On the heels of both discursive and visual practices of the nineteenth-century which, as expressed through realist/naturalist literature and also in landscape paintings, had rationalized the consumer of art's symbolic power over the seemingly passive earth, one Latin American author in particular penned a number of captivating short stories whose central concern was precisely this intimate connection between the 'natural' and the 'cultural.'

The stories of mining life written by the Chilean author Baldomero Lillo (1867-1923) and published in a collection titled *Sub terra: cuentos mineros* (1904) function simultaneously as both a document of the squalid conditions of his surrounding social context, and also as a critique of socio-economic practices he believed could and should be changed. Yet, complementing the idea that his stories served as a faithful representation of life in Southern Chile, Lillo's work constitutes not merely an eloquent call to arms, but an admirable and complex fusion of both naturalist and modernist literary styles. Combining sparing prose and simple but compelling plots with a flair for poetic description and enduring images, *Sub terra* delves underground in order to advance a dialectical understanding of human work. Lillo's triumph in these stories is to deliver an elaborate picture of how the immaterial socio-cultural notions which guide our production of the landscape create a built environment which then, in turn, impacts the way we think about ourselves. Like the Marxian dialectical premise holding that we transform ourselves

Chapter 1 - EARTH

though our work, the stories in *Sub terra* comprise a lengthy meditation on the importance of seeing our own reflection in landscape—now seen not merely as the passive object of contemplation, but rather as playing an active role in our development. They ultimately provide the opportunity to revalue and internalize the reconciliation of our seemingly 'natural' material realities with our purportedly 'cultural' immaterial thoughts.

Lillo, of course, was neither the first thinker nor the first author to suggest an intimate connection between these seemingly discrete areas of experience. The reconciliation of the natural and the cultural was one of the key legacies of nineteenth-century thought, broadly speaking. From the philosophical-economy of Marxist dialectics to the contemporary praise of nature by American authors associated with *The Dial* (Thoreau, Whitman), from Darwin to later even the 'philosopher of poetry' Henri Bergson, a gamut of mid-to-late nineteenth-century thinkers worked to reconcile the inner processes of humankind with their external environments. In no way, however, did this far-reaching conscious reconciliation come to constitute the bedrock of western societies. This fact is, lamentably, the unfortunate consequence of a pernicious mode of human thought whereby the thinker from the outset separates him or herself from his environment. As internationally renowned urban geographer David Harvey (1998) has recently explained, such thinking has strangely come to subtend many strains of modern environmental movements themselves, such that ecological processes are quite shortsightedly if not altogether incorrectly seen to be discrete from human processes. He writes that:

> For although [much ecological discourse] claims that everything relates to everything else, it does so in a way that excludes a large segment of the practical ecosystem in which we live. In particular, it excludes the ecosystemic character of human activity in favor of a curious separation, inconsistent with its own biocentric vision, of human activity. If, after all, biocentric thinking is correct, then the boundary between human activity and ecosystem must be collapsed, and this means not only that ecological processes have to be incorporated into our understandings

of social life; it also means that flows of money and of commodities and the transformative actions of human beings (in the building of intricate ways of urban living, for example) have to be understood as fundamentally ecological processes. (330-31)

One of the reasons it has proven to be so tempting to subtract human activity from ecological processes may in fact be due to the enduring legacy of nineteenth-century visual practices, which have adhered strongly to our now twenty-first century social consciousness. Whereas the landscape art of centuries past provided the bourgeois a commanding view of a pre-existing and virgin nature to be exploited if not at least visually possessed, the enduring cultural legacy of such viewing practices lives on in more widespread understandings of today's rural and urban landscapes. Furthermore, the aesthetic visual consumption of yesteryear's landscape is today infused with a more explicitly capitalist character, as this chapter explores.

The practices of landscape production most visible in the urbanized world of the advanced capitalist countries today center on channeling the visual consumption of urban landscapes this way or that, providing an infrastructure for its development and encouraging city-dwellers, urban tourists, local governments and multinational corporations to conceive of city-space itself as a product destined for consumption—an investment in-and-of itself (Harvey 1996, 2000). Landscape continues to be something to be appreciated aesthetically, as if it were the flat-background of experience; a product to be possessed just as the nineteenth-century bourgeois learned to visually possess the viewed image through landscape portraiture; the passive ground for our human activity. Nevertheless, the accumulated wealth used to reproduce today's landscapes more in the image of the immediate if shifting goals of capitalistic speculation remains tied to an accumulation of material wealth and raw materials (both pre-existing and simultaneous) that takes place quite far indeed from today's urban centers of consumption in the advanced capitalist countries. Historically speaking, one of the most significant sources of this accumulated wealth is, interestingly enough, mining activity. As a counterweight to the way in which human activity is routinely whitewashed from the landscape by today's social and even

Chapter 1 - EARTH

explicitly ecological discourses, this chapter returns to the social and literary landscape of the dawn of the twentieth century by way of a discussion of one of that time period's most celebrated Latin American authors. It thus ultimately seeks to reconcile the presentation of mining activity in the short-stories contained in *Sub terra* with the insights of contemporary theories of landscape from drawn from human and cultural geography.

Although Lillo's literary output should not be approached purely through recourse to his biographical information, there is much of interest to be unearthed there. He was in fact born in the mining zone of Concepción—an area that critic Fernando Alegría (1959a) has called "dinámica y progresista" (247)—in a small town named Lota. His father, José Nazario Lillo had travelled to California for two years during the gold rush of the mid-nineteenth century, and Baldomero spent much time as a youth living and even working in and around the mining camps of Southern Chile. To a certain extent, his stories translate the physical and social landscape of his upbringing to the written page. Although Lillo did indeed start work on a novel titled 'La huelga' that was never completed, he wrote and published numerous short stories and articles that were published in such venues as *El Mercurio*, *Zig-Zag*, *Pacífico Magazine*, *Las últimas noticias*, *Revista Cómica*, and which he himself later grouped together in order to form *Sub terra* and subsequently *Sub sole* (1907, to be discussed in chapter four of this book). A closer look at the environment of his youth will help to orient the reader of these pages before getting into the stories collected in *Sub Terra* themselves and subsequently questions more literary and geographical.

Although references to the area appear in records of the Conquistadors dating back to 1550 (Aztorquiza 73), Lota was founded in 1662 as Santa María de Guadalupe on the gulf of the Arauco on the western coast of southern Chile. George J. Mills reported in 1914 that "Coal-bearing strata are found along the Chilean coast from about 36° S. lat. Southwards into the Magellanic lands. Those which have been explored so far and are now being vigorously worked lie between the bays of Talcahuano and Arauco, and the most important mines are at Coronel, Lota, Curanilahue, and Lebu" (Mills 154). Population increased with the advent of mining in the area and Lota became a town in 1875, and a city in 1881. Lota was ultimately to become one of the most important mining locations in the country. As Octavio Aztorquiza describes it in the important work *Cien años del carbón de Lota (1852-septiembre-1952)* (first published in 1952, recently republished in Santiago by Orígenes, 2005), coal production at Lota was "el nervio que anima la marcha del país" (11). The Compañía Carbonífera e Industrial de Lota was formed the 9th of September, 1852, by Don Matías Cousiño (1810-1863), described as "un visionario que soñó con los ojos abiertos" (11). The site was first manned by 125 operators and yielded an initial production of 7,815 tons of coal (Aztorquiza 11, 13). The coal-mining industry begun by Don Matías, the "Visionario del carbon" (Aztorquiza 37), was carried on by Don Luis Cousiño and later Don Carlos Cousiño—who together came to constitute what the critic calls a "Magnífica trilogía, ejemplos de chilenos de empresa" (Aztorquiza 61).

Production skyrocketed as dependency on coal increased, and the mining companies of Lota and Coronel went on to produce 294,000 tons of coal in 1906, and 494,000 tons in 1919 (Chavarri 7). Not surprisingly, the wealth produced in the mines of the area did not at once bring a stable economy or a notable increase in quality of life. As Gilbert Butland notes in his *Chile: An Outline of its Geography, Economics, and Politics* (3rd ed., 1956), the area was at one time a place where "one-fifth of babies die before they reach one year of age" (22). The epic tone of the volume *Cien años del carbon de Lota*, content as it is to uncritically praise the visionary qualities of Cousiño, the laudatory state of the education of miners in 1952 and the replacement of miners by machines that now do the work of a thousand men (13, 14), is somewhat predictably dismissive of Lillo's literary work. One of the book's selections from the first printing of 1952 by one of Chile's top critics who went by the name, in the original Spanish, 'Alone,' bemoans what is, effectively, *Sub terra*'s lack of boosterism.[2] Alone's brief description of a trip down through the mines of Lota and up again (15-20) is a transparent attempt to elide a century's history of conflict. Already in 1952, the critic prefers an image of Lota without struggle, where exaggerations and legends have lamentably replaced hard-working men aiding in the construction of a modern industrial Chile. Near the end of his piece, after a tour of the mines has come to an end, he moves so far as to relate that:

Chapter 1 - EARTH

Ninguna lamparilla alumbró en parte alguna espectáculos siniestros, muchachitos pálidos y atados, llorando; caballos ciegos, operarios consumidos por la obscuridad, restos de catástrofes dramáticas y peligros amenazadores. ¿Qué se hicieron las víctimas? ¿Están en el pasado? ¿O nunca existieron? (20)

The implicit intertext for his statement is, in fact, constituted by stories authored by Lillo and discussed in more detail over the course of this chapter: the "espectáculos siniestros" of the tale "Juan Fariña," the "muchachitos pálidos y atados" of "La compuerta número 12," the "caballos ciegos" of "Los inválidos." Similarly, in the same volume (Aztorquiza 1952) the Chilean writer and contributor Luis Durand describes the ill effects of mining as merely transitory, disappearing with the light of day. The mine's workers are, he admits, skinny and pale—an admission followed by a significant qualification: "Su palidez es impresionante. Sin embargo, es solo el efecto de la prolongada estada en la obscuridad. Pronto el aire, la tibieza del sol, el calor de la comida con que los esperan allá en el hogar, les reconfortan y los transforman" (24). Bring them out of the mines, and all is better. Later, with their hair neatly combed, he continues, the miners are hardly recognizable as such. Both Alone and Durand unfortunately provide a history of the mining zone of Lota that is too tidy, too superficial to be accurate. Driven by a suspicious boosterism—the need to project a cleansed image of the mining region—Aztorquiza's volume tends to accentuate the positive without presenting the pervasive and significant negative aspects of the lives of the area's coal miners.

Certainly there were non-systemic positive outcomes of the coal industry—profits were used "en la realización de grandes obras públicas: se abren caminos, se construyen ferrocarriles," and Don Carlos Cousiño famously left 9 million pesos to charities upon his death (Aztorquiza 45, 63). Yet these 'grandes obras públicas' are, of course, meant to provide the infrastructure for increasing coal production, and likewise Cousiño the capitalist would have not had 9 million pesos to donate had it been shared more equitably with the people mining the coal. When read against the backdrop of such convenient histories of mining as those in Aztorquiza's volume, the testimonial aspect of Baldomero Lillo's literary output becomes all the more significant. Where Alone's historical memory approaches its limits, where Durand's analysis is insufficient, Lillo's stories step in to supply a necessary corrective. Contrary to what many apparently believed in 1952 (if Aztorquiza's volume is any guide) life in Chile's mining communities was and is hard. As Lillo saw so clearly, its risks were many, and its ill-effects lasted a lifetime, if they did not ultimately cut that life short.

Just as did Chile's social reality, the geography of Chile also directly influenced Lillo's life experience. To gain an initial appreciation of the way his socio-geographical context motivated Lillo's writings, it is informative to take brief look at a paper published the same year as *Sub terra* (1904) by J. Russell Smith in the *Bulletin of the American Geographical Society* titled, appropriately, "The Economic Geography of Chile" (1904). The article reveals a curious parallel between the geographically material and immaterial in the Chile of Lillo's time. The geographical contrast between the country's icy mountainous highs and expansive desert plains ("Chile is a country of geographic extremes," 1), parallels a steep discrepancy in social wealth between rich and poor ("The property of the country is in the hands of a few," 4). Smith writes of the Chilean mining class that "the unlettered and shiftless labourers are in a state of semi-serfdom because of continuing indebtedness" (4-5). The trials and tribulations of such workers, trapped as they are in a system of semi-serfdom, comprise the narrative action of Lillo's stories just as they earlier had for Zola's classic mining novel *Germinal*.

Likewise, Smith mentions that Coronel and Lota (as per Millán 1972, two of the places where Lillo lived) are the shipping ports for "the only mining centre of importance [which] is between Concepción and Levu" (19). Smith continues: "Some of the mines are directly on the seashore, and coal is actually raised from under the Pacific. The mines are from 500 to 1,000 feet deep, and working veins from 2 to 5 feet thick" (19). Already in Smith's report one can see the raw materials for Lillo's literary exposition. Into *Sub terra* figure the class conflict of the region as well as the peculiar mining landscapes particular to the area. In the extra-literary Chile as in the Chile of Lillo's stories we witness the construction of mines under

Chapter 1 - EARTH

the sea itself—which will figure in the stories "Juan Fariña" and "La barrena"—but also the literary potential of the landscape to evoke a contradictory modernity. The dual nature of this Chilean region's landscape is reflected, on the one hand, through the mining stories of his *Sub terra*, and on the other, through his water stories of *Sub sole* and, posthumously, *El hallazgo y otros cuentos del mar* (1956). Because Lillo himself seems to have organized his own work along these lines, I have pursued the earth stories in this chapter, while the water stories I leave for a later chapter.

Even if one admits a rudimentary correspondence between Lillo's stories and his own socio-geographical environment, it would nonetheless surprise many of Lillo's international readers (and critics) to learn of how his stories connect with specific places and events. The gate at the center of "La compuerta número 12," for example, quite likely his most well-known tale, was taken directly from a site Lillo visited in the mine known as Buen Retiro.[3] Similarly, in "La barrena," Lillo references a digging competition amongst miners from Playa Negra and Playa Blanca, two locations on the gulf of Arauco (see Aztorquiza, map insert between pages 112 and113). Then there is also the story "Juan Fariña," which as a note published in the original version of the story in the *Revista Católica* (1903) states, was written as a fictionalized explanation to the very real collapse of the mine of Puchoso Délano in Coronel (see Bocaz 2005). Finally, "El Chiflón del Diablo," the title of one of his most engrossing stories (61), foregrounds a common regional term used to denote 'mine' ('chiflón'), and as discussed later in this chapter, is in fact a name subsequently given to a mining area in Lota (the glossary titled 'Diccionario de vocablos mineros' included in Aztorquiza's book defines Chiflón as the "Galería principal de la mina" 270). Certainly the story's title suggests a more literary origin, as 'the Devil's whistle' is an enviably evocative moniker, summoning up for the reader not merely the visual image of the wind whistling harshly through the mining tunnels, symbolically reflecting the intense work experience suffered by the miners, but also by contributing to a haunting dramatic expectation in the reader's approach to the story. To wit: in the tale "El Chiflón del Diablo," the mere mention of the pit's name causes the reassigned miners of Lillo's story to imagine their own deaths: "Entre morir de hambre o aplastado por un derrumbe, era preferable lo ultimo: tenía la ventaja de la rapidez" (63). It is important, in this regard, that the reader of Lillo's stories today approach them not merely through the terms of a metaphorical journey, on par with Dante's descent into hell (one critic has noted that *Sub terra* depicts an abstract realm of "hell on earth," Ball Jr. 1989), but rather the hellish aspects of a specifically Chilean reality.[4]

Although Lillo remains one of the most frequently recognized Chilean writers within the field of Latin American literature, broadly conceived, sustained critical interest in his work outside of Chile has proved to be disproportionate to the level of name-recognition he enjoys as an author. Moreover, critics writing in English have been particularly slow in exploring his work, and thus slow in introducing readers of English to his ideas and works. Although the year 2009 marked fifty years since the first English publication of the stories in *Sub terra* as *The Devil's Pit and other stories* (1959, eds. Esther S. Dillon and Angel Flores), to-date there has not been a noteworthy attempt to explore his work in either language. To wit: a relatively recent and admirable bibliography of Lillo published by Jorge Román-Lagunas in the *Revista Chilena de Literatura* (1991) points to only three doctoral dissertations and one masters thesis written on Lillo in the United States since 1924,[5] and among the numerous article-length publications devoted to Lillo specifically, only eight have been published in the United States and Canada—and among those only four are written in English. In this context, returning to Lillo's work as presented in his most lauded collection (*Sub terra*) today constitutes an attempt to give the author's stories the sustained critical attention they have deserved but nonetheless never enjoyed.

Reading *Sub terra*, it is important to keep in mind critic Rafael Millán's (1972) contextualization of the stories collected therein as the product of two of Lillo's educational influences – knowledge gleaned from reading works of literature, and the author's direct knowledge and experience of the mining environment of the Chilean South.

Las largas noches lluviosas del sur chileno, tan frecuentes, las ocupó con la lectura de sus autores preferidos: Zola, Maupassant, Dostoiewski, Tolstoi, Flaubert, escritores que—unos más, otros menos—tendrían posteriormente

Chapter 1 - EARTH

marcada influencia en la obra de Lillo; y es evidente que la lectura de los más realistas, unida al conocimiento de primera mano que de la tragedia cotidiana de los trabajadores de las minas de carbón y de sus familias, su miseria, las condiciones en que viven y mueren allá abajo—sub terra—(Baldomero bajó a las galerías, ojos y oídos atentos, aunque de tarde en tarde y como visitante nada más), serían los ingredientes básicos de su obra futura; (8)

Moreover, blending literary analysis with advances in the field of contemporary human and cultural geography allows a chance to dwell on the intimate connections between human work and the land, between thought and representation. This inquiry necessarily requires a doubled comparative approach. First and foremost, there is the more traditional comparative approach engaged through exploring the foundational influence of Emile Zola's seminal novel *Germinal* (1885) on Lillo's stories. Although a handful of critics have explored this literary influence—and more often than not only briefly (Durán Luzio 1994: 916; Durán Luzio 1988: 64; Chavarri 1966: 8, Alegría 1959a, Sedgwick 1944)—I want to bring the connection between Lillo and Zola to bear in a close-reading of the stories in *Sub terra*. Significantly, this approach goes beyond a standard naturalist comparison to enfold and appreciate the more lyrical, poetic and modernist aspects of the Chilean's work. Lillo in fact admirably blends the social preoccupation of much naturalist literature with a deeply rich symbolic imaginary more characteristic of Latin American Modernism—an aspect of his work which has been seemingly neglected by the vast majority of critics.

Second, there is the more novel comparative approach launching from Lillo's work toward a reconciliation of disciplines (literature / geography).[6] These two approaches are themselves not irreconcilable. Ultimately, the revised literary recontextualization—of Lillo as betwixt and between both naturalism and modernism—works alongside a geographical reading of his works. The Chilean author masterfully portrays the earth not merely as the passive ground for human activity but, drawing upon a metaphor used also by Zola in his naming and description of the mine 'Le Voreux,' as an active even monstrous creature, much as even contemporary critics of have envisioned capitalism itself to be a monster (Lefebvre 1992).[7] At the same time, Lillo highlights that, wherever humankind is concerned, the landscape is always already social, coming at once to both express social relationships and also to define and limit them. In many of the Chilean's stories, particularly in "El pago," "Los inválidos," "La compuerta número 12," "El Chiflón del Diablo" and "Juan Fariña," the earth functions not merely as the mirror where humanity comes to confront itself and its ongoing negotiation of priorities, but rather also an evocation of a shifting and contradictory modernity. Although the understanding of modernity invoked throughout the present work is certainly multi-dimensional, in this chapter, I want to dwell on one of its particular manifestations. This is a Marxian notion of modernity, one that is decidedly at once both social and economic, material and immaterial; one that, most importantly, has found a new expression and modulation in the contemporary thought of human geographers.

A greater understanding of the contradictions of this modernity awaits us as we travel underground into the mines, pushed along by Baldomero Lillo's compelling prose. Along the way, this chapter shifts from literary analysis to the larger methodological questions that frame late-twentieth-century and contemporary twenty-first-century human and cultural geography. In this way, I hope to engage the cultural studies tradition as conceived by Raymond Williams. Looking backward in an 1986 lecture titled "The Future of Cultural Studies," Williams characterized the still developing approach as exercising "the refusal to give priority to either the project or the formation – or, in older terms, the art or the society" (152). Curiously, the literary debates that have eschewed Lillo's Modernism in favor of a labeling him a Naturalist suffer from a more fundamental and problematic separation between the socio-cultural activities of humankind and the 'natural' landscape. This separation, as a part of this chapter will assess, is also an inadequate basis upon which to approach a close-reading of his intriguing stories depicting mining life in the late-nineteenth/early-twentieth-century Chilean South. Returning to Lillo's stories in order to underscore their dualistic/dialectical approach ultimately permits a more vivid understanding of the methodological questions at the heart of contemporary research in geography.

Chapter 1 - EARTH

Betwixt and Between: Naturalism/Modernism

By way of an initial and provisional categorization, there can be no doubt that the Chilean author is in many ways a naturalist. Lillo's stories are greatly influenced by his reading of Zola—as Millán makes clear, merely one of many such influences, but perhaps one of the most powerful if not at least one of the most apparent. To wit, Lillo is included in the 'realism and naturalism' section of a now classic *Anthology of Spanish-American Literature* (Englekirk, Leonard, Reid and Crow, 1968). Yet despite this categorization, what is also apparent in Lillo is the infusion of a decidedly Latin American form of literary modernism. Whereas as regards the social struggles of miners, Zola undertakes a certain realist/naturalist approach that has come to be synonymous with the French writer's name itself, Lillo builds upon such a straightforward realism/naturalism with a uniquely complex style that captures Zola's social critique while going beyond the latter's unadorned representational style in *Germinal*. Lillo's captivating narratives layer brutal depictions of a decidedly modern social inequality with more poetic images, uniquely reconciling the French symbolist and Parnassian roots of Latin American modernism's literary inheritance with a Zola-esque Naturalism.

Latin American modernism is a literary movement which, as critics have commonly agreed, spans the period of approximately 1880-1920.[8] Although there is a tendency to discuss Latin American modernism as a literary aesthetic first and foremost,[9] it is more accurate to say that it was itself a unique fusion of literary precepts and overtly political and engaged social critique. The notion of modernism most familiar to the general population of Hispanist scholars is a peculiar stripped-down and aestheticized movement that touted 'art for art's sake' and emphasized the emotive power of abstract colors over local color, form over function, myth over message. Yet as it was developed by its most noted practitioners (e.g. the Nicaraguan Rubén Darío, the Mexicans Amado Nervo and Manuel Gutiérrez Nájera, the Colombian José Asunción Silva, the Venezuelan Manuel Díaz Rodríguez and the Cuban revolutionary José Martí, among others), it was a social, spiritual and political cry that expressed its critique of a rapidly modernizing Anglophone industrialized world that held disproportionate power over underdeveloped countries. Modernists pursued this critique through highlighting the musicality of poetry and a poetic prose that, far from being a mere escape from the 'real' world was a critique of the overly-rational mechanistic thought of capitalism. Manuel Díaz Rodríguez (1908) railed against a superficial understanding of modernism as a mere aesthetic question, signaling the deep spiritual importance of modernism and returning to the idea of modernism as a "doble reacción en literatura contra el naturalismo ilusorio y contra el cientificismo dogmático" (434). José Martí, a well-known figure of the long Cuban revolution who also became one of modernism's most prominent poets, provided an image in one of his speeches that can be easily appropriated to reflect the relationship of art to social and political realities. In a speech made in Tampa, Florida published as "Los pinos nuevos" (1891), Martí crafted the image of a tree planted on top of a buried cadaver: "El árbol que da mejor fruta es el que tiene debajo un muerto" (374). As my appropriation of Martí's statement suggests, even those poetic images of Modernism that are most seemingly irreconcilable with the idea of social justice are to be grounded in an understanding of Latin American social and political realities.

Critic Ned Davison's now classic work *The Concept of Modernism in Hispanic Criticism* (1966) appropriately states that "The critics are generally agreed that Modernism was a rejection of naturalism, philosophical positivism and moralistic verse" (19). The commonplace simplification of modernism as 'art for art's sake' perhaps owes less to Hispanist critics who have engaged the rich imagery and complex forms that characterized its poetry than it does to the institutionalized forms of literary criticism which were in vogue during modernism's exegesis and subsequent development—namely a certain variant of formalism. Modernist poetry has thus been institutionalized as the movement's canonical mode of expression, with prose being acknowledged only rarely and as of marginal interest. In many instances, Modernist prose is not addressed by critics—and where it is addressed, is often enjoys less critical interest than poetry.[10] To give an example, Naomi Lindstrom's (1994) first chapter on modernist prose is easily the shortest chapter in her magnificent book on *Twentieth-Century Spanish-American Fiction* (and once again the reader finds Lillo mentioned only briefly [40-42] as part of the

Chapter 1 - EARTH

chapter on "Realism and Naturalism: 1900-1930"). Lillo's stories, rooted as they are in the social realities of miners and not in the world of fairy tales that so preoccupied many of the movement's more renowned authors, surely seem to be of marginal interest to study of *modernismo*. Yet once a simplistic canonical understanding of modernism is cast aside, the Chilean's dual emphasis on both striking and poetic images and powerful social critique is squarely modernist, and superbly so.

Caution is certainly in order: I do not want to replace Lillo's naturalist label with a modernist one—certainly his naturalism is an important and even indispensible aspect of his work. According to author and critic Enrique Anderson Imbert (1963), it is from Zola that Lillo learned to relate and denounce at the same time (256). There can be no doubt that Lillo's stories appropriate a naturalist approach to denounce—Armando Zarate revealingly includes Lillo's story "La compuerta número 12" in his anthology of *Literatura hispanoamericana de protesta social* (1994: 267-73). Yet it should be noted that his stories not only denounce, they also connect with the key tenets and tropes of modernism, even if this aspect of Lillo's stories is often less visible to the critic or perhaps deliberately overpowered by the more naturalist aspects of his work. I also want to make clear that I am not the first to suggest a modernist aspect to the Chilean's work. Víctor M. Valenzuela argues in a brief mid-twentieth-century essay titled simply "Baldomero Lillo and Modernism" (1956) that four of Lillo's stories in particular show "the marked influence of the techniques of Modernism" (89)—yet none of the stories he mentions are from *Sub terra*, a fact that encourages a strict—and I believe inaccurate—division between his naturalist mining stories and his modernist water stories. Likewise, critics have often noted the emotive power of Lillo's prose, but they have most frequently stopped short of connecting this aspect of his work with modernism (Chavarri 12). An article by Carmelo Virgillo (1978) is perhaps one of the only places (if not the only place) where the a critic has made a sustained attempt to offer an alternative to a canonical naturalist reading of Lillo: "En general, lo que más se ha estudiado es su valioso papel de retratista de la realidad social chilena a fines de siglo. El presente estudio destaca, por otro lado, la técnica expresionista de Lillo" (142). Even here, however, modernism is not even mentioned, despite that the stories in *Sub terra* had been written and published during a time in which the movement was very much in vogue. Importantly, Lillo's stories are composed and read during the first half of the rise of modernism, if not at its apogee, understandably fusing naturalist intent with modernist flourishes. Durán Luzio (1988) makes a point of showing how Lillo goes beyond Zola, but nevertheless limits this move to merely incorporating the social reality of Latin America, preferring not to speak of modernism.[11]

The story "El pago" provides a splendid introduction to the way in which Lillo folds naturalism and modernism together, even though each approach is here clearly more discretely delineated than in other stories. "El pago," as its title indicates, is concerned with a single pay-day marking the end of a fortnight's work, and centers on one miner, Pedro María, and his family's anticipation of his earnings. The story develops along classically naturalist lines, emphasizing the social and physical context of mining work and the way in which it determines and even stifles the development of the protagonist. Lillo emphasizes that there is little to eat and mentions how the provisions purchased by the miners are controlled by the company through monopolistic practices (50, 53). Here, the mine as a physical environment—a place of unbearable heat and scarce ventilation (49)—mirrors the social limitations faced by those living in the mining village. But Lillo perhaps most clearly engages a characteristically Zolaesque naturalism in the attention he places on faithful descriptions of the drudgery and hard labor of mining work itself, as in the following typical example:

> Apoyado en el codo, con el cuello doblado, golpeaba sin descanso y a cada golpe el agua de la cortadura le azotaba el rostro con gruesas gotas que herían sus pupilas como martillazos. Deteníase, entonces, por un momento, para desaguar el surco y empuñaba de nuevo la piqueta sin cuidarse de la fatiga que engarrotaba sus músculos, del ambiente irrespirable de aquel agujero, ni del lodo en que se hundía su cuerpo, acosado por una idea fija, obstinada, de extraer ese día, el último de la quincena, el mayor número posible de carretillas, y esa obsesión era tan poderosa, absorbía de tal modo sus facultades, que la tortura física le

Chapter 1 - EARTH

hacía el efecto de la espuela que desgarra los ijares de un caballo desbocado. (48)

Squaring with the naturalist aims of the story's author, here, Lillo's description of the miner's everyday activity evokes, in a larger sense, the confinement wrought of routine behaviors and the limitations of social possibilities. Through Lillo's prose, Pedro María is in fact completely defined by and through these mundane actions as the narrator painfully reduces the complexity of human experience to task-related minutia—work is all, all is work. Waiting for the payout, Pedro's name is not called, and as the narration reaches its close, the miner and his family are still without money for food. Hammering the point home is the climax, when it is revealed that not only will the miner not receive his pay, but that instead he even owes money to the office. The man responsible for the pay-outs tells Lillo's protagonist: "—Tienes diez pesos de multa por cinco fallas y se te han descontado doce carretillas que tenían tosca. Debes, por consiguiente, tres pesos al despacho" (57). Instead of receiving his pay, Pedro is tragically notified of an outstanding debt.

This brutal naturalist world sculpted by Lillo is undoubtedly faithful to his own direct experience of life in mining communities—a life where, if the individual is not crushed physically through his punishing labor (as happens to a young boy in the story "La compuerta número 12," discussed below), he is nonetheless crushed economically by a system of accumulation that cares not for his well-being but only for his productive capabilities. The miner is indebted to this system for life as an indentured servant if not as, in many senses, in fact, a slave. From this perspective, the narrator's consistent description of harsh winds blowing and hard rain falling throughout the story reflect and support the naturalist core of Lillo's story itself. The story's message has a fatalist tone—it is useless to struggle, all aspirations come to nothing in the end as realities external to the individual determine his possibilities for development. Although this—as will shortly become clear—is an incomplete summary of the story, "El pago" begs in part to be understood as a classically naturalist story centered on the harsh realities of mining work. Here there is, seemingly, no evidence of the characteristic tropes of Modernism. The latter did, of course, often invoke subterranean worlds as was accomplished through the pen of Darío ("El rubí"), but the Nicaraguan did not tackle the workspaces of hard labor, but instead created a fantastic world of necessary if convenient escapism, of precious metals in abundance, of creatures like gnomes and fairies, of the power afforded dreams as a counterweight to the overly rational world of industrial capitalism and the crippling legacy of Latin American colonization.

Yet delving further into Lillo's story shows that the Chilean author moves beyond a simple naturalism as the story incorporates selected elements of the Modernist literary aesthetic—even if in a limited capacity. Completely beaten down by his work in the mine and moreover worn out by his own anticipation of a pay-out that will never come, Pedro María declines an invitation to drink with other miners and instead finds a place to lie down: "Una inmensa laxitud entorpecía sus miembros y habiendo encontrado un lugar seco se tendió en el suelo y muy pronto un sueño pesado lleno de imágenes y visiones extraordinariamente extrañas y fantásticas cerró sus párpados" (58). Significantly, for the final two pages of the story, Lillo's protagonist does nothing but dream. He dreams that he is working in the mine, a mine that has become "rojiza, blanda, gelatinosa" (58). His consciousness merges with that of generations of past miners (58-59), and the sweat from his body becomes "púrpura" (59). A giant crucible excretes rivers of gold over the countryside, and "Al contacto del oro la tierra se estremecía y, como al galope de una varilla mágica, brotaban de su seno palacios y moradas espléndidas" (59) as music fills the air and the earth itself begins to dance. Then the music and dance stop abruptly, diamonds fall from around women's necks and from their hair to become tears on their shoulders, and rubies leave stains of blood and the palaces, "tomando un tinte rojo, violáceo, horrible, parecían de sangre coagulada" (59).

One could certainly argue that because the modernist element of the story is restricted to a dream sequence the story itself remains naturalist through and through—that the dream merely drives home the incontrovertible truth of social determinism.[12] But more powerfully, the incorporation of the tenets and tropes of modernism through a dream sequence as narrated un "El pago" has the effect of mirroring the very origins of Latin American Modernism as a movement. Modernists decried the deeply uneven distribution

Chapter 1 - EARTH

of material wealth that was, for Latin America, a direct consequence of the conquest and enduring patterns of colonization and set out to imagine worlds that were inherently different from the current one as a way of charting a course for a better world. Dreams were at the core of this critique and their yearning for a better world through the practice of art. Engaging Victor Hugo's statement that blue was the color of daydream, the Nicaraguan Rubén Darío titled one of the most important works of Modernism *Azul* (1888)—a work that included both prose and poetry. In its intercalation of a dream sequence imbued with modernist aesthetic, "El pago" concisely if discretely represents the tension between naturalism and modernism that characterized the literary landscapes of Lillo and his contemporaries.

Elsewhere, however, Lillo's incorporation of both modernist and naturalist aspects is seldom so clearly delineated as it is in "El pago." I want to continue to explore the Chilean's use of both naturalism and modernism in the stories contained in *Sub terra*. This necessitates grounding interpretation of Lillo's work first and foremost in one of his greatest literary influences, Emile Zola in order to see how the Chilean moves far beyond the limits of Zola's naturalism. Although a study of Lillo's work cannot rest purely on the latter's relationship with Zola's earlier novel *Germinal*, it is important to appropriately acknowledge this influence. As others have suggested briefly or in passing (Brown 1950, Chavarri 1966, Durán Luzio 1994, Sedgwick 1944), Lillo has adapted aspects of Zola's seminal novel to a Chilean social reality, and yet he has also infused those elements with a (more broadly Latin American) modernist literary aesthetic that is understandably lacking in Zola's work and less frequently acknowledged than is his naturalist inheritance. This modernist aspect of his work has most often been overlooked by scholars of Latin American literature, who have been more content to see Lillo's work more as an expression of a realism/naturalism, an interpretive tradition that perhaps owes more to the primacy of Zola's legacy and the interpretive biases of scholars inclined to laud European literature over the 'peripheral' literatures of underdeveloped countries than it contributes to an understanding of Lillo's stories. Certainly there are similarities and obvious direct appropriations made visible by even a cursory comparison of work by the Chilean and the Frenchman, as this section will make clear. And yet there are also striking divergences quite pertinent to the question of literary style. Whereas, in comparison, Zola's use of figurative language is quite limited and his relatively infrequent employment of metaphor and imagery tends to engage a rather straightforward social critique, Lillo prefers a more open-ended approach, foregrounding aesthetic matters and yielding a text whose aesthetic qualities are rather more complex than what is found in *Germinal*.

The most frequent appearance of figurative language in *Germinal* is the consistent personification of the mine itself, which, while it is certainly effective, remains yet somewhat programmatic. In addition to naming the mine 'Le Voreux,' the narration highlights its monstrous nature again and again in splendid, sometimes extended passages. The pit of the mine is described as "some monstrous and voracious beast crouching there ready to gobble everyone up" (7); the "insistent puffing" of the mine's pump sounds "as though the monster were congested and fighting for breath" (8); all in all the mine is likened to a demonic beast: "And Le Voreux, crouching like some evil beast at the bottom of its lair, seemed to hunker down even further, puffing and panting in increasingly slow, deep bursts, as if it were struggling to digest its meal of human flesh" (15). Many passages draw out the ravenous appetite of this demon "the pit could swallow people in mouthfuls of twenty or thirty at a time, and with such ease that it seemed not even to notice the moment of their consumption" (27). It gorges upon people, its entrance the beast's maw, the shaft its digestive system, "its giant bowels capable of digesting an entire people" (28). After the strike is begun by the workers, the now lifeless mine is compared to a dying man (236), and after it is flooded by the anarchist Souvarine, "It was all over: the vile beast squatting in its hollow in the ground, gorged on human flesh, had drawn the last of its long, slow gasping breaths. Le Voreux had now vanished in its entirety down into the abyss" (482). The same simile and metaphor through which Zola likens the mine to a voracious beast is also used to denounce, by extension, the landowning class, in the form of a "squat and sated deity to whom they all offered up their flesh but whom no one had ever seen" (14, also 532).[13] Now conceived more abstractly the monster is neither the physical mine nor the landowning class but instead capital itself and

Chapter 1 - EARTH

the set of social and economic relations that has earned the name capitalist. As one character (Deneulin) puts it "you're just sharpening the monster's teeth so it can devour us faster. And devour us it will, make no mistake!'" (213). Some invocations of the metaphor remain somewhat more ambiguous and can apply at once to both the mine and capital equally.[14]

Very rarely does Zola's use of figurative language move beyond this simple manifestation—but there is one place of consequence where Zola develops a lasting even poetic image, this time of landscape. This occurs at the beginning of the novel and is of great relevance to present concerns. In the opening paragraph of *Germinal* Zola writes of the desolate character of the mining zone traversed by his main character Etienne as an ocean (combining both metaphor and simile).

> Out on the open plain, on a starless, ink-dark night, a lone man was following the highway from Narchiennes to Montsou, ten kilometers of paved road that cut directly across the fields of beet. He could not make out even the black ground in front of him, and he was aware of the vast, flat horizon only from the March wind blowing in broad, sweeping gusts as though across a sea, bitterly cold after its passage over league upon league of marsh and bare earth. Not a single tree blotted the skyline, and the road rolled on through the blinding spume of darkness, unswerving, like a pier. (5)

The plain is a sea, the horizon is oceanic, the road is a pier. This rare foray into poetic prose that in some respects is at odds with the goal of the straightforward naturalism frequently attributed to Zola as one might expect has a larger purpose in the context of the novel as a whole. The Frenchman introduces his novel with a captivating visual metaphor for the superimposition of ocean and land precisely as a foreshadowing of the work's catastrophic end—the anarchist coal-miner Souvarine will flood the mine with water.[15]

Nevertheless, Lillo goes far beyond Zola's limited use of metaphor and imagery complementing the naturalist intent motivating *Germinal* with a distinctly Latin American form of modernism as his story "La compuerta número 12" shows quite effectively. The focus of the masterful second story of *Sub Terra* is the introduction of a young boy, age 8, to the harsh reality of the mine. Lillo's inclusion of this detail reflects not merely his first hand experiences of mining work in his native Chile, but also his own literary education through reading *Germinal*—where the old man Bonnemort curiously relates having started work in the mine at age 8 ("I wasn't even eight years old the first time I went down in a mine. It was Le Voreux, as it happens," 11).[16] Certainly the denunciation of child labor as a social issue to be remedied constitutes the heart of the story's narration. The story depicts Pablo, 8, taking over the job of an equally young boy José who was crushed one day earlier while on the job (15). Lillo's sparing naturalist dialogue reflects the father's awareness that reluctance to work has no place in the world of a mining community when he hands the boy over to the foreman: "—Señor, aquí traigo el chico" (14). The factual details sketched out by Lillo in his presentation of an accurate and believable mining environment are just as somber: there are six members of Pablo's family and only one works. The boy's fate is to be a miner, just as his father has been, and the sooner the better, especially given that his father is himself in jeopardy of being fired for underproduction (15).

Just as in Lillo's story "Los inválidos" (below), the narration in "La compuerta" points out how the mine uses people up, wearing them out before their time, referencing "el fatal lindero que una vez traspasado, convierte al obrero viejo en un trasto inútil dentro de la mina" (16) and pointing out that Pablo is not the only young one to suffer this fate ("pués había en la mina muchísimos otros de su edad, desempeñando el mismo trabajo," 19). Certainly, description of the cord by which the father physically ties the son to his work post needs no literary flourishes to emphasize how trapped the boy is (20). Yet elsewhere, Lillo frequently goes beyond sparing elaboration and a paucity of isolated but penetrating details in his description, which is better described as lyrical. In his evocation of the foreman's reaction to the young boy, Lillo's prose is by contrast inspired:

> Sus delgados miembros y la infantil inconsciencia del Moreno rostro en el que brillaban dos ojos muy abiertos como de medrosa bestezuela, lo impresionaron desfavor-

Chapter 1 - EARTH

ablemente, y su corazón endurecido por el espectáculo diario de tantas miserias, experimentó una piadosa sacudida a la vista de aquel pequeñuelo arrancado a sus juegos infantiles y condenado como tantas infelices criaturas a languidecer miserablemente en las húmedas galerías, junto a las puertas de ventilación. (14)

Here there is also the basic metaphor of the mine as a creature that ran throughout Zola, as Lillo writes of the "entrañas de la tierra" (16) and of the mine as a "monstruo insaciable" (20) that "no soltaba nunca al que había cogido" (20),[17] but also a vocabulary that is more attentive to mood than you would perhaps expect from strictly naturalist prose, emphasizing, particularly at the beginning, the dark ambiance of the mine through repeated instances of words such as "lóbregos/as" (13, 14, 16), "negro/as" (13, 13, 14, 21), "cripta" (14), "carbón" (21), "penumbra" (13), "sombra/as" (13, 14), "oscura/o," "oscuridad," "a oscuras" (14, 15, 17, 18, 18), "el color de hollín" (14), "macilento" (14), "tinieblas" (17) and "opaca" (15). Although a handful of critics have drawn attention to the emotive power of Lillo's prose (Chavarri 1966; Preble 1976; Singer 1975), guided by an over-arching interest in literary periodization, they have nevertheless proved reluctant to see this in terms of a modernist aesthetic. Durán Luzio (1988), for example, envisions the lexicon of "La compuerta" as a reflection of "el código estético naturalista" (75)—to support his claim he notes how Lillo frequently reduces humans to animals (75-76). Ellen Singer's brief four-page note titled "Atmosphere in 'La compuerta número 12'" (1975) is in many ways an ode to Lillo's use of the color black. She begins her essay in *Romance Notes* with the question "Why do we give a pejorative significance to the color black?," answering that "There are, of course, many reasons, and most of these can be cited in an analysis of the atmosphere in 'La compuerta número 12,' a short story by Baldomero Lillo" (526). She does not exaggerate. Here Lillo pursues the color black with singular purpose much as other Modernist authors pursued the transcendent meaning of other colors (*Cuentos de colores* by M. Díaz Rodríguez [1899], for example). While the Chilean's story may certainly be, as Richard E. Ball Jr. (1989) suggests, an attempt to depict a people "condemned to work in a hell on earth without hope of salvation"

(333), he accomplishes this not only through a faithful description of the harsh realities of the mining world alone but simultaneously though a rich even lyrical prose that contrasts sharply with the austere descriptions and the sparing use of metaphor found in *Germinal*. Singer is correct to suggest that "Like a true artist, Lillo carefully chooses his words and suggests, rather than states, makes us feel rather than tells us" (529). Here he moves beyond the sober style associated with strictly naturalist prose of Zola, who conceived of literature in terms of scientific experimentation and more or less straight-forward denunciation (Zola 1880).

Lillo's "La compuerta número 12" retains *Germinal*'s emphasis on the dehumanizing nature of mining work through the use of numbers which come to stand in for human beings. The short story's title refers metonymically to the boy Pablo through his work location just as in Zola's workers lived not in a town with a more conventional name but rather in Two Hundred and Forty (15, 129)—substituting a mere number for a complex human referent. Yet the depiction of mining work itself is much more dour in Lillo than in Zola, due of course to the Chilean context, which as one critic puts it prompts Lillo to express "un pesimismo natural" (Chavarri 8). As in the Frenchman's novel, in the Chilean's story, mining work is the horrific means whereby the individual is necessarily sacrificed to the idol of wealth accumulation. In *Germinal*, the children workers form merely a side-story, and even then we are told almost exclusively of their non-work escapades, whereas Lillo places child labor as the central preoccupation of the story, even using biblical references to suggest that the father has sacrificed his son as Abraham intended to do to Isaac (Pablo is "más desdichada que el bíblico Isaac," 21). In "La compuerta," the narrator directly denounces that "Los pequeñuelos, respirando el aire emponzoñado de la mina, crecían raquíticos, débiles, paliduchos, pero había que resignarse, pues para eso habían nacido" (20). Lillo goes so far as to underscore that the rebellion that drives Zola's novel, as well as the hope that is not entirely extinguished by the novel's close, has no place in his native country. In "La compuerta," rebellion is squelched before ever being voiced by the father who is well aware that life in Southern Chile is already too fragile: "pero aquel sentimiento de rebelión que empezaba a *germinar* en él, se extinguió repentinamente ante el recuerdo de

Chapter 1 - EARTH

su pobre hogar y de los seres hambrientos y desnudos de los que era el único sostén" (20, emphasis added).[18] In a world where children, too, must be sacrificed to the monstrous mine, there can be no hope, a judgment confirmed by Lillo's curious use of the word "lápida" (17) to describe the tunnel door (number 12) operated by the young Pablo—a word that is more often used to refer to the headstones of graves. Lillo's story is, like Zola's novel, at once a denunciation and a warning. Nevertheless, it goes further than *Germinal* in its attentiveness to the creation of mood, atmosphere.

Likewise, the whole of Lillo's work *Sub terra* is not so much a mere echo of Zola but rather a literary experimentation that builds upon *Germinal*, filling in the spaces left unexploited by the French naturalist and seeking to give his stories a more poetic quality in tune with the developing aesthetic of a Latin American Modernism.[19] Looking at the significant figure of the horse in Zola's novel of 1885, and a similar event in one of Lillo's stories, provides an opportunity to assess one example of how the Chilean accomplishes this. Horses, of course, comprise a significant part of the mining world, being lowered into the pits in the same cages that carry the mine's workmen or the latter's bosses. Yet the life of a mine horse differs substantially from the life of the human miners and even more so from the lives of the overmen or pit bosses; in that whereas men live above ground, the horses were actually stabled there, sometimes living out their entire lives in a quiet darkness beneath the surface of the earth. Although Zola makes reference to an unnamed horse or horses on a number of occasions (e.g. 8, 13, 58), he invokes the lives of two beasts of burden in particular as a parallel to the narrative of Etienne's experience in Montsou. Just as he gives us the newcomer Etienne, Zola likewise introduces us to the horse Trumpet, newly introduced to the mine and greeted by one of the mine's most experienced workhorses, Battle. Zola's text describes Battle as "a white horse with ten years' service and something of an elder statesman." He continues the description as follows:

> He had spent the ten years down the mine, occupying the same corner of the stable and doing the same job every day up and down the roadways; and not once in that time had he seen daylight. Very fat, with a gleaming coat and

a good natured air, he seemed to be living the life of a sage, sheltered from the misfortunes of the world above. Moreover, down here in the darkness, he had become very crafty. The roadway in which he worked had now grown so familiar to him that he could push the ventilation doors open with his head, and he knew where to stoop and avoid getting bumped at the places where the roof was too low. He must have counted his journeys too because when he had completed the regulation number, he flatly refused to start another and had to be led back to his manger. Old age was now approaching, and his cat-like eyes sometimes clouded over with a look of sadness. Perhaps he could dimly remember the mill where he had been born, near Marchiennes, on the banks of the Scarpe, a mill surrounded by broad expanses of greenery and constantly swept by the wind. There had been something else, too, something burning away up in the air, some huge lamp or other, but his animal memory could not quite recall its exact nature. And he would stand there unsteadily on his old legs, head bowed, vainly trying to remember the sun. (59-60)

This brief story of Battle's own increasing familiarity with the mine must be read against story of Etienne's increasing confidence in navigating the problematic terrain of the mine.[20] Battle becomes something of a role-model for Trumpet—a newcomer just as is Etienne—at least for Zola's intermittent interest in things equine, and both are personified to great effect in the narration of their first meeting underground (59-61). Like many a trapped miner, each horse eventually becomes fodder for the mine's voracious appetite—Battle dying (502) as part of the narration that chronicle's the frustrated escape of Etienne and others after the anarchist Souvarine sabotages Le Voreux as many more horses are extinguished in their stables (500). As the above quotation from *Germinal* drives home, the horses function as a dramatic accompaniment to the destitute lives of the miners who work the pits at Montsou, allowing Zola to extend his presentation of the horrors of life underground, providing both a fuller more 'realist' picture of the mining world's ins and outs and, through the literary technique of animal parallelism, heighten-

Chapter 1 - EARTH

ing the reader's grasp of the novel's social critique.

And yet, when read against Lillo's short story "Los inválidos" (included as the powerful introductory story of *Sub Terra* 1904), one notices that for all Zola's effort, the Frenchman has not fully exploited the possibilities offered by his own emphasis on the parallel world of the mine horse. One such scene in *Germinal* whose dramatic and social potential Zola has left unexploited concerns an evocative narration of the death and subsequent lifting of the horse Trumpet to the surface in one of the cages of Le Voreux. "As the swelling band of strikers was becoming more threatening, a large door opened at ground level and some men appeared, hauling the dead animal, a sorry bundle still wrapped in its rope net, which they then abandoned among the puddles of melted snow" (426). Near the end of the work, Zola returns to an extended personification of the horses Battle and Trumpet, implicitly invoking the close mentoring relationship found amongst mineworkers—Trumpet, it is implied, like many new to the mine, has crumbled from the pressure and deprivation that characterizes the life of all miners.

> He had never been able to accustom himself to life underground. He had always looked miserable and never wanted to work, as though tormented by longing for the daylight he had lost. Battle, the doyen of the pit horses, had tried in vain to pass on some of his ten years' accumulated compliance by rubbing up against him in a friendly way and nibbling at his neck. Such caresses had only made Trumpet more miserable, and his coat would quiver as he received these confidences from his elderly comrade who had grown old in the darkness. […] In the stables they shared a manger and spent their time together hanging their heads and blowing into each other's nostrils, sharing their constant dream of daylight, their visions of green grass and white roads and yellow brightness stretching into infinity. Then, as Trumpet lay dying in the straw, bathed in sweat, Battle had begun to nuzzle him, in despair, with short snuffles that sounded like sobs. He could feel him getting cold: the mine was taking away his one last joy in life, this friend who had come down from above all full of

lovely smells that recalled the days of his own youth up in the fresh air. (426)

Zola's sympathetic treatment of the dead horse, and by extension, his sympathetic treatment of all of the miners suffering at Montsou, continues as Trumpet is roped to the bottom of a cage and is then "suddenly being whisked away into the darkness, lost for ever up the black hole" (427). The scene is narrated from below through the animal consciousness of the elder horse Battle, as an inversion of what a worker on the surface of the earth would experience as his deceased comrade were lowered into a dark grave. Zola thus writes from Battle's perspective: "And as he stood there craning his neck, the animal could perhaps dimly remember the things of this earth [...] His legs started trembling, and he began to choke on the fresh air coming down from those distant landscapes; and as he plodded slowly back to his stable, it was as though he were drunk" (427). The narrative voice explores the horse's consciousness notably from the perspective of a human worker grieving for his dead human companion. Battle faces his grim reality with a superficially stoic posture, hearing the distinctly human call of the mine worker's vice (alcohol). Yet Zola's sympathetic and reconciliatory exploration of this mixture of horse and human consciousness is cut short as the narrative jumps abruptly to the scene above ground. We are given to understand—merely in passing—that Trumpet's body lies on the ground adjacent the mine's mouth, and the reader is then immersed once again in the struggles of the striking workers. What Zola has neglected to exploit—and what has not escaped Lillo, himself an informed and impressed reader of *Germinal*—is the dramatic possibility contained in the description of the scene whereby the horse is physically extracted from the mouth of the mine. Such a scene in fact begins the Chilean's story "Los inválidos" and more importantly constitutes its most enduring image.

    In contrast with that of *Germinal*, Lillo's portrayal of the link between human workers and horses benefits from his having chosen the format of the short story. Certainly this restricted format is flattering to a realism/naturalism that seeks to drive home not only realistic detail but also a fundamental insight into the nature of experience—in this case the plight of the worker under a capitalist

Chapter 1 - EARTH

system of inequalities that exploits him. The limited space of the short story leaves little room for distraction from the central role of this link between human worker and horse, as opposed to Zola's characteristically long novel format. Nevertheless, Lillo's writing itself is more concise and his presentation is also more direct, as the first sentence of the story makes clear: "La extracción de un caballo en la mina, acontecimiento no muy frecuente, había agrupado alrededor del pique a los obreros que volcaban las carretillas en la cancha y a los encargados de retornar las vacías colocarlas en las jaulas" (5). The importance of the extraction is highlighted by Lillo's exploitation of dramatic effect. The reader witnesses the scene from outside the mine along with the workers described in the story:

> Todos esperaban silenciosos la aparición del caballo, inutilizado por incurable cojera para cualquier trabajo dentro o fuera de la mina y cuya última etapa sería el estéril llano donde sólo se percibían, a trechos, escuetos matorrales cubiertos de polvo, sin que una brizna de hierba ni un árbol interrumpieran el gris uniforme y monótono del paisaje. (6)

Whereas in Zola's novel, the horse and the men are subjected to similar forces but described separately, with each comprising a separate focal point for the narration, in Lillo's story, the men and the horse are described together and in relation to one another through the same shared landscape of the mine. In *Germinal* this relationship is moreover less complete due to the role played by the forest in relation to the striking workers. The woods have historically been a place of refuge for those on strike, a place to plan out of earshot of the mine's overmen, off the map both literally and figuratively. The focus of the narration on this forest-geography is essential to the Frenchman's novel, and not just from the perspective of plot. Certainly the forest reflects the Western European landscape at the heart of the novel, but more importantly, the forest/mining village dichotomy continues the presence-absence zero-sum game incarnated in the general strike at Montsou as a response to the unsympathetic exercise of power on behalf of the mine owners. The woods underscore Souvarine's (if not Zola's) belief in the possibility of a more equitable future for workers—they serve as a reminder that capitalism has not yet, and particularly so at the end of the nineteenth century as compared with twenty-first-century capitalism today, colonized everywhere. (Lefebvre wrote that capitalism survived throughout the twentieth century "by producing a space, by occupying a space," 1973: 21). Likewise, the absence of the woods in Lillo's story, or a comparable space of possibility or organization—particularly in light of his close reading of *Germinal*—although perhaps indicative of the geography of the area of Southern Chile where the stories in *Sub terra* likely take place, reflects also the distinct and comparative lack of hope for Latin American miners (if Aztorquiza's cleansed narrative, free from conflict between labor and management, is any sign) as opposed to organized European workers at the end of the nineteenth century.

To a certain point, dovetailing with accounts of other connections between the two writers, Lillo has taken much from Zola's literary exploitation of the mining horse. The horse whose story is narrated in "Los inválidos" has been underground for a period of ten years (5), just as Zola's elder-statesman horse Battle has 10 years of experience (1885, 59). Like the Frenchman, the Chilean is well aware of the important role carried out by the mine-horse. Nevertheless, he has also changed much. In Zola, Trumpet is dead before being taken out of the mine, whereas in Lillo, the horse is alive when lifted out of the mine and even at the story's end. In themselves, these similarities and differences lend little to an analysis of Lillo's fiction. Yet from a perspective that acknowledges the foundational importance of Zola and *Germinal* specifically to Lillo, the somewhat subtle differences in the narration of a horse's death reveal a radically different approach to literary composition. Whereas Zola'a use of the mine-horse was limited given his focus specifically on the working lives of miners and his sparing naturalist style; in Lillo, the horse becomes a transcendent being coming to fold the miners into the landscape, and representing also the Chilean's more poetic, modernist emphasis on imagery in contrast with a brute realism alone. For Lillo the fate of horses is not merely parallel to the fate of men, as Zola's alternating narration ultimately suggests, but one and the same, as the narrator of "Los inválidos" underscores:

Chapter 1 - EARTH

—¡Pobre Viejo, te echan porque ya no sirves! Lo mismo nos pasa a todos. Allí abajo no se hace distinción entre el hombre y la bestia. Agotadas las fuerzas la mina nos arroja como la araña arroja fuera de su tela al cuerpo exangüe de la mosca que le sirvió de alimento. ¡Camaradas, este bruto es la imagen de nuestra vida! Como él, nuestro destino será, siempre, trabajar, padecer y morir. (8)

Whereas Zola presents us with the dead horse (Trumpet) and soon leaves things equine for the human drama of the strike, here in a poetic twist Lillo extends the moment of the horse's death to occupy the whole of the short story, thereby mythologizing it as if it were now a prose poem. Although the horse is as good as dead—not even flies want his flesh (10-11)—Lillo's story is in fact more powerful precisely *because* he makes it out of the mine and gets a chance to revisit the outside world that he did not see for so long. The dénouement of the story (in fact, the story might be more properly understood as itself one continuous dénouement), constructs a lasting image of the permanence of death, and by extension, the lack of hope that pervades the mining landscape of Southern Chile. In place of Zola's pure naturalism, we have Lillo's animistic landscapes where Tobler's First Law of Geography (1970) holds true: "Everything is related to everything else."[21]

In a sense, Lillo's story is more ambitious than *Germinal* in that it attempts at once to deal with both the legacy of colonization and at the same time the fate of a Latin America held back by an economic colonialism that reduces the more luminescent aspects of human experience to a hollow rationalism. Against the brute mechanism of industrialization and the plodding advance of Western capitalism, the death throes of Lillo's horse—appropriately named Diamante—are at once the last sighs/protests of a Latin America that has become the object and not the subject of its own history. Diamante is wrapped up not only in the wealth accumulation to which every mining landscape is directed but also through a Modernist symbolism—focused as elsewhere on precious metals and subterranean worlds—but is also himself a product extracted from the mine, much as the miners of Zola as well as Lillo's fictional worlds are reduced to mere numbers. The carefully-chosen and symbolic name Diamante communicates through contrast the unsettling irony that instead of being valued as a precious metal, the horse is in fact pulled from the mine and left to die on his own in the countryside, unproductive and therefore unwanted, a sacrifice to the callous capitalist enterprise that sees life itself as expendable or only in terms of a use-value harnessed to the triumph of exchange.

The story "El Chiflón del Diablo" continues Lillo's theme of the mine as a voracious consumer of human and animal life, and in parallel of mining as itself a dehumanizing activity. The story narrates two days in the life of a presumably typical miner who goes by the nickname Cabeza de Cobre on account of his reddish-hair. Using indirect and underhanded tactics, the foreman manages to re-assign the protagonist and another miner to the dreaded "Chiflón del Diablo" under the implicit threat of being left without a job at all. The pit so-named—deceptively called Chiflón Nuevo in the double speak of the mining company's management—gets its moniker from the fact that it boasts the most injuries and deaths in the area—"La galería del Chiflón del Diablo tenía una siniestra fama" (64). As one character puts it, those forced to work there were living on borrowed time ("los que trabajan allí tienen la vida vendida," 67):

> Continuamente había que extraer de allí un contuso, un herido y también, a veces, algún muerto aplastado por un brusco desprendimiento de aquel techo falto de apoyo y que, minado traidoramente por el agua, era una amenaza constante para la vida de los obreros, quienes, atemorizados por la frecuencia de los hundimientos, empezaron a rehuir las tareas en el mortífero corredor. (64-65)

In tune with Zola's appropriated base naturalistic style, the story emphasizes the complete lack of benefits for the company's injured miners (67), pointing out the workers have no hope to request reassignment lest they be fired and reduced to begging (64). In fact, they would rather die fast—while working—than slowly on account of hunger (63). But moreover, as the narrator points out in the lexicon of naturalism, assignment to "El Chiflón" is their destiny ("estaban resueltos a seguir su destino," 63). As in *Germinal*, here too the social content of the story is clear, even if the possibility of strike or

Chapter 1 - EARTH

rebellion seems superfluous in the Chilean context. The protagonist wonders: "¡Cuántas veces en esos instantes de recogimiento había pensado, sin acertar a explicárselo, en el porqué de aquellas odiosas desigualdades humanas que condenaban a los pobres, al mayor número, a sudar sangre para sostener el fausto de la inútil existencia de unos pocos!" (66).

Against the background of a naturalist style, once again Lillo turns to elements of a Modernist aesthetic for the crucial elements of "El Chiflón del Diablo." First, there is the abrupt ending of the story. Faced unexpectedly with the death of her son in the company's deadliest pit, Cabeza de Cobre's mother ends her life by allowing herself to fall into the same pit that has killed her son. Clearly separated by lines within the text, the story's last paragraph reads:

> Jamás se supo cómo salvó la barrera. Detenida por los cables niveles, se la vio por un instante agitar sus piernas descarnadas en el vacío, y luego, sin un grito, desaparecer en el abismo. Algunos segundos después, un ruido sordo, lejano, casi imperceptible, brotó de la hambrienta boca del pozo de la cual se escapaban bocanadas de tenues vapores: era el aliento del monstruo ahíto de sangre en el fondo de su cubil. (73).

Lillo's use of the straightforward metaphor of the mining pit-as-monster clearly has its antecedent in Zola, yet here its application by Chilean is somewhat less conventional. Two pages earlier in the story, he refers to this monster in a metaphor that evokes a more concrete and disturbing image, showing a Modernist-inspired preference for emphasizing expression over meaning alone: "bajo las arcadas de cal y ladrillo la máquina inmóvil dejaba reposar sus miembros de hierro, en la penumbra de los vastos departamentos, los cables, como los tentáculos de un pulpo, surgían estremecidos del pique hondísimo y enroscaban en la bobina sus flexibles y viscosos brazos" (71). An octopus with flexible even viscous arms, Lillo's metaphorical description of the mine seems to go beyond merely underscoring its voracious nature, approaching a disturbing and colorful image of a monster from another world entirely.

Second, in "El Chiflón" there is the appearance of a *paisajismo* reminiscent of that used by Latin American Modernism's Peninsular contemporaries the so-called Generation of '98. Marking an hour after Cabeza de Cobre has gone to work at the company's deadliest pit, Lillo's narrator intercalates a poetic description of the landscape that will endure throughout to ring in stark cacophony with the story's troubling end.

> Cuando una hora después de la partida de su hijo, María de los Angeles abría la puerta, se quedó encantada de la radiante claridad que inundaba los campos. Hacía mucho tiempo que sus ojos no veían una mañana tan hermosa. Un nimbo de oro circundaba el disco del sol que se levantaba sobre el horizonte, enviando a torrentes sus vívidos rayos sobre la húmeda tierra, de la que se desprendían por todas partes azulados y blancos vapores. La luz del astro, suave como una caricia, derramaba un soplo de vida sobre la naturaleza muerta. Bandadas de aves cruzaban, allá lejos, el sereno *azul*, y un gallo de plumas tornasoladas desde lo alto de un montículo de arena, lanzaba un alerta estridente cada vez que la sombra de un pájaro deslizábase junto a él. (68, emphasis added)

Lillo's attentive description to the landscape is not solely significant for being an indication or foreshadowing of María's son's death—whether it has already occurred or whether it is impending. It is also a more poetic passage whose lyricism works to highlight the intense contrast between a beautiful above-ground landscape and the harsh realities of the mines underground, and simultaneously of the dialectical tension between leisure and work (the former, as Henri Lefebvre notes in *Rhythmanalysis*, only gaining meaning in relation to the latter). The poetic quality of Lillo's description, used sparingly and pointedly in "El Chiflón," strikes a counterpoint to the bare naturalism of the story as a whole, and subtly pays homage to Darío's (and Hugo's) praise of the color blue/*azul*, connecting with Modernist symbolism much as occurs in the dream sequence from "El pago" (above).

In the introduction to the English translation of Lillo's work

Chapter 1 - EARTH

titled *The Devil's Pit and Other Stories*, Fernando Alegría (1959b) in fact points out "the marked influence of Rubén Darío that is found in certain landscape descriptions in *Sub Terra*," although he leaves the question of which landscape descriptions unanswered (xix).[22] José A. Ramos (2001) argues similarly that certain stories of Lillo's "poseen características predominantemente naturalistas, *y que no falta en ellos ciertos rasgos románticos e incluso modernistas*" (334, emphasis added), although his discussion of these characteristics is quite limited in Lillo's case (the article is devoted to two other authors as well). In fact, the modernist aspects of his stories are often fundamental, in the sense that the are not merely peripheral elaborations, but instead in one way of another instrumental in moving the plot forward ("El pago"), commenting on major events of the story through symbolism ("El Chiflón"), or in the case of the most pervasively modernist story of Lillo's ("Juan Fariña") in fact the story's central core. Most importantly, these modernist aspects aid in Lillo's construction of a more nuanced prose.

"Juan Fariña," a prize-winning story originally published in "Revista Católica" in 1903, strays perhaps the farthest from the Chilean's naturalist center, coming to be the most powerfully modernist story of Baldomero Lillo's. The story begins with the arrival of an unknown worker to an unnamed mine near the Chilean coast. Although the newcomer is blind, he seems to be capable, and the foreman asks him to join the company. The new miner quickly earns a solid reputation for good work, but he is also progressively shrouded in mystery. There are many who believe the man to be in partnership with the devil, if not the devil himself, "Aquel obrero infatigable, del que se hablaba en voz baja y temerosa, no era sino el Diablo que vagaba de día y de noche en las profundidades de la mina" (102). This reputation is supported through unexplained events that happen beneath the earth, particularly at night. Two watchmen charged with patrolling the ventilation corridors of the mine at night find an unknown worker in the blind miner's assigned section. As the unknown miner furiously works the rock, some lit firedamp—the dangerously explosive natural gas pervasive throughout the mines—illuminating him in a blast of flames. The next day, the two watchmen are found dead in a badly ventilated section of the mine, and as the narrator tells us, "desde ese instante, nadie dudó en la mina de que un tenebroso pacto ligaba al aborrecido ciego con el espíritu del mal" (103). The narrator reaffirms this again on page 104, stating that "De un hombre que tenía pacto con el Diablo no podía esperarse nada bueno." At the end of the story, after Juan states that "—Cuando yo muera, la mina morirá conmigo" (105), he uses carefully placed dynamite to destroy the reinforcements that hold back the waters of the sea—remember that in this part of Chile, the mines are being drilled under the ocean itself (as in "La barrena," to be discussed later). Ultimately, as the narrator relates, "el agua del mar llenaba toda la mina y subía por el pozo hasta quedar a cincuenta metros de los bordes de la excavación" (109).

There are obvious parallels to Zola's *Germinal* in terms of the most significant plot events. Juan, like both Etienne and the anarchist Souvarine of the French novel of 1885, is a newcomer to the area who drastically changes the tenor of the culture of the mines. Also, Juan recapitulates the destructive actions of Zola's Souvarine, who also floods the mines. Similarly, there is indeed a social message in the story, faithful to the naturalism which is indispensible in interpreting Lillo's literary production but which is nevertheless merely one aspect of a more nuanced project. This project, as we have seen, goes beyond a strict naturalism to incorporate the lyricism, dream worlds, striking colors and poetic dimensions characteristic of modernism. Yet, despite the naturalist aspects and the parallel invocation of Zola's novel of 1885 (perhaps the most blatant in many ways, in others perhaps the most subversive), it is the fantastic aspect of "Juan Fariña" that subtends the story's naturalism, and not the other way around as perhaps can be said of the other stories in the collection (as above, "La compuerta número 12," "El pago," "Los inválidos," "El Chiflón del Diablo" etc.). Here Lillo places even more emphasis on mystery and ultimately on the fantastic. The very start of the story diverges from Lillo's more straight-forward presentation of the specific social realities of Chilean mining communities in other stories by deliberately shrouding the tale's location in mystery. The name of the mine itself is left curiously unspecified: "se ven hoy las viejas construcciones de la mina de . . ." This omission is quite curious when compared with his other stories, especially the title of the story "El Chiflón del Diablo," which suggests a specific name for a mining location, one that lives on in the name of a specific mining

Chapter 1 - EARTH

location in the very area of Chile explored through Lillo's stories.

In "Juan Fariña" as in "El Chiflón," Lillo indeed evokes the subterranean world of the mines as indeed "hell on earth" (Ball, Jr. 1989) through reference to the devil himself. Nevertheless, the interesting thing about "Juan Fariña" is its use of the very "espíritu del mal" himself to denounce capital and the greed of the mining company. Although the workmen of the story fear the devil—as represented/suggested by the blind miner—the story underscores the connection between the devil and the company's reckless and dehumanizing pursuit of wealth. This wealth, as evidenced by Lillo's depiction of the living conditions of miners throughout *Sub terra*, never trickles down to benefit the miners themselves, but rather as in Zola's *Germinal* sustains first and foremost the capitalist class of mine owners and subsequently the mid-level managers and foremen who carry out these owners' wishes. Read in this context, the devilish figure of "Juan Fariña" is a bit more ambiguous than the workmen, steeped in Christian religious tradition, might be capable of realizing. The narrator, for one, seems to think that Juan has done the men a public service of sorts—that he has even liberated them from a form of indentured servitude. Toward the end of the story, the narrator writes that: "El nombre de Fariña estaba en todos los labios y nadie dudó un instante de que fuera el autor de la catástrofe que los libertaba para siempre de aquel presidio, donde tantas generaciones habían languidecido en medio de torturas y miserias ignoradas" (109). From this perspective, the story chronicles Juan's' final act of rebellion against the forces of evil as personified in the land-owning capitalist class and metaphorically in the mine.

An additional clue buried in the text supplies evidence for this interpretation—the form of a cross. As the unnamed figure extracts load after load of coal from the mine's veins, "de pronto un pedazo arrancado con fuerza del inmovible bloque derribó dos trozos de Madera de revestimiento apoyados en la pared, los que al caer el uno sobre el otro, formaron, por extraña casualidad, *una cruz* en el húmedo suelo del corredor" (103, added emphasis). This image of the cross is subtly repeated later in a description of Juan's 'crossed' arms (107). This interpretation is encouraged by the fact that none are killed as a result of the devil's actions, a destructive act affecting only the mine itself—the built environment for capital accumulation. Even the death of the two watchmen who stumble upon the unnamed figure in the darkness may be attributed directly either to a devilish force that may not in fact be Juan (this is left unclear in the text), if not to the danger inherent in the mine itself. Most importantly, whereas in *Germinal* the anarchist Souvarine's destructive act also kills many of the workmen and horses who are trapped in the mine (and even the protagonist's love interest, Catherine), here not a single miner is injured, let alone killed, when the mine is flooded—a fact that makes it easier to hold a grudge against Zola's anarchist than against "Juan Fariña." Perhaps destroying the mine is not the act of the devil at all, but an act performed in the best interests of the miners who have suffered there a most dehumanizing work. Moreover, afterwards, every year the figure of Juan is said to manifest itself in the ocean, as if on a recurring Saint's Day:

> Todos los años, en la noche del aniversario del terrible accidente que destruyó uno de los más poderosos establecimientos carboníferos de la comarca, los pescadores de esas riberas refieren que cerca del escarpado promontorio, en la ruta de las naves que tocan en el puerto, cuando suena la primera campanada de las doce de la noche en la torre de la lejana iglesia, fórmase en las salobres ondas un pequeño remolino hirviente y espumoso, surgiendo de aquel embudo la formidable figura del ciego con las pupilas fijas en la mina desolada y muerta. (110)

The sad part is that, in direct opposition to what is suggested by the story's narrator, the workmen still demonize Juan and avoid the yearly manifestation of his apparition (110). Although the mine is destroyed, the imprint of the capitalist landscape has not been washed from the miners' consciousnesses.

In their refusal to embrace either a strict naturalism or an escapist modernism, Baldomero Lillo's stories perform a reconciliatory act that ultimately squares with the methodological intentions of contemporary human and cultural geography. For many geographers, capital is neither an idea, nor a fixed reality, but instead both at once. Destruction of the physical environments for capital production alone cannot be the sole solution to social and economic inequalities. Neither can winning over the minds of the working class itself be enough to change processes of wealth accumulation. Lillo's stories work to emphasize the dialectical relationship between 'hand and head' (see Sennett *The Craftsman* 2008), or as urban philosopher Henri Lefebvre put it, the triadic relationship between land-labour-capital (*Rhythmanalysis*).

Dialectics, Contradiction, Reconciliation

Critical consensus maintains that Baldomero Lillo's fictional stories were in great measure intended as an instance of naturalist social critique, even if they have transcended the frame of naturalism to incorporate aspects of modernism, as has been discussed above. He cared deeply about the fate of the miners who worked on, beneath and within the land, not merely as beings who shed light on an abstract 'human condition' of frailty, but specifically as workers necessarily participating in an international capitalist system of production and wealth accumulation on location in Chile. Fernando Alegría (1959a) admirably describes this period in history:

> Ese mundo minero, tal como lo conoció Baldomero Lillo, fue durante una época fuente de grandes riquezas, que no siempre sirvieron para el progreso del país. Sus dueños, ambicionaban el poder y la fortuna para incorporarse a la lujosa decadencia europea de fines de siglo. Cuando quisieron trasladar ese lujo a la tierra nativa e incrustarlo como una corona sobre el pequeño imperio negro de sus minerales, el país había adquirido ya conciencia de sus contradicciones sociales y económicas. (247-48)

Still, the characteristic decadence of the late-nineteenth-century industrializing transatlantic west had a flip side. Whereas centralized governments and explosions of capitalistic enterprise saw the accumulation of vast amounts of wealth, this came at a cost to the capitalists, as Alegría goes on to explain: "el absoluto dominio político que ejercía una clase social privilegiada, llevaron a las masas del país a interesarse en los programas revolucionarios que patrocinaban el socialismo y el anarquismo europeos" (249). Although Lillo himself was not a declared socialist during the period of revolutionary process spanning from 1890 to 1920 (see Alegría 249), his stark depictions of mining life were consistent with the claims of both socialists and anarchists that a better quality of life and a fairer distribution of wealth were necessary. In fact, Lillo was a celebrated figure among socialists and those pushing for reform. To wit, José Santos González Vera (1964) tells us that "Este libro [*Sub Terra*], además de señalar un avance en la literatura chilena, fue bandera del socialismo naciente, y se presume que influyó en el mejoramiento de los mineros. La edición se agotó en tres meses" (266). It is easy to find resonance with such ideas in Lillo's text. In the story "La compuerta número 12" he composed a poetic salvo against the evils of child labor. In "El Chiflón del Diablo" he railed against the lack of benefits suffered by miners in his contemporary Chile. Across a number of stories he spoke to the very real risk of injury and even death faced by the miners both poetically through descriptions such as that of the horse Diamante facing his own death ("Los inválidos"), and more succinctly through the miners who are abruptly killed in mining tragedies (involving gas in both "Juan Fariña" and "El grisú," being crushed in "La compuerta"). Accordingly, his stories reflect not merely questions of literary style (whether modernism, naturalism or, as I have argued above, both at once) but moreover the struggles Chilean miners faced at the time.

From the perspective of human geography, there is much to be gained through an exploration of the stories in *Sub terra*. This work –just as does its precursor, Zola's *Germinal*– treats the land dialectically as both the product of human work and at the same time a galvanizing force for a particular reshaping of humankind's social reality. In the story "El Chiflón del Diablo," for example, Lillo manages to draw out the intimate relationship between human beings and the earth with a literary flourish. The Chilean writes of one worker's cough with the lexicon of the mining environment as "una tos breve y cavernosa" (69). Immediately afterward, the man produces "un escupitajo negro como la tinta" (69), symbolically (and through synecdoche) reproducing the image of the mine producing and hauling up the mined black coal—which could then be made into ink, to give just one example, and sold. In addition to these and other such artistic embellishments, the more consistent description of the mine

Chapter 1 - EARTH

in terms of human activities (above, throughout both *Sub terra* and of course its precursor, *Germinal*) contributes most to emphasizing this relationship. Just as does Zola's aptly named 'Le Voreux,' Lillo's mines relentlessly gobble up life after life—not merely the miners themselves, but also their families and their children.

In "El Chiflón," however, there is yet another way in which Lillo goes beyond Zola in his appropriation of the metaphor mine=voracious human being. The main character of the story, known as Cabeza de Cobre is killed in a mining accident in the treacherous title mine. Once his dead body is finally brought to the surface of the mine and into the light of day where a crowd of villagers is gathered, the narrator relates that: "Por entre los pliegues de la tela que lo envolvía asomaban algunos mechones de pelos rojos que lanzaban a la luz del sol un reflejo de cobre recién fundido. Varias voces profirieron con espanto: —";El Cabeza de Cobre!" (73). His hair constitutes the man's most recognizable trait, but here also evokes the routine procedure through which—whether coal, copper, or other such substance—precious materials are routinely produced and expelled from the mine. This time, however, the 'product' is not coal, but rather the cadaver of a miner, stressing the emotional impact of the reality that deaths and accidents are in fact an unsurprising outcome of such a dangerous job. The only difference between this human product and any other is effectively the howling scream of Cabeza de Cobre's mother, who herself produces "un clamor que no tenía nada de humano" (70) before throwing herself to her death in the very same pit.

Lillo is far from committing the fallacy of much ecological thought noted by geographer David Harvey (1998, above). The earth is not merely the backdrop for human struggles—instead, it is one part of a negotiation that goes on between human beings themselves. Ultimately, in reshaping the earth, as Lillo's stories suggest and as Marxist dialectical thought holds, the people in Lota are in fact reshaping their own social relations and are ultimately recreating themselves. The newly created society is, as Lillo's stories document, a quite horrendous one, showing how the value of human life is necessarily and quite brutally devalued in the pursuit of wealth accumulation. As the land is mined and destroyed, so too are the men who destroy it also destroyed in the process. "El Chiflón" mentions that a miner named "Juan" has just died there (66), and that benefits for the mine's workers are at this time non-existent (66, above). The mining landscape of Lota, refashioned by the mine owners in their quest for wealth, is the third term in a Lefebvrian triad (land-labor-capital) that (re)produces a class distinction—one class rises to power only on the backs of another. Lillo is quite conscious of this sort of exploitative relationship, as he makes clear in his text: "¡Cuántas veces en esos instantes de recogimiento había pensado, sin acertar a explicárselo, en el porqué de aquellas odiosas desigualdades humanas que condenaban a los pobres, al mayor número, a sudar sangre para sostener el fausto de la inútil existencia de unos pocos!" (66). The workmen must pay for their daily bread by in fact risking their lives ("[sus] vidas eran el precio, tantas veces pagado, del pan de cada día!" 66). Appropriately, just as did the Frenchman before him, the Chilean here (albeit more indirectly) references the socialist struggle against capital that must come to inform any treatment of the realities of twentieth-century landscape—even if this is more overt in Zola's chronicle of the burgeoning socialist consciousness of the main character of Etienne, the newcomer to 'Le Voreux' who soon finds himself at the head of a general mining strike.

Notably, however, the frustrations of Lillo's fictitious workers do not lead to any sort of collective action—a fact that somewhat faithfully represents the Chilean context during Lillo's time. *Sub terra* was published in 1904, but it was not until 1920, in the wake of the general strikes of 1918-19 that reverberated throughout numerous Western countries, that Lota had its first strike. Perhaps resonating with the political complexity of Zola's *Germinal* more deeply than with the reluctance of Lillo's work to explicitly embrace a political agenda, the miners in Lota were divided amongst two groups that Chavarri (7) identifies as 'Reds' (anarchists / Zola's Souvarine) and 'Yellows' (more moderate socialists / Zola's Etienne). It seems that the very absence of organizing activity in Lillo's stories is not merely a tactic used to emphasize his acceptance of a stylized naturalist literary aesthetic, but instead a faithful representation of what was going on (or what was not going on) at the time. *Sub terra* is—to return to a point made earlier—at once both a literary experiment and a social document.

Lillo was undoubtedly influenced by his upbringing and sur-

Chapter 1 - EARTH

roundings, and yet reciprocally, his literature also had an enormous effect on working conditions in the country. This unique situation presents with a curious opportunity to overturn the methodological direction of traditional literary criticism. The possibility exists of seeing not only how Lillo's prose reflects his social environment, but also how it in turn shapes that environment. Yet this opportunity is best understood as a chance to close the dialectical circuit of literary criticism. Within both Marxism and contemporary cultural geography, humankind's activity reshapes the land which then has the effect of recreating humankind's social relationships, which again feed back into the subsequent production of landscapes to square with a given (and evolving) set of social relationships. Lillo's stories are thus equally a part of a dialectical circuit. His literary landscapes serve as reproductions (and modifications) of a given extra-literary social environment only to then modify the social relationships which gave rise to the stories (his celebration by socialist reformers in Chile). Extra-literary reality helps to shape literary production which then aids in refashioning that very extra-literary reality. To use simplistic terms, society shapes art, which shapes society.

Literature has always been able to influence 'real' life, but in Baldomero Lillo's case, this relationship is particularly interesting. The critic Jorge M. Chavarri, for example, gives Lillo much credit for the social advances in Chile since 1924, beginning shortly after his death in 1923. Although Lillo had not offered any plan for improvement (9), Chavarri argues that in the critic's mind the author of *Sub terra* should receive "direct credit" for the progress made after the publication and divulgation of his stories (7-8). As he explains:

> Es difícil darse cuenta de la influencia formidable que Baldomero Lillo tuvo en las masas trabajadoras, y entre los representantes de ambas cámaras, para adoptar leyes protectoras, especialmente en lo que se refiere a las condiciones del trabajo en las minas de carbón. Por eso es que ya en 1924, Chile pasa su primera ley social, con énfasis en el liberalismo socioeconómico, que aporta grandes beneficios a la clase media y al pueblo en general.
>
> Se formula un reglamento de salarios, horas de labor, trabajo de la mujer; se prohíbe la labor infantil; hay

protección para accidentes, para la salud y la vejez. Se reconoce la legalidad de los gremios de trabajadores y el derecho que tienen a la huelga. Se legalizan las sociedades cooperativas, y, en un dos por tres, gracias a la influencia de Lillo, Chile llega a ser el primer país en este hemisferio de crear un sistema de seguro social, el más avanzado que hay, aunque constituye un peso formidable en su estricta economía nacional. Lillo fue el primer escritor chileno que se preocupó en sus cuentos de los problemas sociales de los mineros. (5)

Lillo's prose is here directly credited with advances in the rights of Chilean miners. His stark depictions of the base conditions in which miners worked and lived had a lasting legacy—despite the fact that he was so infrequently mentioned throughout the work *Cien años del carbon en Lota* ([1952]2005, 16, 23),[23] a book that unfortunately replaces history with boosterism, instead of speaking more accurately of the social conditions of miners in the area.

Although Baldomero Lillo's case is in itself interesting, it speaks more broadly to a fundamental notion of engaged literary criticism. There is a larger point to be made regarding dialectical scholarship. In many disciplines, there is a fundamental operating principle that involves reconciling two areas of experience that are never found in isolation—immaterial and material aspects of experience. For Marx, the built environment (a material reality) and the existing material conditions of life had a significant effect on immaterial realities (non-material social relationships) just as immaterial realities had a significant effect on the production of material realities. In the urban philosophy and cultural geography of self-proclaimed Marxist Henri Lefebvre, this dialectical emphasis was maintained, just as it has been for more recent theorists. For example, as Alan Latham and Derek McCormack (2004) express so succinctly in their article "Moving Cities: Rethinking the Materialities of Urban Geographies," what is needed in approaching cities is "a notion of the material that admits from the very start the presence and importance of the immaterial" (703). I want to suggest that Lillo's incorporation of both modernist and naturalist literary principles and themes serves as an acknowledgement of the complexity of this type of

Chapter 1 - EARTH

dialectical relationship between immaterial and material forces. As this chapter has addressed above, modernism supplied Lillo with an immaterial world where qualities sought to supersede quantities, where sentimental descriptions of landscapes ("El Chiflón"), an acknowledgement of the power and social impotence of dreams ("El pago"), the less-tangible aspect of a story's mood ("La compuerta") and the poetic image of a horse's death ("Los inválidos") were in no uncertain terms contrasted with the limitations of existing social environments proffered by naturalism.

Through its core properties, the excessive description of and dominating presence of the earth itself in Lillo's stories suggests through implied counterpoint another world of immaterial qualities. The pervasive mining activity depicted in *Sub terra*, the obsessive carving of material realities through creating tunnels in the earth, begs explanation only through an immaterial process of careful thinking that is curiously absent. Whereas Marxist praxis, for example, emphasized the intimate connection between thought and action, capitalist activity must proceed unhesitatingly toward the goal of wealth accumulation. Lillo's focus on obsessive mining activity itself functions as a critique of the pernicious rational accumulation practices of industrial capitalism—which during the time of the Modernists was gaining a substantial foothold in Latin America. The story "La barrena," which although not included in the original 1904 edition of *Sub terra* was appropriately included in subsequent editions, serves as the Chilean's most direct indictment of this process.

As in other stories in the original edition of *Sub terra*, the narrative action of this tale takes place below the ground in the mines. In "La barrena," two competing mining groups take ever more drastic measures to outmaneuver each other and thereby gain exclusive access to an as of yet unmined area. As the old unnamed narrator tells to a boy who is presumably his grandson: "Entonces fue cuando los de Playa Negra quisieron atajarnos corriendo una galería que iba desde el bajo de Playa Blanca en derechura a Santa María. Nos cortaban así todo el carbón que quedaba hacia el norte, debajo del mar" (127). The old man describes his own bosses who unhesitatingly take on the role of military strategists, "Entretanto, nuestros jefes no se contentaban sólo con mirar. Estudiaban el modo de parar el golpe, y andaban para arriba y para abajo, corriendo desaforados con unas caras de susto tan largas que daban lástima" (128). The old narrator is soon directed to choose his ten best men and begin drilling at Alto de Lotilla. This arrangement is made specifically in order to outwork the other group and win access to the prized wealth more quickly:

> lo que exigía de nosostros [...] era abrir un pique en el sitio donde estábamos y en seguida una galería paralela a la playa que cortase en cruz la línea que traía la de Playa Negra. Pero para que tuviese éxito este plan, era necesario llegar al cruce antes que los contrarios. Y aquí estaba lo difícil, porque la distancia que ellos debían andar era menos que la mitad de la que nosotros teníamos que recorrer para ir al mismo punto por debajo del mar. (128-29)

The work is brutal, the heat underground intense, the pace furious; but even so the miners are willingly driven to the brink of exhaustion in order to cut off the other group's tunneling trajectory and lay claim to the as-of-yet unmined area ("Algunos se desmayaban y cuando el pito del capataz nos indicaba que había concluído el turno, una niebla nos oscurecía la vista y apenas podíamos tenernos de pie" 129-30). The miners' strong competitive urges push them on to victory, and when the other (losing) team's drill breaks through their own existing if freshly-dug tunnel, there is a surprise lying in wait. All the victorious miners scramble out of the mine as the foreman tosses a fistful of chili on a hot pile of coal. Safely outside, they celebrate as they watch the workers from the "enemy mine" ("la mina enemiga") brought up to the surface at a distance, reeling from the effects of the aspirated chili: "una extraña tos los sacudía de pies a cabeza" (134). The victory, however, is fleeting. The chili is so slow in dissipating that the tunnels collapse before work at either camp can be resumed: "El techo de la galería, apuntalado a la ligera, se derrumbó, dando paso al agua del mar" (135). There the story abruptly ends.

Certainly, given its decidedly naturalist style, the tale effectively functions as a parable of capitalist accumulation—much as other stories of modernism did (Darío's "El rubí," for example). Also, however, Lillo's "La barrena" moves ultimately not in a naturalist arc but in a modernist one. In contrast to delivering a harsh

Chapter 1 - EARTH

indictment of factors external to humankind—as naturalist authors did by charting the determinist influence of psychological, social truths through literary experimentation—Lillo's story clearly (and in a more immediate sense) pits one group of men against another. The story does not, for example, document the exploitation of a young boy by devastating socio-economic factors beyond the control of his father ("La compuerta"); nor does it reference the severe inequalities of the pay system at the mine ("El pago"). Here the Chilean's crisp writing and his expert exploitation of a genre more apt at developing a single thought or image (the short story) packs a punch. What it does show clearly is how two groups of miners who are, in point of fact, equals, each working for their respective foremen, take it upon themselves to compete, and how that competition leads to injury and ultimately to destruction of the working environment itself.

Through this story, as through many others, Lillo establishes a multifaceted critique of the many internal contradictions of modernity. First, as Marx sought to divulge, it is contradictory that a system of wealth accumulation should contribute so little to those who actually make the accumulation of wealth possible, leaving them mired in poverty and facing an uncertain death ("El pago," "Los inválidos"). Lillo's work as a whole speaks strongly to this Marxian critique even if it does so implicitly rather than explicitly. Here is a group of stories that brings to life the writings of self-proclaimed Marxist philosopher Henri Lefebvre, who maintained that capital was a monster, and that the people worked inside the monster itself, not seeing its true dimensions (*Rhythmanalysis*). Lillo's miners are so mired in the day-to-day struggle of earning money for food ("El pago") that they have little time and energy for questioning the unfair operating procedures and inequities of the society in which they are immersed.

Second, it is contradictory that whereas Chile as a nation may have benefitted from the growth of the coal industry started by Don Matías Cousiño, it was able to do so only at a great cost to its people. It is this very cost that is so suspiciously absent from *Cien años del carbon de Lota*, and it is this same cost that forms the foundation of Lillo's stories. Cousiño is persistently portrayed in saintly or heroic[24] terms, as in the following typical (and lyrical) example:

Pero es 1852 la fecha decisiva para la industria carbonífera nacional, cuando don Matías Cousiño, con resolución inquebrantable, sin desaliento ni vacilaciones, inicia en vasta escala la explotación de los yacimientos carboníferos de Lota, introduciendo en las minas las primeras máquinas, contratando los primeros técnicos adecuados y fundando la ciudad actual y sus principales servicios, revelando con ello extraordinaria visión del futuro. Merced a sus esfuerzos, la industria carbonífera es hoy una gloria para su estirpe, un orgullo para la técnica y el capital chilenos y una fuente de riqueza y de progreso para la patria. (98-99)

Throughout the book there is no discussion of the serious problems of mining, of the tuberculosis from which Lillo, as well as numerous Chilean miners who worked long shifts underground, died. Instead, we find an unproblematic, even triumphant description of Cousiño as himself a conquistador, rapidly luring fishermen and campesinos to abandon more traditional forms of life and become miners.[25]

The book is motivated by a boosterism that seeks to celebrate, for example, the Company's 90th anniversary, Lota's triumphant survival of the earthquake of 1939, and the visits of Chilean President González Videla and earlier American vice president Henry A. Wallace to Lota (on the 3rd of November, 1947; on the 30th of March, 1943). At times it is a self-congratulatory yearbook, having a number of sections devoted to the administrators of the Company, replete with photographs (127-48). Accordingly, there is a brief and obligatory attempt at praising a select group of loyal workers: a list of miners who have worked more than 30 years of service (149-50), an award given to "el minero más meritorio" (151). Despite the fact that the book seeks to take on 100 years of mining activity in Lota, the discussion, where it is not reduced to pure hagiography (of the trinity of Cousiños), concentrates on a more modern period of the mine's history. Even this focus on the last 20-30 years recurs to statistics only when flattering. There is even a pie chart depicting the injuries and deaths at the Lota company during the year 1951 stating that only 0.27 percent of accidents were fatal, 2.24 percent were serious, add 97.49% were merely light (232)—the percentages themselves seem quite cold and abstract, and the decision to use percent-

Chapter 1 - EARTH

ages over numbers in the graph seems to be hiding an ugly reality.

Where can one turn for a glimpse of this ugly reality? To Lillo's *Sub terra*, of course. Lillo's stories were written and presumably take place not during the early years of Cousiño's Compañía but during one of the first periods of remarkable growth: "De 100 mil toneladas de carbón que se extraían anualmente al iniciarse sus tareas, la explotación llegó a 318.000 toneladas en 1905" (Aztorquiza 112)—one year after the publication of his collected stories in 1904. Even Aztorquiza's laudatory volume mentions from the perspective of 1952 that the attempt to reach a "solución de los problemas obreros," to vastly improve Social Welfare through the construction of libraries and schools, and to create "más favorables condiciones de trabajo" was only the focus of "los últimos treinta años" (i.e. since 1922; 116). It turns out that the book's author, Octavio Aztorquiza, was, in fact, the director of Bienestar Social for 25 years, ending in 1948 (198), a fact that may almost certainly compromise the volume's purported objectivity. This perhaps explains the high level of praise for the Dept. of Social Welfare and the suppression of the sordid details of mining life both before and after the creation of the department. "El Departamento de Bienestar es […] el crisol sonde se plasma el porvenir de días mejores" (197). The graph included in the text that charts the development of Bienestar Social runs only from 1942 to 1951, squaring with the text's own admission of the relatively-late development of a concern for the miners as not only workers but human beings in their own right—"Con la experiencia de los años se ha llegado a la conclusión de que una de las bases de la estabilidad de la industria la constituye el bienestar social que hoy, prácticamente, vela por el trabajador desde su nacimiento hasta su muerte" (195).

The story "La barrena" is also, however, an allegory for the internal contradictions inherent to capitalism. As Marx, and later Marxist thinkers such as Lefebvre and Harvey have all emphasized, the self-interest of capitalists routinely leads to crises in capitalism. As capitalists strive to accumulate wealth, this wealth is only partially reinvested into the circuits of capital—too little reinvestment and there is too little work or remuneration for workers, which leads to crises of overaccumulation/underproduction. Due to a systemic individualism, both capitalists and labor often work against their own interests. Capitalists often work in direct opposition to their class interests merely by accumulating too much wealth and thus limiting opportunities for work, and moreover limiting the buying power of the very class that sustains their production from below. Similarly, workers often go against the interests of their own class, either by siding with capitalists or management of being forced to accept whatever working conditions prevail due to the fact that their lives are more rooted in place (see R. Williams and Harvey on 'militant particularism'). As an allegory for these contradictory proceses, in "La barrena" the drive for accumulation actually leads to a crisis where accumulation is, in fact, short-circuited. Neither can the capitalists reap the benefits of the unmined area, nor can the workers be employed there—each camp loses as the competitive system destroys the built environment for production[26] and surplus capital lies stagnant.

The contemporary landscape of Lota offers further reason to dwell on the contradictions characteristic of modernity. It is strange that the very spot which was once the site of back-braking labor is now the leisure destination of many tourists to Chile. It is the landscape of Lota itself that is the text for the boosterism of tourism. As is clear from Don Mitchell's landmark text *Cultural Geography* (2000), such a process is not particular to Chile, but is instead a strategy of the modern post-industrial world where locations that were once hubs of production attempt to remake themselves as a product to be sold on the international market. In what may be considered a classic example representing a more general process, Mitchell considers the case of Johnstown, Pennsylvania in depth. Toward the end of the nineteenth century, Johnstown was one of the most important steel-producing cities in the United States. By the 1980s, however, the steel industry famously left for more advantageous locations. This occurred during a time marked by a more flexible model of capital accumulation (see Harvey 2000). Upon visiting Johnstown today, the tourist finds hardly a trace of the area's history of worker exploitation. There is hardly a reminder of the chaotic relation between labor and management that shaped the industrial landscape of the area. Instead, the history that Johnstown chooses to sell to tourists is that of the city that survived the Great Flood of 1889. The story now sold is that of a city that was able to

Chapter 1 - EARTH

reconstruct itself from the very mouth of disaster. Mitchell writes:

> Visitors to Johnstown today can see the site of the broken dam (which is a National Historical Park), and then work their way down the path of the flood, through the various villages that were destroyed in 1889, and into the city itself, where an impressive Flood Museum tells the history through artifacts, photographs, oral histories, reconstructions of scenes, and so on. The film made by historian David McCullogh and the Flood Museum from McCullogh's book on the flood (and broadcast as part of McCullogh's American Experience television program) is available for viewing. The Flood Museum also dedicates a portion of its space to telling the industrial history of Johnstown, tracing its development from a small farming community, to innovative steel-center, to a landscape of deindustrialization. Outside, visitors can follow a "flood trail" around the city, seeing surviving buildings, imagining the size of the mountain debris that built up behind the stone bridge, riding an incline plane to the plateau above the city, and visiting the cemetery where the unidentified bodies are buried. In the museum and in the landscape itself, visitors can learn how Johnstown rebuilt after the flood, becoming once again one of the foremost steel-producing cities in the country. Despite the somewhat forlorn aspect the landscape projects now that the mills are quiet, visitors can feel for themselves why Johnstown bills itself as a "city of survivors." (95)

The turbulent history of the struggle between labor and capital—which once dominated the landscape—has been wiped away and replaced with the flattened image of a vague and distant industrial past.

Lota has similarly recreated itself as a product. In contrast to the brute physicality of the mining world of early twentieth-century Chile—a world of quantities, of bottom-lines, of sweat, toil and physical hardship for the working classes, of physical luxury and possessions for the landowning classes—the discourse of the mining region of Lota that exists today (the signifier), has been curiously uprooted from the material world of the mines (its signified). All that is solid melts into air. The Lota that was once a hub of Chilean production had, of course, initially been seen as a model city, representative of the early twentieth-century industrial modernity. Mills (1914) writes of the area's evolution toward such a productive hub in triumphant terms: "The development of Lota from a fishing village to a busy mining and manufacturing town of 15,000 inhabitants, a model of its kind, is one of the romances of Chilean enterprise and organising power, and deserves a more detailed description" (154-55).[27] This triumphant view has certainly not been an uncommon one over the years as Chile has struggled to gain recognition in a fickle and constantly-shifting world market. Yet beneath this image of a successful Lota, as Lillo's stories show, there was always another world where men were rendered beasts, where both beasts and men spent much of their lives working underground in dangerous and dimly-lit passages without seeing sunlight, where each was essentially a cog in the great machine of production, where pay was scarce and making a living was a constant struggle.

After the closure of the once highly successful Lota mines, just as in the case of post-industrial Johnstown, there has been an attempt to turn the chaotic history of the mining area into a tourist destination. Perhaps out of joint with their subject matter, Toby Green and Jani Janak, the authors of a popular travel guide for Chile, write of the area somewhat candidly: "Even before the mine's closure in April 1997, the town was known to be one of the poorest in Chile and, although the government has invested in retraining for the miners and trying to open up Lota to tourism, the city still suffers greatly from poverty and neglect" (296). As one might expect, tours of the coal mines, which run almost entirely under the sea, are now offered by former miners to curious visitors. An interesting manifestation of this post-industrial tourist interest in Lota can be found, also, online. Clarence Fisk (2004) has posted a fifteen-paragraph commentary in Spanish on his trip to the area, ending it with a cheery "¡Vamos todos a Lota!" Data about the mining area's history, dimensions and locations are interspersed with practical travel advice—for example, "Este paseo [a Lota] debería hacerse en dos o tres visitas para conocerlo bien." One paragraph is devoted to the

Chapter 1 - EARTH

Museo de Lota, from which Fisk supplies tourist photos that await his readers just a click away. But the center of the short piece is a description of the trip into the mines. "La parte más interesante de este paseo es la bajada a una Antigua mina de carbon llamada, ahora que es atracción turística, 'El Chiflón del Diablo'. Con este nombre bautizó los socavones y piques de la mina Don Baldomero Lillo en su obra magistral 'Sub Terra.'" The descent, of course, as anyone who has visited a mine will know, requires donning the miner's outfits, complete with hats and lamps ("cascos y lámparas a batería"). A sense of authentic experience pervades Fisk's narration, as when he writes that "Me encuentro con ropa de calle dejada por los mineros colgada de rondanas en los tejados (no existían los lockers)." The guide for Fisk's experience is, Don Roberto Rojas, a former miner for 18 years who became a tour guide when the mine closed in 1997.

The production of leisure space in Lota, interestingly, was already in process under the initial reign of Cousiño's mining company:

> Much of the Cousiño fortune has been spent on the creation of the great park above the town, one of the wonders of Chile, and among the most beautiful in the world. It contains trees and plants from all quarters of the world, with wild animals, a great aviary, lakes, fountains, and statues (including the well-known statue of Caupolican, by Nicanor Plaza). In the centre Señora Cousiño built, at enormous expense, a magnificent palace, which, though roofed at her death was unfinished internally, and has since remained unoccupied, a melancholy example of a great dream unfulfilled. (Mills 1914, 155-56)

This contrast between the Lota of leisure and the Lota of work was the explicit point of introduction highlighted by Fernando Alegría (1959a) in an academic introduction to Lillo's work.

> En el sur de Chile, en las cercanías de la dinámica y progresista ciudad de Concepción, hay una costa de dramáticas configuraciones: allí se ven Colinas plantadas de pinos, lujuriosamente verdes, cubiertas por viejos helechos,

acantilados abruptos, suaves y escondidas playas bañadas por una marea tupida de cochayuyo y otras algas marinas, apacibles botes pescadores trenzados en una vasta acumulación de redes; allí las gentes transitan en una atmósfera de paz y lejanía, y, a menudo, se pierden en dunas solitarias. En ciertas zonas se alzan construcciones gigantescas donde reina una actividad que el observador no identifica de inmediato. En la cima de unas amplias colinas existe un parque fabuloso: el Parque de Lota; y entre plantas de vieja alcurnia chilena hay una fastuosa mansión del más depurado estilo dieciochesco. La mansión está permanentemente vacía. Nunca fue ocupada por sus dueños. Entre los senderos floridos se divisa un muelle. Una inmensa maquinaria lleva, entre el fragor de grúas y cadenas, la carga que se van tragando lentamente los barcos: el oro negro, el carbón chileno. Esa mansión vacía y ese muelle sumido en nubes de vapor y de hollín, son el símbolo de un mundo que encontró su expresión en la obra del escritor más patéticamente vigoroso que ha producido la literatura chilena: Baldomero Lillo. (247)

Ultimately, the landscape of Don Matías Cousiño's Lota was riven through by contradiction—what is often referred to by geographers as the 'uneven geographical development' of capitalism. "A poca distancia del hermoso parque y de la principesca mansión, existía un mundo de diferente carácter, dantesco en las proporciones de su miseria: era el mundo de los mineros" (Alegría 1959a, 248). As Lefebvre writes in *Rhythmanalysis*, work and leisure must be understood as two abstractions wrought of a dialectical pairing. There can be no measured quantification of the working day (such as the spatialization of time denounced by Marx) without an implicit conception of leisure as the night side of work. Just as there was to be a built environment for production, there was also, necessarily to be a built environment for leisure.

Ultimately Lillo's stories capture the contradictions of modernity. Certainly he drew attention to this through a naturalism that sought to denounce the plight of humankind more generally, but also through a more place-bound denunciation of the ills brought

Chapter 1 - EARTH

by a growing capitalist industrialization to Chile. On top of this, he incorporated modernist elements into his stories that more poetically heightened the force of this denunciation by pointing to an escape to a world of qualities and dreams that subsequently injected the possible into Chile's literary and even social landscape. Contradiction was, of course, at the very core of modernism itself as Ned Davison's seminal work explored: "The aesthetic of Modernism is, in its essence, contradictory" (6). But moreover, Lillo's stories acknowledge the fundamental complexity of worlds, like our own, that are at once material and immaterial through the contrast he evokes between naturalism and modernism, achieving a literary rendering of the very uneven landscape that motivated his stories. Pointing to the contradictions between rich and poor, work and leisure, the co-existence of hope and despair, the environments we have created versus those which we might have alternatively created, *Sub terra* speaks at once to all of these contradictions of modernity. Nearly one-hundred years later, Lillo's stories still speak to us of the inequalities that continue to structure the uneven landscapes of our cities and post-industrial tourist creations.

Yet most importantly, the unique fusion of denunciation and hope we find in Lillo's collection implicitly taps into Marx's vision of a new society. Zola—in *Germinal*—had explicitly spoken to this vision:

> A new society would emerge in a single day, as in a dream, a great city shining like a vision, in which each citizen would be paid the rate for the job and have his share of the common joy. The old word, already rotten, had crumbled to dust; and humankind, newly young and purged of its crimes, would be one nation of workers, with the motto: "To each according to his deserts, and to his deserts according to his works." And the dream would grow ever grander and more wonderful, and the higher it reached towards the impossible, the more beguiling it became. (Zola 171)

In *Sub terra*, however, Lillo evokes a landscape that is at once material and immaterial, the product of suffering, imbued with hope. It is this fairly basic aspect of his work that is the real triumph. In refusing to portray the subjugation of humankind to capital as definitive, he bucks the naturalist tendency to show how we are definitively shaped by the current contours of our physical and social environments. *Sub terra*'s modernist inflections expose a world which coexists with that of the naturalist, one in which the possibility of an alchemical change of perspective is very real. He poignantly uses the earth itself as a mirror held up to society. In shaping the earth, humankind re-shapes itself. Lillo's description of mining life shows us the depth and breadth of our own productive power. Delving underground, thought that is driven by the phantom of wealth production shows us how such activity leads only to great destruction, of the worker, of the mine, of our humanity itself. Yet it is in reaching the surface that Lillo shows us the poetic dawn of a new world forming. It is our imagination that must provide the spark that will lead us to collective action.

2

FIRE: AN EXPLOSIVE MODERNITY (LILLO/LUGONES)

There is, in Centralia, Pennsylvania an underground coal-mine fire that has been burning for almost 50 years now. In 1962, a coal seam was accidentally lit by a trash fire and could not be extinguished, causing the abandonment of the mine and eventually the town itself. By the 1980s, the carbon-monoxide surging from the underground fire had ultimately prompted Centralia's evacuation.

> Over 47 years and 40 million dollars later the fire still burns through old coal mines and veins under the town and the surrounding hillsides on several fronts. The fire, smoke, fumes and toxic gases that came up through the back yards, basements and streets of Centralia literally ripped the town apart. Most of the homes were condemned and residents were relocated over the years with grants from the federal government although some diehards refused to be bought out and some still remain in the town. Today Centralia is a virtual ghost town with only a few remaining residents.[1]

It is this type of destruction that has long captivated humankind's attention and established fire as not only a devastating physical force, but also a powerful symbol. Of all the symbols of change, perhaps none is as primal, as powerful and as enduring as that of fire.

For early humans fire was a rich source of ritual and imagery. For alchemists and early chemists it occupied a privileged position not merely as a catalyst but as something akin to a life-force. The Copernican revolution had the effect of installing a ball of fire at the center of our known world, and contemporary cosmology retains a fascination with the power of flames and hot gases. Richard Wrangham, the Ruth Moore Professor of Biological Anthropology at Harvard University, in his recent book *Catching Fire: How Cooking Made Us Human* (2009), even argues that the adaptation of producing cooked food spccfically prompted widespread "changes in anatomy, physiology, ecology, life history, psychology, and society" (14). Nonetheless, even if our understanding of fire and our awareness of its significance is now more nuanced we are still in many ways at its mercy, as the example of the coal-mine fire at Centralia shows.

Not surprisingly, the elemental power of fire figures heavily in the work of early twentieth-century Latin American authors Baldomero Lillo and Leopoldo Lugones. There are certainly surface differences among the literary products of each—regarding subject matter and style. Nevertheless, in both cases, fire expresses or symbolizes a fundamental change in the whole, in the totality of life, the fabric of being. Each author taps into the primitive roots of our fascination with fire to emphasize that life as we know it can and often does fundamentally change. The fire appearing in Lillo's *Sub Terra* runs from the slow burn of coal to the quick explosive flare-up of 'firedamp' ('el grisú'), natural gas seeping out from the mine's walls and ceilings that is easily ignited by the flame of mining lamps ("El grisú," "Juan Fariña"). In Lugones' *Las fuerzas extrañas*, it appears as both the soft-glow of occult forces harnessed by pseudo-scientific investigation ("El psychon") and as a harsh and mysterious apocalyptic fire-rain ("La lluvia de fuego"). In both cases, the authors use such clemental symbolism to depict the fundamental uncertainty and contradiction at the base of the modern experience. Fire symbolizes, for each author in his own way, the possibility of a sudden upheaval that holds the possibility of forever changing the material

Chapter 2 - FIRE

and immaterial conditions of our everyday lives.

The Chilean and the Argentine, however, approach this apparent (and apparently modern) contradiction between the material and the immaterial each from a different position. Lillo's stories use fire first and foremost to portray the material dangers of the mining experience, and secondly to point to the more elusive intangible dangers of immaterial processes—the consequences of a drive for accumulation indistinguishable from excessive greed. Tending toward the pole of pure materiality, they question the excess of action and material forces unguided or untempered by careful thought processes directed toward social ends. Lugones' stories, on the other hand proceed inversely, locating fire at the very threshold of human knowledge, as a gatekeeper of the unknown itself. Tending toward the pole of pure immateriality, they question the unrestrained immaterial force of a thought that drives toward absolute knowledge with little regard for produced material consequences. When read against one another, Lillo and Lugones's works point to a dialectical circuit whereby thought and action might move together adequately—the immaterial process of thought is thus appropriately informed by the material consequences of its precepts and goals, while material action is infused by an appropriately hesitant and responsible thought.

Through their common focus on power of fire, *Sub terra* (Lillo) and *Las fuerzas extrañas* (Lugones) suggest that when this dialectical circuit is severed, abused or ignored, the consequences may become quite dire, indeed. In this chapter I explore how each author uses fire toward his own end separately, but with an eye to the complementary nature of their literary explorations. In "El grisú" and "Juan Fariña," Lillo uses fire as a destructive elemental force unleashed by irresponsible human actions and concomitant with other inhumane consequences of somewhat inhumane systems of production. Lugones's "El psychon" uses the soft-glow of flame-like human auras to point to the contradictory unity between material and immaterial realities, while his "La lluvia de fuego" admonishes against reducing immaterial human consciousness to a merely material essence. In every case, the authors invoke the notion of a modernity riven throughout by contradiction and danger, by shifting and unpredictable, explosive changes—a notion that squares with the melting modernist vision of Marx himself in one way or another: "All that is solid melts into air, all that is holy is profaned, and men at last are forced to face...the real conditions of their lives and their relations with their fellow men" (*The Communist Manifesto*, qtd. in Berman 21).

Lillo's *Sub terra*: Underground Fire and Revolution

The way we make sense of the use of fire in Lillo's classic text depends to a large extent on the approach taken. From the perspective of a nineteenth-century literary realism, underground coal fires, firedamp gas explosions and the illumination devices that often caused such catastrophes were an inevitable outcome of the consistent danger faced by workers while working a lifetime in the mines. The use of fire in Lillo's story "El grisú" undoubtedly accurately reflects the social context in which his mining stories were written (discussed in more detail in chapter one). Nevertheless, through superb literary craft Lillo expertly illuminates the imaginary of the mine revealing it to be allegory for all kinds of human struggle. Fire comes to symbolize human anger and human suffering at the same time it connotes warmth, welcome and the possibility of a different future. It is, in a way, a symbol for the explosive tempers that threatened mine work and at once the powerful vital force that made this work possible. We saw in chapter one how Zola evoked the mine itself as a fire-breathing monster and how Lillo continued to build upon this metaphor. For the Chilean as for the Frenchman, underground fire represents not only hatred but also the driving force of passion, coming to represent a range of opposing forces that subtend and provoke human action, and notably also the possibility of revolution itself.

Read through a literary naturalism, fire becomes more than a displaced expression of or mirror for human emotion. Emile Zola's *Germinal* (see chapter one), for example, clearly turns to fire repeatedly to reference the coming socialist/anarchist conflagration that will supposedly wipe inequality away. The novelist's description of his protagonist's adaptation to mining life is notably phrased in terms of a 'becoming-molten,' "as though he himself had somehow become molten and could pass through chinks in the rock where

Chapter 2 - FIRE

once he wouldn't even have ventured his hand" (138). Etienne's literary reconciliation with the properties of fire underscores his awareness of the explosive potential of ideas, of a newfound flexibility and a more pointedly-directed of his efforts and energy. Later, he even survives an underground explosion to emerge as if reborn at the novel's close. The novel is rife with symbolism of fire as anger, hatred (410, 434), yet moreover, fire is imbued with the power to completely transform society: "By fire, sword and poison" (245), by way of "burning and killing, of a glorious apotheosis" (293), by "set[ting] fire to the whole bloody lot" (399), the bourgeoisie will be incinerated "by the fires of heaven" (439). Zola's work consistently equates the symbolic power of fire with "the workers' revolution, whose conflagration would engulf the dying years of the century in flames as crimson as the morning sun which now rose bleeding into the sky" (530).[2] At the novel's climax, explosive charges set by the character Souvarine do away with the mine central to the action of the novel *Germinal*, symbolizing just such a spontaneous and violent social upheaval disrupting the bourgeois forces of production that subtend mining work of the late nineteenth century.

Later, during the mid-to-late twentieth century, fire was of course still being used to speak of the complete socialist transformation of society, as can be seen in the apt English title of Henri Lefebvre's book on the events of 1968: *The Explosion* (the complete French title reads: *L'irruption de Nanterre au sommet*). Nevertheless, the more-recent appearance of this type of imagery is in fact rooted in Marx's earlier conception of a rapidly transforming modernity. He captured the sudden modern transformation of mid-nineteenth-century urbanizing society splendidly in the phrase, taken from *The Communist Manifesto*, "All that is solid melts into air." Marx's understanding of modernity placed emphasis, above all else, on the contradictions that structured modern society, all connected to the triumph of exchange-value over use-value. More and more extensively, as his work suggests, the transformation of society was driven by the creation, destruction and reproduction of environments designed to facilitate capital accumulation. This process would notably be reflected in self-declared Marxist philosopher Henri Lefebvre's dictum that capitalism "has survived throughout the twentieth century by occupying space, by producing space" (*The Survival of Capi-*

talism, 1973: 21). Marshall Berman's celebrated book of 1982, which takes as its title Marx's concise characterization of modernity (*All that is Solid Melts into Air*) teases out the paradoxical unity of these chaotic times grounded in the sea-change wrought by a specifically nineteenth-century modernity:

> To be modern is to find ourselves in an environment that promises us adventure, power, joy, growth, transformation of ourselves and the world—and, at the same time, that threatens to destroy everything we have, everything we know, everything we are. Modern environments and experiences cut across all boundaries of geography and ethnicity, of class and nationality, or religion and ideology: in this sense, modernity can be said to unite all mankind. But it is a paradoxical unity, a unity of disunity: it pours us all into a maelstrom of perpetual disintegration and renewal, of struggle and contradiction, of ambiguity and anguish. To be modern is to be part of a universe in which, as Marx said, "all that is solid melts into air." (15)

Berman's work appropriately and famously invokes a Marxian framework to focus on contemporary urban shifts and the built environment of the city. Yet long before the infrastructures of today's modern cities were thoroughly colonized by contemporary urban planning—in Lefebvre's understanding an arm of modern capitalism itself—the sea-change wrought by changing accumulation strategies was at work deep beneath the surface of the earth, engaged in the production of another built environment. This environment was none other than that of the underground mines.

Although class struggle is an implicit part of the stories of *Sub terra*—as seen by Lillo's resonance with socialist and labor movements in Chile following his death in 1923 (discussed in chapter one)—their author is also deeply fascinated by the more mysterious, destructive and transformative aspects of fire. This fascination does not, however, overshadow his naturalist critique of working conditions, but rather coexists with it. Fire for Lillo is not merely a reality of underground mining life, but also a metaphor for modernity itself, an expression of the terribly turbulent nature of a contradictory

Chapter 2 - FIRE

time that became a focal point for numerous turn-of-the-century authors in Europe and Latin America. What better place, what better context or environment, than the underground mines to evoke the tremendous sense of upheaval that was palpable at the time?

Lillo's fascination linking fire with the notion of social upheaval can be seen most clearly in the story "El grisú." This well-crafted tale relates the events leading up to a massive underground explosion resulting from the title gas ('firedamp'). The narration heightens the effect of the story's final explosion by beginning the story with a description of the mine's uncharacteristic silence and immobility: "En el pique se había paralizado el movimiento" (23). At the same time, this opening sentence conveys the possibility of future explosive violence through the humanizing lexical choice of 'paralyzed'('paralizado') to connote stoppage—simultaneously reinforcing the idea of the mine as a giant creature (as per Zola). Sudden movements follow: the rapid arrival of the English-speaking engineer 'Mister Davis' on the scene ("*De improviso* el ingeniero apareció en la puerta de entrada," 23, emphasis added), the sudden arrival of workers to a tense labor meeting ("*De pronto,* allá a la distancia, apareció una luz seguida luego por otras y otras hasta completar algunas docenas," 29, emphasis added), for example, all foretelling the sudden, violent eruption to follow. Lillo also builds on the suspense implicit in the tale—the wait preceding the final explosion—through descriptions that show the workers tensely awaiting some unannounced event or another, as when they tensely await the arrival of Mister Davis: "Los obreros fijaban una mirada recelosa en cada lucecilla que brillaba en las tinieblas, creyendo ver a cada instante aparecer aquel blanquecino y temido resplandor" (24).

One of the true successes of the story is Lillo's development of the chiaroscuro interplay between light and shadow, made possible by the story's mining setting. The story takes place almost entirely underground, coming to constitute an inverse companion to *Sub terra*'s "Los inválidos," where we witness the extraction of a dying horse from the mine largely from a vantage point on the surface (discussed in chapter one). In "El grisú," Lillo creates an eerie underground mood by almost obsessively referencing lanterns, accentuating the sharp visual contrast of the underground scene. The beginning of the story draws the reader's attention to the pervasive darkness underground through a simple opposition between the strong outdoor sunlight and the necessarily insufficient use of lanterns below the surface of the earth. The carefully positioned last sentence of the first paragraph contrasts with the previous description of the capataz standing next to the elevator "con su linterna encendida" (23) by opposing the seemingly weak power of underground lamps to that of the daytime sun: "En lo alto el sol resplandecía en un cielo sin nubes y una brisa ligera que soplaba de la costa traía en sus ondas invisibles las salobres emanaciones del océano" (23). Throughout the story, the narrator continuously draws attention back to these lanterns every few paragraphs in order to remind the reader of the realities of the underground mining world, to emphasize the oppressive atmosphere of the mine as foil for the physical, biological and social determinism stressed by the naturalist and perhaps most innovatively to continuously exploit the poetic possibilities offered by the lasting image of soft underground light (23, 23, 24, 28, 28, 29, 29, 30, 31, 32, 34, 35, 35, 37, 37…). For example, a lantern is carried by the mine's intimidating engineer when he is first described for us, and customarily punctuates his arrival when meeting with the workers ("llevaba en la diestra una linterna," 23; "su presencia anunciada por la luz de su linterna era más temida en la mina que los hundimientos y las explosions del grisú," 24). This interplay constitutes another layer of the story as Lillo characteristically crafts a tale that, like others in his collection, is just as attentive to mood and imagery as it is to social concerns and circumstances.

Yet the continuous mention of lanterns does more than work to establish mood and accurately reflect the mining conditions of the time. Light is, for Lillo, a precious resource (perhaps akin to the way gems and precious metals were invoked by the modernists – see Fraser 1992, Lodato 1999) that, while used by both upper-management and miners alike, comes to reflect the inequality of the social relationship between the capataz and the head engineer on one side and the lowly workers on the other. For example, the lantern is associated with inequality when the intimidating Mister Davis—who on account of "su orgullo de raza" believes the lives of the workers are undeserving of the attention of a "*gentleman*" (the word is left in English in the text, 24, original emphasis)—decides to punish a young boy for his inability to pull the corpulent engineer through a

Chapter 2 - FIRE

difficult section of the mine as would a workhorse.[3] It is by the "light of his lamp" that the capataz writes down the order from Mister Davis not merely to fire the boy but rather to evict both him and his remaining family from their house (the boy's father has already died, presumably from the tough working conditions): "trozó en ella, a la luz de su linterna, algunos renglones," 28). When the miners arrive en masse for a meeting to discuss working conditions in the mine, their lanterns signal their approach by way of "la larga hilera de lucecillas" (29). But while the workmen also have access to the resource of light underground, Lillo takes the opportunity to distance their access to light from any symbolic power over the conditions of their own lives, in the process underscoring the correlation he develops between light and the power of the engineer: "Y a pesar del considerable aumento de luz, las sombras persistían siempre y en ellas se dibujaban las borrosas siluetas de los trabajadores, como masas confusas de perfiles indeterminados y vagos" (30). The miners may have light, but as Lillo soon makes clear, this light does not have, for them, the power it gains from association with the mine's privileged engineer. They remain in the shadows, a group of confused and vague profiles. When the miners arrive, Mister Davis shines his own light on the group as if an inspector upon a group of suspects being interrogated: "Este levantó la linterna a la altura de su cabeza y proyectó el haz luminoso sobre el grupo del cual se destacó un hombre que avanzó, gorra en mano, y se detuvo a tres pasos de distancia" (31). The engineer forcefully refuses to negotiate with the miners, who are left dumbfounded and unable to say a word (33). In Lillo's well-crafted description of what follows, the lanterns move rapidly and sympathetically with the agitation of the disappointed miners ("En la lobreguez de la sombra agitáronse las luces de las lámparas, moviéndose en todas direcciones," 34). In anger, a young miner—convinced there is no remedy to the situation (34)—explodes: "estalló la lámpara en el muro donde se hizo mil pedazos" (35).

The anger subsides and the narration cuts sharply to a section of the new tunnel being dug in the mine. This new section abounds with the deadly natural gas of the mine or 'firedamp'/grisú, a danger carefully made explicit by the story's narration. As one of the older miners explains to a younger one, "Una chispa, una sola y nos achicharramos todos en este infierno. [...] es el grisú [...] La galleria debe estar llena del maldito grisú" (36). Raising a lamp upward reveals that its flame grows suddenly on account of the amount of highly flammable gas present in the mine (37). In this new section of the mine, a confrontation between a young resolute miner who goes by the nickname of Viento Negro and the engineer (and the capataz) turns physical. Implicitly indebted to Zola's *Germinal*, Lillo describes his young miner's anger as "una mirada de fiera acorralada, en la que brillaba la llama sombría de una indomable resolución" (39). He is forced to work against his will and, investing his emotion in his work, makes the necessary repairs. In so violently hammering away at the mine's infrastructure, however, he creates many large and dangerous sparks (40). Ultimately it is here that the story delivers its climactic payload:

> Una llama azulada recorrió velozmente el combado techo del túnel y la masa de aire contenida entre sus muros se inflamó, convirtiéndose en una inmensa llamarada. Los cabellos y los trajes ardieron y una luz vivísima, de extraordinaria intensidad, iluminó hasta los rincones más ocultos de la inclinada galería.
> Pero aquella pavorosa visión sólo duró el brevísimo espacio de un segundo: un terrible crujido conmovió las entrañas de la roca y los seis hombres envueltos en un torbellino de llamas, destrozos de maderas y de piedras, fueron proyectados con espantosa violencia a lo largo del corredor. (40-41).

The "formidable explosión" that ensues as the firedamp is ignited by the angry young miner's hammerstrikes, one which is compared to "la repentina erupción de un volcán" (41), has been foreshadowed through, among other things, an earlier "*explosión* de risas" (39, emphasis added) released by those watching the engineer taunt the young lad. Similarly, prior to this Lillo has had an older miner directly address the possibility of a huge firedamp explosion in the mine directly: "estamos, vaya el caso, dentro del cañón de una escopeta, en el sitio en que se pone la carga [...] Al menor descuido, una chispa que salte o una lámpara que se rompa, el Diablo tira el gatillo y sale el tiro" (37). The long-awaited explosion central to "El grisú" and

Chapter 2 - FIRE

intimated by its very title soon occurs—the 'devil pulls the trigger' at last—and the resulting blast is so powerful that its effects are felt even above ground, as retold by the story's narration, cross-cutting to the surface. Later, a group of men searching for those injured by the blast finds of the workmen and capataz only bodies blown to pieces (44); the head engineer is found hanging from the wall, his stomach impaled by a metal rod (45). Here, Lillo ends the story by stressing the compassion of the miners as they carefully take Mister Davis down and bring his body out of the mine, seemingly no longer bearing him any ill-feelings.

Squaring with the Modernist's rejection of transparent didactic narratives, there is a sense in his stories that not only is Lillo denouncing a particular Chilean form of capitalistic enterprise whereby accumulation trumps the lives of workers but simultaneously an inherent crack in the capitalistic base of our frail human experience. For Lillo, the capitalist system is—as it was for Marx, although this is often forgotten by scientific-Marxian tendencies toward 'pure' economism/materialism[4]—a crushing social system that gravely affects our contemporary lives. This system is, of course, as Marxian thought recognizes, nonetheless the product of human beings who nurture it over time. Appropriately, Lillo closes the story with the scene of the workmen carrying the dead body of the engineer—strangely enough the only body that has survived the blast intact—out of the mine: "respiraban con fatiga bajo el peso aplastador de aquel muerto que seguía gravitando sobre ellos, como una montaña en la cual la Humanidad y los siglos habían amontonado soberbia, egoísmo y ferocidad" (45). The workers maintain their humanity precisely by treating the dead engineer with the respect he had perhaps earned only through intimidation in life. But nevertheless, Lillo points to the past and future perpetuation of an unfair system incarnated in the cadaver which 'continues to weigh on them.' Surely there will be someone to take his place, and perhaps in gathering his body the miners continue to show they are trapped within the strict class-structure necessary for the form of capital accumulation that subtends their lives in the mines. Yet as the Chilean's story emphasizes, the current situation of capital accumulation is both the outcome of a long-standing inheritance ("los siglos") and also an effect that humankind ("la Humanidad") continues to (and in a way chooses to) produce. The possibility for change lies in a concordance between 'nature' and man-made action, as suggested by Lillo's naming the young miner 'Viento Negro' (twice on p. 40) and then using the same term to refer to the dangerous mine gas (*"viento negro,"* 43, original emphasis).

Yet we must be careful in restricting the Chilean's literary output by attempting to fit it squarely within the boundaries of one literary movement/style or another. More than a chance to denounce specific conditions of his native Chile, Lillo also undoubtedly saw in the mining life of his fellow countrymen a chance to grapple with a universal frailty of humankind. Suggesting yet another connection with the Modernists, for whom fire was an elemental force that pointed to the inherent interconnectivity of the universe (drawing upon Pythagoras's discussion of such properties), the real protagonist of Lillo's story is the explosive power of fire itself. Despite all Lillo's naturalism, the key motivation underlying "El grisú" is not merely a faithful representation of the social conditions of mining life in southern Chile but also an attempt to grapple with violent and strange forces which are beyond the complete control of humankind. The attention Lillo pays to creating a mood, the central role he gives to light, fire and gas, his suspenseful drawing-out of the story's climax all point to the possibility that, while the story's social aspects were important, he simultaneously sought to paint a more general picture of change. Most importantly, as can be seen in the soft ending of "El grisú," however much his stories were rightly credited with being the motor force for changes in Chilean coal-mining, the Chilean is himself hesitant to turn the story into purely a revolutionary call to arms. Although he is certainly sympathetic to such a position, as critics have pointed out, it is worth noting in this regard that instead of having the coal-mine explosion serve for a complete transformation of the forces of production, by intensifying the conflict between the mine's workers and its managers and leading to a general strike, for example, the explosion actually results in a display of human compassion that straddles the deep stratification that characterized the Chilean mining world at the time. From this perspective, Lillo is able to foreground both the destructive power of disasters and our necessarily human responses to them more generally.

Chapter 2 - FIRE

Although the notion of a complete and even violent upheaval concerning the whole of social life is perhaps best fictionalized in the powerful fire-imagery of "El grisú," Lillo tackles the same idea in other stories of the original *Sub terra* volume. In the latter story we saw a miner attribute the power to make the firedamp explode to the Devil himself ("Al menor descuido, una chispa que salte o una lámpara que se rompa, el Diablo tira el gatillo y sale el tiro," 37). In the story "Juan Fariña," however, instead of being equated with bad luck, chance or unpredictable immaterial forces, the devil's presence in the mine is rendered material in the title character. Juan, a blind newcomer to one of the mines on the Chilean Gulf states simply upon his arrival to the mine that "Me llamo Juan Fariña y quiero trabajo en la mina" (98). Although I have discussed this story in more detail in chapter one (above), it is the powerful explosion at the story's climactic ending that is of interest here.[5] Whereas "El grisú" ends with a massive explosion and cave-in that destroys part of the mine in question and kills a number of workers caught underground, Juan manages to explode the entire mine, rendering it henceforth unusable, much as the anarchist character Souvarine does in Zola's novel *Germinal*.

In moving slowly but surely toward this final great explosion, the story "Juan Fariña" may in fact have at its center an act of contestation. In *The Explosion* (1968), Henri Lefebvre defines contestation in treating it as relevant to the student movement and upheaval of 1968.

> Contestation is first of all a refusal to be integrated, with full awareness of what integration entails with respect to humiliation and dissociation. Contestation is an all-inclusive, total rejection of experienced or anticipated forms of alienation. It is a deliberate refusal to be co-opted. The movement was born from negation and has a negative character; it is essentially *radical*. Contestation is by definition radical. It does not arise out of a partial "subject" or out of fragmentation. It derives its radical character from the fact that it originates in the depths, beneath the roots of organic, institutional social life—below the "base." Contestation thus brings to light its hidden origins; and

it surges up from these depths to the political summits, which it also illuminates in rejecting them. (65)

In Lillo's story, the outsider who comes to work at the mine is—speaking quite literally, given the story's fantastic trajectory—demonized, both by the other mine workers and also, although perhaps more questionably, by the narrator of the story himself. Nevertheless, this is precisely the reaction expected from a bourgeois-sympathizing work force who, certainly for a variety of reasons, are unable to stand up to the mining company for their own rights. Juan Fariña shakes the working life of the miners to the very core, quite literally from working deep in the mines, below the 'base' of the highly organized social structure of the mine. Juan's action is truly radical —in the Lefebvrian (Marxian) sense of the word—an all-inclusive, total rejection of the alienation he attributes to the realities of mine work. Significantly, the narrator's final summary of the events put in motion by Juan Fariña's destructive action is ambiguous, playing at once to both the fear of the people and Juan's underappreciated role as 'liberator.' As he puts it succinctly, "El nombre de Fariña estaba en todos los labios y nadie dudó un instante de que fuera el autor de la catástrofe que los libertaba para siempre de aquel presidio, donde tantas generaciones habían languidecido en medio de torturas y miserias ignoradas" (109). The implication is that Juan has managed to do on the miners' behalf what they have proved unable to do.

There is an interesting relevance here to what is referred to as the "theory of the spark" by Lefebvre (1968, 112) and others. Vladimir Lenin famously held that once the flame of revolution was ignited in a given location, it would spread from one country to the next in an explosive chain-reaction. Certainly Lillo does not dialogue explicitly with this "theory of the spark," but, on the other hand, he does manage to chronicle the insufficiency of individualist approaches to radical social change. From today's perspective, "Juan Fariña's" short-lived discrete revolutionary action and what follows forms a chain of events familiar with the contemporary trend toward the capitalistic management of marginal attempts at revolution. Looking to the student movements of 1968, Lefebvre points to the importance of collective action, and of the necessity for many groups to have bridged theory and practice—i.e. for such a

Chapter 2 - FIRE

movement to be both collective and political in its very origins (112). Lillo's devilish figure Juan does not engage the other miners as do Etienne and even to some extent Souvarine of Zola's *Germinal*, he does not challenge them to work with him or to, in Lefebvre's words "think the unthinkable" (113). Instead, he engages in a solitary contestation of the capitalist underpinnings of the mining system in Chile at that time, and is accordingly demonized by the population, doing away with the notion that the actions of a critical minority might be able to turn the tide on their own, unaided by a massive swell of support.

Whether or not this theory holds elsewhere, Lillo's text gives us no reason to believe that the explosion of a revolution which is literally underground will lead to more extensive revolutionary activity in the southern Chile represented in *Sub terra*. Even after Juan succeeds in exploding the mine, he becomes institutionalized as a social pariah or a common taboo, a mere devilish myth or remnant of a superstition whose work in the name of the population has been completely forgotten. With the first stroke of the clock at midnight on the anniversary of the great mining explosion,

> fórmase en las salobres ondas un pequeño remolino hirviente y espumoso, surgiendo de aquel embudo la formidable figura del ciego con las pupilas fijas en la mina desolada y muerta.
>
> Junto con la última vibración de las campanas se desvanece la temerosa aparición y una mancha de espuma marca el peligroso sitio, del que huyen velozmente las barcas pescadoes impulsadas por sus ágiles remeros y ¡ay! De la que se aventure demasiado cerca de aquel Maelstrom en miniatura, pues atraída por una fuerza misteriosa y zarandeada rudamente por las olas, se verá en riesgo de zozobrar. (110)

It is important to note, in this regard, that as the narrator ends the tale with the above superstitious warning, he has deliberately left out any discussion of the effects of the mine's closure upon the community. It may be reasonable to assume that other mines were opened nearby, or that miners were relocated to other already-existing projects (as in the fearful tale "El Chiflón del Diablo," for example), yet what is also clear is that Lillo has not wanted to problematize the story any further, thus keeping the superstitious community itself as the story's primary focus.

As opposed to other stories where he more clearly denounces the standard operating procedure of the mining company ("El Chiflón," "El pago," "Los inválidos"…), here the Chilean takes a wider view and shows how the workers themselves are complicit in their own exploitation. In this light, it is more significant than ever that Lillo has subtitled his story a 'legend'—the tale's complete title reads "Juan Fariña (leyenda)." The addition of the parenthetical 'leyenda [legend]' foregrounds not the facts of the tale itself but the *perception* of truthful events, mitigated by a specific group of people. The story can in this sense be taken as a commentary on a group of Chilean workers who are not merely unable to take up revolution due to pressing material concerns (the crushing poverty, eternal debt and inadequate pay of "El pago," for example), but who are moreover unable to escape tired patterns of an immaterial mode of thought that is mired in subjugation. Ultimately, the population's tendency to demonize outsiders, to work unquestioningly in the interests of the mining company, to allow superstition to trump a square assessment of their working and living conditions is more resistant to change than even the infrastructure of the mine itself. In a sense, this story is much more brutal than Zola's *Germinal*, where the population is eventually on the whole willing to stand up for their rights (albeit with more than a few complications).

Through the dramatic incorporation of underground explosions, both of Lillo's stories ("El grisú" and "Juan Fariña") capture the reality of spontaneous changes and their disastrous effects. In fact, much of the volume deals with perhaps the most important change in a human life—the suddenness of death. Of the eight stories included in the original text of *Sub terra*, only two are content to merely present chronic harsh working conditions (child-labor in "La compuerta" and indentured servitude in "El pago") while five of the remaining six treat death itself: in "Los inválidos" there is the impending death of a horse, in "El Chiflón del Diablo" Cabeza de Cobre dies underground and his mother subsequently throws herself into the pit, in "El pozo" a man in buried alive through another's

Chapter 2 - FIRE

trickery, "Juan Fariña" two night watchmen are killed in the mine, in "El grisú" a number of men are killed by a firedamp explosion. As a volume riven through by sudden changes, violent explosions and of course, death, *Sub terra* splendidly portrays the contradictory and multidimensional nature of modernity. There is a sense in his stories, as in the stories of other modernists of the time, of the fragile nature of structures, of the contradictions that lie underneath seemingly solid systems. For the Chilean, these contradictions take physical form in the shifting layers of rock exposed by mining activities and from which the dangerous firedamp gas oozes. In Lillo's stories one can perceive the importance of spontaneity. This importance is, to reverse chronology, reminiscent of Lefebvre's assessment of the revolutionary surge of the 1968 student movement. "Movement flares up where it was least expected; it completely changes the situation, which now emerges from the mass of facts and evaluations under which it had been hidden" (*The Explosion* 7). In a way, Lillo's focus on the apparent solidity of the mines and its disruption can be read as a physical foil for the immaterial qualities and spontaneity that coexists within any given set of social structures.

As Lefebvre writes, "There are imbalances and gaps everywhere, which sharpen or veil (these two effects may be superimposed) the already existing contradictions and antagonisms" (13). Through an eloquent mixture of overt physical dangers and subtle social critique *Sub terra* points to the ephemeral nature of a modernity riven through and though with and in fact constituted by contradiction. Although Lillo may not make an explicit call to arms in the name of socialism, the key contradiction of the volume is, of course the very same capitalistic contradiction later denounced in 1968 by Lefebvre. The French philosopher asks "As for the contradiction between private ownership of the means of production and the social character of productive labor, considered basic by Marx, can we maintain that it has been resolved, that it can be relegated to a secondary place?"; and Lefebvre's reply is, "Certainly not" (14).

If this was true in Lefebvre's industrialized European context of the 1960s, it was doubtless true in Lillo's Chile, which was still reeling from a period of intense militaristic and economic colonialism. Lillo's volume is (as discussed in both chapter one and the present chapter, above) in fact grounded in a criticism of the conditions of the class of workers who operate the mines in Southern Chile. There is a rift between those working in the mines themselves and the managers and mine bureaucrats who remain indifferent to their needs ("El pago"), between the poverty of a class of people who must work tethered to their work site from a young age ("La compuerta") and the opulence of the class represented by the portly Englishman Mister Davis ("El grisú"). And yet Lillo's workers have recourse neither to forms of collective action nor to disalienated forms of consciousness that would make such collective action feasible, as do the organized workers in Zola's *Germinal*. It is perhaps for this reason that the spontaneity requisite of collective anti-bourgeois action is lacking from *Sub terra*. In the place of such immaterial conditions for revolutionary spontaneity, the reader finds only the physical reification and reduction of such activity posited by false consciousness; instead of revolution, there is merely the material explosion of the firedamp, a physical change that stands in for an elusive social change that would be at once physical and mental. The internal contradictions of the mining system are not visible to the mine's workers. Without consciousness of these contradictions, there can be no "sudden extension of the movement" such as there would be in the case of 1968; there can be for Lillo's miners, no "intense, rapid, and lucid perception of immediate possibilities" for change (Lefebvre 113).

Whereas in Lillo we find sudden and destructive physical changes described without a corresponding shift in the consciousness of the miners themselves who experience them, the stories of Leopoldo Lugones are attentive to the alienation of individuals caught in the maelstrom of a rapidly changing modernity without a clear understanding of the social dimensions of the experienced events themselves. Where Lillo's stories stress the devastating events of a material reality, Lugones's tales focus on individual consciousness. As we will see, however, in both cases the effect is to portray the turn-of-the-twentieth-century experience of modernity as one in which the individual struggles to connect with others. Although both authors fail to portray the dialectical link between consciousness and material conditions, taken together Lillo and Lugones succeed in pointing to the importance of connecting material events with social and collective understandings.

Chapter 2 - FIRE

Lugones's *Las fuerzas extrañas*: The Apocalyptic Power of Fire

Fire was, for Lillo, a point of entry into all manner of materialist critique. For Lugones, on the other hand, fire was a more diffuse symbol for the unknown. As critics have shown (H. Fraser 1992), the Argentine proved to be—as were other modernists of the time—fascinated by apocalyptic symbols, changes that threatened to refashion a completely new reality. In this way, he invoked the unpredictable and contradictory forces of that nineteenth-century modernity of which Marx had remarked "All that is solid melts into air." Lugones's characters are witnesses to and often victims of extreme shifts in reality, taking the notion of an uncertain modernity (perhaps put most eloquently by Marx, but certainly not unique to his work) and pursuing it quite literally. Many stories from *Las fuerzas extrañas* depict pseudo-scientific investigations that draw upon the occultism popular at the time (and particularly the spiritualism of H.P.B., a.k.a. Madame Blavatsky, as will be discussed in the next chapter). These investigators set out to discover and harness the hidden but powerful forces in the cosmos and are subjected to the contradictory and explosive forces of a modernity that takes a less than compassionate stance toward the human pursuit of knowledge.

Two stories in the Lugones's collection of short fiction are notable for integrating fire into their exploration of a turbulent modernity. The final story in the collection *Las fuerzas extrañas*, "El psychon" works to establish the soft-glow of human auras and light (forms akin to fire) as a point of entry into the interconnectivity of the universe. Moreover, Lugones's well-crafted tale echoes the preoccupation with change that motivated Marx and other nineteenth-century thinkers. Here, it is not the solid that melts into air, but the seemingly ethereal, immaterial process of thought itself that congeals into a tangible form of matter. The title substance of the story—named 'el psychon' by its discoverer—is in fact thought rendered in physical form through pseudo-scientific research and experimentation, experimentation which results in some rather unfortunate circumstances. The second story, "La lluvia de fuego," deals more directly with the apocalyptic power of fire—the harsh manifestation of a non-human world which we may never completely understand. As described by a decadent bourgeois narrator-protagonist, a rain of burning copper falls intermittently upon his urban locale, seemingly without explanation. Here fire also expresses an intimate connection with fundamental and unknown forces of the universe and similarly provides a warning of the sea-change to come. Yet more importantly, fire becomes a way to address the notion of alienation which Marx outlined and which Henri Lefebvre continued to explore.

Scholars of the nineteenth-century well know that Marx regarded alienation most of all as a product of the eventual triumph of exchange-value over use-value. In brief, workers were progressively alienated from the fruits of their own labor and moreover from the real conditions of their own lives and of their relationships with others due to structural social and economic changes. Ideology then functioned as a veil, as an impediment to developing class-consciousness—an awareness of the changing deep structure or economic base of modern life. Whereas there has been a tendency to consider Marxian alienation in strictly economic terms, Henri Lefebvre has rightly recovered the global relevance of the term, noting in his *Critique of Everyday Life* (v. 1) that alienation is at once economic, philosophical, social, political, and ideological (249).

In a sense, all of the fantastic stories included in Lugones's volume have at their base a fascination with alienation that can be considered uniquely modern. The fact that so few of them deal directly with class relations (as we will see, "La lluvia de fuego" does), should in fact be interpreted as a displaced alienation itself—an implicit triumph of the ideology that obscures the real conditions of everyday life. Instead of addressing the sharp changes which have been noted by scholars of modernity—for example, the shift of the city from use-value to exchange value (covered by Lefebvre in *The Right to the City*) that took place over the eighteenth and nineteenth centuries, or the progressive industrialization and construction of a built environment for production (such as the mining infrastructure depicted in Lillo's *Sub terra*)—Lugones explores an imaginative allegorical foil for the deep shifts that came to characterize a modern sensibility. In short, the stories in *Las fuerzas extrañas* evoke the real conditions of a shifting and uncertain modernity not merely through

Chapter 2 - FIRE

their fantastic plots but more importantly through their omissions.

"El psychon" opens with a short academic biography of one Doctor Paulin, "ventajosamente conocido en el mundo científico por el descubrimiento del telectróscopo, el electroide y el espejo negro de los cuales hablaremos algún día" (135). The doctor, we are told by the story's unnamed narrator who manages to become his assitant in Buenos Aires, is "un físico distinguido" and a disciple of Wroblewski at the University of Cracovia: "habíase dedicado con preferencia al estudio de la licuación de los gases, problema que planteado imaginativamente por Lavoisier, debía quedar resuelto luego por Faraday, Cagniard-Latour y Thilorier" (136). The doctor's name is, we are informed, a necessary invention: "Nuestros médicos y hombres de ciencia leerán correctamente el nombre del personaje, que disimulo bajo un patronímico supuesto, tanto por carecer de autorización para publicarlo, cuanto porque el desenlace de este relato ocasionaría polémicas, que mi ignorancia no sabría sostener en campo científico" (135). Most importantly, the supposed 'Doctor Paulin' is, by his own admission, a spiritualist (136). The story mentions in passing such phenomena as 'dirigación' ("acción modificadora ejercida por la voluntad sobre determinadas partes del organismo" 136), thus touting a significant power of the mind over the body ("El espíritu es quien rige los tejidos orgánicos y las funciones fisiológicas, porque es él quien crea esos tejidos y asegura su facultad vital" 136). He also insists, somewhat fantastically, "que las exhalaciones fluídicas del hombre son percibidas por los sensitivos en forma de resplandores, rojos los que emergen del lado derecho, azulados los que se desprenden del izquierdo" (137). Doctor Paulin explains to the narrator that on one occasion, a 'sensitive' saw a yellow flame flare up from his occiput and grow to thirty centimeters in height (137). He then worked with a sensitive (Antonia) to conduct experiments which led him to believe that this light is obstructed by the growth of hair, but also that there is some connection between the lights atop the heads of people and the Earth's northern lights or aurora borealis: "habría una identidad curiosa; pues la raya 5567, coincidiría exactamente con la hermosa raya número 4 de la aurora boreal..." (139).[6] By explicitly analogizing the auras of human beings to the earth's lights, Lugones uses the soft glow of flames to suggest a mysterious connection between humankind and the universe itself at a more elemental level.

The elemental relationship signaled by Lugones's use of fire is merely a step toward a more thorough reconciliation of humankind with the cosmos. Building on studies of the liquefaction of gasses, the doctor manages, he believes, to produce 'pensamiento volatilizado' (142). Although thought is immaterial, its manifestations must be fluid, he reasons (142-43). The subsequent attempt to render thought in a physical form that he refers to as 'el psychon,' however, produces some unforeseeable events. After a presumably successful experiment, the doctor decides to let the volatized thought escape from the test tube through evaporation:

> la idea de que sería una inconveniencia estúpida saltar por encima de la mesa, acudió a mi espíritu; mas, apenas lo hube pensado, cuando ya el mueble pasó bajo mis piernas, no sin darme tiempo para ver que el doctor arrojaba al aire como una pelota su gato, un siamés legítimo, verdadera niña de sus ojos. El cuaderno fue a parar con una gran carcajada en las narices del doctors [...] Lo cierto es que durante una hora, estuvimos cometiendo las mayores extravagancias, con gran estupefacción de los vecinos a quienes atrajo el tumulto y que no sabían cómo explicarse la cosa. (145)

The story ends quickly, with the narrator noting that the doctor disappeared the next day, and that he is currently in a German asylum.

In "El psychon" it is the soft glow of fire which suggests a connection between what we now know and knowledge that lies just beyond our grasp. Fire comes to express the intimate interconnection of things, a relationship that finds its way into the texts of Modernists through the theorems of Pythagoras, as critics have noted (see Gullón 1968). Importantly, even in this intimate connection there is a danger. Lugones's stories tap into the social imaginary of upheaval to which late-nineteenth and early-twentieth-century modernists responded, a world constituted at its base by contradictory and unstable forces, an atmosphere of constant uncertainty. As Marshall Berman (1982) writes, "This atmosphere—of agitation and turbulence, psychic dizziness and drunkenness, expansion of

Chapter 2 - FIRE

experiential possibilities and destruction of moral boundaries and personal bonds, self-enlargement and self-derangement, phantoms in the street and in the soul—is the atmosphere in which modern sensibility is born" (18). Such an atmosphere is the bedrock of the stories in *Las fuerzas extrañas*, wherein Lugones seeks purposely uproot the modern reader from any feelings of solidity and thrust him or her into a world that is scarcely recognizable.

"El psychon" provides a notable example of this characteristic atmosphere, venturing into a world that functions as an allegory for the ever-shifting relations of late-nineteenth-century capitalist society. Marx famously chided the bourgeoisie for being akin to sorcerers: "Modern bourgeois society, a society that has conjured up such might means of production and exchange, is like the sorcerer who can no longer control his spells" (qtd. in Berman 101). Lugones's scientists are perhaps another similar metaphor for a trepidatious approach to the modern. Like Marx's sorcerers, they create experiments that go awry, ending in at best insanity ("El psychon"), at worst in death (see the discussion of "La metamúsica" in the following chapter). Yet even in this dangerous experimentation there is something redemptive about being able to tap into the undercurrents of modern life, to experience the power of the fundamental unity of things, a unity that has been progressively partitioned by what Henri Lefebvre calls the characteristic fragmenting of bourgeois society (*The Urban Revolution*). While the scientists are unable to sustain such a profound connection with the base of modern life, this may, strangely enough, be yet another one of modernity's contradictions

Whereas in "El psychon" fire functions as a mere point of entry into a fantastic world where everything is connected, in "La lluvia de fuego" Lugones portrays fire as an apocalyptic power that is mysteriously connected with man's sense of alienation from the conditions of his own life and from those of others. Progressively threatening rains of fire interrupt the hum-drum everyday life of an urban-dwelling bourgeois narrator-protagonist. Appropriately, the story begins on a relatively normal day, as emphasized in its first line reading "Recuerdo que era un día de sol hermoso" (39). After a mere three sentences which quite unremarkably describe the weather and the narrator's view from his terrace ("la recta gris de una avenida..."), the mood abruptly shifts as a new paragraph begins with the shocking declaration that: "A eso de las once cayeron las primeras chispas" (39). The event is incongruously narrated in a quite blasé manner, as if delivered as a product of rote-memorization. The fuzzy precision regarding the time of the event tends to reproduce the exaggerated objectivity of a news-report. Thus the rain of fire begins: "partículas de cobre incandescente que daban en el suelo con un ruidecito de arena" (39). Lugones's narrator is detached enough to be relieved that the destruction does not immediately impact him more directly ("Por fortuna la brisa se levantaba, inclinando aquella lluvia singular hacia el lado opuesto de mi terraza," 40). He takes pleasure in not being disrupted from his 12 o'clock-noon lunch schedule ("En fin, aquello no había de impedirme almorzar, pues era el mediodía" 40). It is crucial to the story that the narrator and protagonist is a bourgeois land-owner who has a slave who reads to him exciting his imagination through travel narratives of exotic places (40) as well as several servants, owns a mansion with a garden, is held in esteem by important folk of the city and informs the reader he is entitled to a municipal bust. He hates both men and women, laments the ten years passed since his last orgy and considers the place where he lives a "vasta ciudad libertina." When his slave is hit in the back by a drop of burning copper falling from the sky, he merely complains that his appetite is ruined ("Bruscamente acabó mi apetito"), but he nevertheless continues eating so as not to offend the help (41).

The sounds of the city and its regular traffic soon cease (41) as the rain builds: "Las chispas venían de todas partes y de ninguna. Era la inmensidad desmenuzándose invisiblemente en fuego. Caía del firmamento el terrible cobre—pero el firmamento permanecía impasible en su azul" (42). Upon initially considering the possibility of fleeing, the narrator's concerns are instead directed toward his possessions "Pensé con horror en mis possessions." The effective punctuation of this moment with the frequent invocation of the possessive pronoun "mi/mis" (e.g. "*mi* mesa, *mis* libros, *mis* pájaros, *mis* peces [...] *mis* jardines [...] *mis* cincuenta años de placidez," emphasis added, 42; also 40) emphasizes the narrator's selfishness and the overarching importance of his comfortable bourgeois lifestyle.

When the rain of fire stops, the city comes back to life ("[la ciudad] despertaba de su fugaz atonía, doblemente gárrula," 43). The entrepeneurial spirit of its denizens revives as many of them rush to

Chapter 2 - FIRE

collect, market and sell the cooling copper lying all about, left behind as a result of the rain of fire ("Muchachos afanosos, recogían en escudillas la granalla de cobre, que los caldereros habían empezado a comprar," 43). Similarly, the city's sexual economy revives: prostitutes immediately return to selling their wares ("un equívoco mancebo [con su] tunica recogida hasta las caderas en un salto de bocacalle [...], Las cortesanas, con la seno desnudo según la nueva moda"), an old man drives by selling dirty pictures, and a eunuch sells stimulating fabrics (43). The decadent city is invigorated now due to enduring the threat of death: "La ciudad, caprichosamente iluminada, había aprovechado la coyuntura para decretarse una noche de fiesta [...] El césped de los parques palpitaba de parejas..." (44). When the deadly rain of fire returns, however, awakening the narrator during the night, the trees have all been charred, and the servants and horses have all fled. Making his way to the cellar under a metal bathing tub, the narrator—forever a decadent—drinks a bottle of wine, and extracts a poisonous wine from its secret hiding place ("Todos los que teníamos bodega poseíamos uno," 45).

The misanthropic narrator almost rejoices in the suffering around him "Quemada en sus domecilios, la gente huía despavorida, para arderse en las calles, en la campiña desolada; y la población agonizó bárbaramente, con ayes y clamores de una amplitud, de un horror, de una variedad estupendos. Nada hay tan sublime como la voz humana" (46). Only after a lengthy paragraph describing the apocalyptic effects of the rain does the bourgeois narrator break down into an emotional response "me acometió de pronto un miedo que no sentía—estoy seguro—desde cuarenta años atrás, el miedo infantil de una presencia enemiga y difusa; y me eché a llorar, a llorar como un loco, a llorar de miedo, allá en un rincón, sin rubor alguno" (47). After the burning copper rain stops for the second time, the city has been destroyed ("la ciudad ya no existía [...] hedía como un verdadero cadáver" 48). An enigmatic boatman (Noah? Charron?) comes to visit the narrator, and a great number of lions creep in from desert to invade the city, after which the rain of fire begins yet again. The story ends with the bourgeois narrator committing suicide by imbibing his poisonous reserve, refusing to resign himself to a world devoid of the decadence of material wealth and worldly things. Now immersed in some fresh water from a cistern in his cellar—his funeral bath ("mi baño fúnebre)—and "apenas turbado por la curiosidad de la muerte," his final thoughts are a testament to his inability to think outside of the bourgeois existence to which he has become accustomed: "El agua fresca y la oscuridad, me devolvieron a las voluptuosidades de mi existencia de rico que acababa de concluir. Hundido hasta el cuello, el regocijo de la limpieza y una ulce impression de domesticidad, acabaron de serenarme" (50-51).

The most obvious interpretive framework for this story, as was noted in the introduction to this book, is surely the biblical one, supported by the quote from Leviticus with which "La lluvia de fuego" begins ("Y tornaré el cielo de hierro y la tierra de cobre" 39). In this way, both the narrator and his city are subject to the wrath of a god who wipes away the sin and corruption of a modern day Gomorrah. Yet appropriately given Lugones's penchant for mysticism, particularly that of renowned Theosophist Madame Blavatsky (to be discussed in the next chapter), there is no direct mention of a godly force, let alone a monotheistic notion derived from biblical texts. If the Argentine pursues a godly punishment, its cause is at best only indirectly discussed through the filter of a self-centered bourgeois narrator and quite more plausibly is absent altogether. Lugones delivers not the didactic reprimand of an old-testament vindictive God who seeks to raise humanity to a higher moral plane, but instead an altogether mysterious event without any explanation whatsoever. Ultimately, Lugones allows the mystery of the story to overshadow any didactic or biblical message, preferring to leave the reader disturbed by the literary destruction of the modern world as he or she knows it.

Coexisting with the biblical imagery of the story, however, there is a rich description and condemnation of a decidedly modern urban culture which affords another interpretive framework for "La lluvia de fuego." In is perhaps just as appropriate to read Lugones's story in the context of a turn-of-the-century urban atmosphere as it is in relation to ancient biblical texts, if not more so. The story describes, to be sure, a modern city with traffic and urban noise (when the rain initially falls, "El cielo seguía de igual limpidez; el rumor urbano no decrecía. Unicamente los pájaros de mi pajarera, cesaron de cantar" 39), a city that is subjected in the story to a progressive take-over by the rural. From this perspective, the story chronicles

Chapter 2 - FIRE

a particularly modern form of urban consciousness through the thoughts of its bourgeois protagonist.

For early twentieth-century urban sociologist Georg Simmel, the urban context required and subsequently produced a necessarily blasé attitude in its inhabitants. In his "The Metropolis and Mental Life" (1903), published only a few years prior to *Las fuerzas extrañas* (1906), Simmel wrote that "The psychological basis of the metropolitan type of individuality consists in the *intensification of nervous stimulation* which results from the swift and uninterrupted change of outer and inner stimuli" (original emphasis). He continues:

> Lasting impressions, impressions which differ only slightly from one another, impressions which take a regular and habitual course and show regular and habitual contrasts— all these use up, so to speak, less consciousness than does the rapid crowding of changing images, the sharp discontinuity in the grasp of a single glance, and the unexpectedness of onrushing impressions. These are the psychological conditions which the metropolis creates. (150)

Necessarily confronting the exacting pace of city-life, Simmel maintains, the "deeply felt and emotional relationships" of small town life are effectively rendered obsolete. A newly urbanized consciousness has thus seen the rise (and the functional necessity) of what he calls a "blasé attitude" where the urbanite must cultivate a "state of indifference" to stay afloat in the rapid current of urban life.

Appropriately, in the story we read not merely of a confusing urban context, the "vasta confusion de techos, vergeles salteados, un trozo de bahía punzado de mástiles, la recta gris de una avenida..." (39), for example, but also of the blasé attitude of an urban dweller such as the protagonist and narrator; a person who retreats from the overwhelming stimulation that characterizes modern city life to a detached even alienated mode of living. This detachment, this alienation, Simmel argues, makes it easier for the urbanite to cope with the ubiquitous oversignification of life in the city. The narrator of "La lluvia de fuego" is in fact portrayed engaging in this struggle to visually assess the rain of fire from within an urban context at the beginning of the story. "Casualmente lo había advertido, mirando hacia el horizonte en un momento de abstracción. Primero creí en una ilusión ótica formada por mi miopía" (39). The fire storm, which the narrator calls "un espectáculo singular" (45) is arguably difficult to discern against the stimulating background of an equally spectacular urban context. The narrator of Lugones's story cultivates what Simmel called a 'state of indifference' throughout—as when sparks fall onto his house, when they hit his slave in the back, and when he seems to relish in the population's suffering (as above).

But the relevance of the story to just such an urban approach can be seen most clearly in the pattern of alienation and disalienation and that obtains in the bourgeois protagonist's own assessment of his shifting situation. Lugones's narrator draws attention to his own alienation from the outset, relating it explicitly to his urban context: "La vasta ciudad libertina, era para mí un desierto donde se refugiaban mis placeres. Escasos amigos; breves visitas; largas horas de mesa; lecturas; mis peces; mis pájaros; una que otra noche tal cual orquesta de flautistas, y dos o tres ataques de gota por año…" (41). Seemingly sick of it all, he is slow to react emotionally to the rain of fire (as above), and never quite develops a deep response to the catastrophe. The narrator is more alienated, still, than other urbanites who are moved by the catastrophe to excessive celebration.

> La gente sentía necesidad de visitarse después de aquellas chispas de cobre. De visitarse y de beber, pues ambos se retiraron completamente borrachos. Yo hice una rápida salida. La ciudad, caprichosamente iluminada, había aprovechado la coyuntura para decretarse una noche de fiesta. En algunas cornisas, alumbraban perfumando, lámparas de incienso. Desde sus balcones, las jóvenes burguesas, excesivamente ataviadas, se divertían en proyectar de un soplo a las narices de los transeúntes distraídos, tripas pintarrajeadas y crepitantes de cascabeles. En cada esquina se bailaba. De balcón a balcón cambiábanse flores y gatitos de dulce. El césped de los parques, palpitaba de parejas… (44)

In the carnavalesque upside-down world of the street festival por-

Chapter 2 - FIRE

trayed in Lugones's story there is not only a temporary inversion of social norms but also an opportunity for a more thorough reassessment of society itself. Significantly, however, this opportunity never comes.

Significantly, Lefebvre writes extensively both of the festival (*Critique of Everyday Life* v. 3, 1981) and more broadly of alienation. For Lefebvre, expanding upon Marx's understanding, alienation is taken to be multiple in nature: at once economic, philosophical, social, political, and ideological (*Critique of Everyday Life* v. 1, 1947: 249). Alienation is not a single unit or entity—in fact there are many alienations (*Critique of Everyday Life* v. 2, 1961: 207). Lefebvre quite astutely takes history itself to be the dialectical movement between alienation and dis-alienation. Considered from this perspective, in "La lluvia de fuego" we witness the rapid passing of time as society jumps from one era to another, eras marked by the burning copper rains. Yet with each periodic rain, disalienation—especially so in the case of the protagonist—is nonexistent. Here is a person who refuses at each step to take stock of his thoughts, desperately clinging to his decadent vision of a world composed by possessions/material goods alone. Abandoned by his servants, his horses—and eventually by his things themselves as they are destroyed by the rains of burning copper—the narrator identifies with his material things to such a degree that he chooses to perish with them by drinking the poisonous wine in the story's final line ("Llevé el pomo a mis labios, y…" 51). Ultimately, Lugones's protagonist pursues a curious reification of himself. His evolution in the story results only in, to appropriate Marx's words, a "stultifying [of] human life into a material force" (qtd. in Berman 20). Similarly, he may seen as one of those bourgeois denounced by Marx who would rather die than face "the real conditions of their lives and their relations with their fellow men" (qtd. in Berman 21).

As opposed to Lillo's massive subterranean explosions ("El grisú" and "Juan Fariña"), Lugones's copper rain charts out a slower-paced but nonetheless portentous and even catastrophic change in "La lluvia de fuego." It is important to note that, whereas the mining-disasters of *Sub terra* are always communal, Lugones depicts tragic events experienced by isolated individuals with few witnesses, if any ("El psychon") or communal events whose importance is limited to the perspective of one person ("La lluvia de fuego"). There is an even more important distinction to make, however. Whereas the Chilean addresses the mutability of physical environments without a corresponding change in thought, the Argentine focuses on the reluctance of patterns of immaterial thought to change. *Sub terra* and *Las fuerzas extrañas* ultimately work together in a complementary fashion to show how a mere change in the built environment for production, how a mere change in the material conditions of society, may mean nothing without a corresponding shift in consciousness. This shift in consciousness needed in order to work for a more just society neither determines nor is determined by physical changes. Both material and immaterial components are required for a fundamental shift in the quality of contemporary life. As the next section explores, recent debates in geography have in a way recuperated the modernist conception of a contradictory world in providing for an approach that conceives of an appropriate methodology as one that admits the conflict between opposing forces—both material and immaterial.

Modernity, Materiality and Immateriality

It is important to remember that, for Marx, the contradictory and uncertain essence of modernity was related to a pattern of human behaviors. Henri Lefebvre maintained this notion in the elaboration of the Marxian concepts he pursued throughout his three-volume *Critique of Everyday Life* (1947, 1961, 1981). Lefebvre pushed Marx's notions of alienation and the spatial nature of capital further than his nineteenth-century predecessor while continuing to articulate a distinctly Marxian understanding of modernity (most explicitly in *Introduction to Modernity* and *Everyday Life in the Modern World*). What allowed Lefebvre to expand so well upon Marx's earlier formulation of modernity as contradictory (so eloquently captured by Marshall Berman in chapter two of his *All that is Solid Melts into Air*, 1982) was the concept of totality. Lefebvre saw this totality in a Marxian way as always uneven (a word incorporated by Lenin into the phrase 'uneven development'), and he stridently sought to depict how a certain form of spatializing bourgeois thought fragmented

Chapter 2 - FIRE

this unitary if uneven reality into seemingly discrete sectors that ultimately supported its own needs. Whereas elsewhere I have more thoroughly explored the relationship between Lefebvre's Marxism and Bergsonian philosophical positions (Fraser 2008), here I want to stress Lefebvre's insistence that a fragmentary mode of thought arises along with significant changes wrought of the nineteenth-century. His numerous volumes centering on the urban problem may in fact be understood as an extended critique of this mode of fragmentary thought.

Lefebvre writes of the fragmenting process of bourgeois thought in numerous works, of which I will give only a few examples here. In *Rhythmanalysis* (1992) he pursues the thought that reifies time as space and fragments totality as a 'general law' of society: "quantified time subjects itself to a very general law of this society: it becomes both uniform and monotonous whilst also breaking apart and becoming fragmented. Like space, it divides itself into lots and parcels: transport networks, themselves fragmented, various forms of work, entertainment and leisure" (74). This posthumously published work throughout advances an alternative mode of perception and critique (centering, namely, on the analysis not of fragments but of rhythms) as an antidote to the pervasive operation of this general law. Similarly, in *The Urban Revolution* (1970), he laments the unfortunate fragmentary contribution of specialized sciences and acknowledges the realities produced through this form of thought (53), but nevertheless pushes beyond fragmentation to suggest a reconstitution of the totality of urban life: "Without the progressive and regressive movements (in time and space) of analysis, without the multiple divisions and fragmentations, it would be impossible to conceive of a science of the urban phenomenon. But such fragments do not constitute knowledge" (49). In *The Right to the City* (1968), Lefebvre devotes a chapter to a concise presentation of this problematic (ch. 5 "Fragmentary Sciences and Urban Reality"), declaring that: "The philosopher does not acknowledge separation, he does not conceive that the world, life, society, the cosmos (and later, history) can no longer make a Whole" (88). Recuperating Bergson's idea of philosophy as an attempt 'to dissolve again into the Whole' (1907: 191), and giving it a more explicitly political inflection, Lefebvre consistently denounces the fragmenting tendency through which bourgeois thought and action has obscured the understanding of modern life as a totality: both in through immaterial conceptions (philosophical, quotidian) and their material expressions (see *The Production of Space*, particularly 20-22).

Throughout his century-spanning life of sustained engagement with the urban phenomenon (b. 1901, d. 1991), Lefebvre charts the development of this characteristic fragmentation through the strict division of human knowledge into separate disciplines. This he does through the spatialized approach to structuring the city, through spatial frameworks that conceptually oppose town to country, public to private space; groups of mental categorizations that stem from a social division of labor (*The Urban Revolution* 60). Most significantly, Lefebvre sees such fragmentary processes of thought as wrought of a nineteenth-century shift:

> During the course of the nineteenth century, the sciences of social reality are constituted against philosophy which strives to grasp the global (by enclosing a real totality into a rational systematization). These sciences fragment reality in order to analyse it, each having their method or methods, their sector or domain. After a century, it is still under discussion whether these sciences bring distinct enlightenment to a unitary reality, or whether the analytical fragmentation that they use corresponds to objective differences, articulations, levels and dimensions. (*The Right to the City* 94)

From the perspective of Lefebvre's recalibrated Marxism, the dawn of modernity may be linked to the thorough imbrication of an instrumentalist tendency of mind in our institutions and everyday life. A particularly pertinent question for Lefebvre is thus: "How can we make the transition from fragmentary knowledge to complete understanding?" (*The Urban Revolution* 56).

It is the nineteenth-century bourgeois mode of thought—connected to the extensive bourgeois reconstitution of social systems where exchange-value comes to trump use-value—that perhaps makes it necessary to reassert the intimate union of everything with everything else. The European occult revival of the early twentieth century (for whom Bergson played an important role, see Grogin

Chapter 2 - FIRE

1988) may be seen in part, as a reaction against the institutionalization of just such an intellectual/analytical fragmentation of the unity of modern life during the previous century. Lugones's stories, in particular, must be seen as springing from this need to connect, to reach an underlying totality which has been obscured by bourgeois spatialization. The research undertaken by Doctor Paulin of "El psychon" and the apocalyptic copper rain of "La lluvia de fuego" both point to this essential unity of modern experience. Furthermore, the need to reestablish a Pythagorean universal harmony underlies the events of other stories from *Las fuerzas extrañas* such as "La metamúsica" and "La fuerza Omega," as will be discussed in the next chapter.

From this perspective, however, Lugones's notion of totality is itself a peculiar one. In Lillo, for example, there is a clear presentation of social differentiation. The lack of a totality portrayed in *Sub terra* is connected to unfair management practices, greedy pit-bosses, careless foremen, unsympathetic and cold cashiers. There is, in short, a human element to the fragmentation and alienation he depicts. Lugones, on the other hand, takes alienation almost as an *a priori* to human experience. His stories deal less with the social realities of alienation but rather with a mystical and even aestheticized (ideological) vision of it. The individual researcher functions as a synecdoche for all humankind, who are similarly alienated from a primordial essence that has the potential to affect them all equally. Yet at the same time that they arguably accept and work from within the characteristically bourgeois fragmentary mode of knowledge, they nevertheless also provide a glimpse of the dangers of this fragmentary approach and point to a fusion of the material and immaterial. Consider the central image of "El psychon" where a psychic element is rendered in physical form.[7] Doctor Paulin's goal to materialize immaterial processes in fact squares with a goal of much recent geographical scholarship. Just as materiality and immateriality were two constitutive aspects of a contradictory modernity articulated through the stories of Lillo and Lugones, contemporary scholarship struggles to connect these two. When such scholarship errs, it errs by overemphasizing either one or the other.

As many geographers now indicate, a proper methodology admits the materiality of the immaterial and the immateriality of the material. As Alan Latham and Derek McCormack write in their

"Moving Cities: Rethinking the Materialities of Urban Geographies" (2004), our approach to urban geography could be improved by acknowledging "a notion of the material that admits from the very start the presence and importance of the immaterial" (703). Moving toward this notion has required an upheaval of sorts from within geography, most significantly a philosophical reassessment of the methods used. As Ali Madanipour so wonderfully states in his *Design of Urban Space* (1996), the concept of space itself is one path into a series of relations of immaterialities and materialities.

> The dilemmas of space appear to lie in the way we relate to it: the way we understand and therefore transform, it. The debates between absolute and relational space, the dilemma between physical and social space, between real and mental space, between space and mass, between function and form, between abstract and differential space, between space and place, between space and time, can all be seen as indicators of a series of open philosophical questions: how do we understand space and relate to it? Does it exist beyond our cognition or is it conditioned by it? Do we relate to it by our reason or our senses? Is space a collection of things and people, a container for them, or are they embedded in it? Is it representing openness or fixity? Do we understand and transform space individually or socially? How do we relate space and time? In our response to these questions, we find ourselves divided between rationalism and empiricism, between materialism and idealism, between objective and subjective understanding, between reason and emotion, between theory and practice, between uniformity and diversity, and between order and disorder. (28-29)

More broadly, theorists in geography such as Dear (2000), Foucault (1975), Harvey (1989; 1990; 1996; 2000), Jessop (1999), Latham and McCormack (2004), Lefebvre (1974), Madanipour (1996), D. Mitchell (2000), T. Mitchell (1999), Marston (2000; 2004), Soja (1996), Thorns (2002) and Tilly (1999) have engaged this problematic explicitly or implicitly, tracing its relevance to a variety of sub-

Chapter 2 - FIRE

relationships that all tie back in to larger questions of the dialectical relationship between the immaterial(mental) and the material(physical). For example: David Harvey (2000) looks "From Place to Space and Back Again," Charles Tilly (1999) advises us to go "toward relational analyses of political processes" (419), Bob Jessop (1999) asserts that the boundaries between the economic and the political are of cultural origin (380), Michel Foucault (1975) looks at the way disciplines originate at the level of the individual and take on the form of repeated spatial practice, Tim Mitchell (1999) argues that the "state effect" arises from the material and provides a framework for a "double-articulation" between the Foucaldian notion of disciplines ascending to more global constructions of power, and Sallie Marston (2004) calls for recognition of the "'nexus' among" and "mutually constitutive nature of the categories" of state, culture and space (38). In "The Social Construction of Scale," Marston (2000) presents an incisive and convincing look into how ideas of scale, itself not ontologically given, become shaped by social practice. As one of the most important names in the subdisciplines of human, cultural and urban geography, Henri Lefebvre's works reasserted the philosophical basis for understanding the production of space, warning of the dangers inherent in simplifying the interaction of both immaterial and material processes.

As I hope to have shown in this chapter, this simple opposition may itself be taken as a particularly significant example of the contradictions of modernity. I suggested that Lillo's stories explore the solidity/physical nature of things, while Lugones's stories delve into the life of the mind, either as it is stultified by a narrator whose 'state of indifference' reduces him to a base materiality ("La lluvia de fuego"), or as it seemingly overcomes the limitations of the material science known as physics, sensing auras and rendering thought itself in tangible form ("El psychon"). In each case, the stories in question call upon fire as an elemental force that leads humankind to deal with a complete transformation of reality. The deliberate use of fire by both authors makes use of a rich and longstanding symbolic tradition. Flames stand at the threshold of materiality and seemingly intangible immateriality. Fire destroys the physical, converts solid to air, and in so doing, as primitive humans recognized through ritual practices, points to a world beyond our immediate perception. It signals the propensity for change from one state to another. Just as the smoldering ash may ignite into flame, this intangibly-unknown could be rendered tangible, the immaterial rendered material, much as the narrator of "El psychon" seeks to prove.

If modernity is contradiction, then Lillo and Lugones point to the problems encountered by approaches that either attempt to focus on the material at the expense of the immaterial (social) relations or on the immaterial powers of thought at the expense of changing material realities (redistribution of wealth, for example). Marx believed that the shifting nature of bourgeois capitalism would lead inexorably through crises to an awareness that would result in a transition to more equitable social relations, as humankind was more broadly able to assess the real conditions of their own lives and their relations with others. For these two authors in particular who were writing during the heyday of Latin American literary modernism, fire symbolized the possibility of this upheaval at the same time that it warned of disastrous consequences. Fire becomes the intersection of two contradictory tendencies of experience, the material and the immaterial, fusing contradiction or perhaps just melting it away. Marx perhaps put it best: "All that is solid melts into air," which brings us to the next chapter.

3

AIR:
THE PLANET OF SOUND
(LUGONES)

> [...] I got to somewhere renowned
> for its canals and color of red
> and lots of guys who shook their heads
> rhythmically to resound
> this ain't the planet of sound [...]
> —The Pixies, "Planet of Sound" (1991)

In a notably cacophonous song by the highly influential and captivating band The Pixies, front-man Frank Black sings of a starship flying space-traveler who bounces from planet to planet searching for the so-called "Planet of Sound." With each planet upon which he touches down in his fission-ignited spacecraft ("I picked me up a transmission / I turned the fission ignition"), he finds that his journey must go on, Goldilocks-style until the right planet is found. On a mars-like red planet of deep canals, "lots of guys" tell him to push on; on another, a "guy in a rover" says the planet of sound is just one more planet over; on another he is simply told to leave—as the chorus emphasizes, in each case, "this ain't the planet of sound." As in many other Pixies' songs, here the lyrics are strangely both humorous and enigmatic. The motivation behind them may certainly be shockingly quotidian, as is the case in the famed "Wave of Mutilation" in which singer Black draws upon a Japanese news-story which discussed the tragic trend of businessmen who would commit suicide by driving off of piers with their families in the car. Whatever the motivation for "Planet of Sound" may be, however, the story narrated through the song's lyrics proves illuminating regarding the state of the debate concerning the place of sound in contemporary geography.

In many ways, geography is a discipline that has historically taken its subject matter to be precisely that—matter itself, the quantifiable materialities of landscapes. In this traditional approach immaterial processes have largely played a limited second role, and the interaction between material and sonorous realities have been neglected. This bias is not merely a disciplinary one—as can be seen in commonly-used phrases which prioritize the more tangible physical world over less material realities ("well-grounded" individuals have their "feet on the ground," and do not have their "head in the clouds"); and action over the sound of mere words ("all bark and no bite"). The reason for this entrenched bias seems to be self-evident and understandable—because we cannot see air, generally speaking, it becomes all too easy to dismiss it. Yet air is not merely some immaterial void, but rather the vehicle for sounds, music and perhaps most fundamentally, speech, all of which play a significant role in the production of our physical realities.

A similar recuperation of the value and importance of sound subtends much of the work of Leopoldo Lugones. Part of his *Las fuerzas extrañas* includes an "Ensayo de una cosmogonía en diez lecciones"—implicitly a tribute to the culture of orality that extends deeply into human history. The Argentine returns to what is perhaps, the birth of the oral tradition—the myths created to explain what would otherwise be left unexplained: our origins and the nature of the universe itself. His Cosmogony is appropriately couched in a frame story that accentuates the oral tradition ("Proemio" 147-48). While walking in the Andes, the narrator comes across a man whose power of speech is entrancing.

> Arrobado verdaderamente por su conversación, confieso que las horas se me iban sin sentirlo, así las ideas expresa-

Chapter 3 - AIR

das por aquellos labios fuesen de las más extraordinarias; pero entre ellas y su autor, había cierta correlación de singularidad que las hacía enteramente aceptables mientras él hablaba. (147)

The narrator feels that he has been chosen, in turn, to communicate the stories he hears to others ("yo fui tomado como agente para comunicar tales ideas, papel que acepto desde luego con la más perfecta humildad" 148). As a recuperation of an oral tradition—a tribute to the power of speech itself—the Cosgmogony functions as both an attempt to use myth to restore a solid ground to a chaotic modern world in constant flux and also as a reminder that this flux is in fact the ground of experience (the expression that 'change is the unchanging'…)—a modernist's idealized notion of a primitive past and at the same time a universalization of the contradictory essence of modernity.

In the Cosmogony's first lesson, life is portrayed as consisting fundamentally of change: "la eterna conversión de las cosas en otras distintas" / "la continuidad de la vida se mantiene en la periodicidad" / "Vivir es estar continuamente viniendo a ser y dejando de ser" (149). In this continuing process of life, that which is material becomes immaterial, and likewise, that which is immaterial takes on material form:

> *lo que viene a ser* se llama *materia, y lo que deja de ser* se llama *energía*; pero claro está que estas cosas figuran aquí como entidades abstractas. No obstante, como las manifestaciones polares de la vida, se permutan, lo que viene a ser, es decir la materia, proviene de la energía y viceversa. (149-50)

Through the voice of his unnamed narrator, Lugones establishes that previous to the founding of our present known universe, there was a universe of pure ether. Through this primordial ether, there ran a movement of a kind not unlike electricity (152-53). In the sixth lesson of the Cosmogony, while charting out the evolution of this universe, he underscores the friction produced in this ether by the movement of atoms acquiring an almost infinite velocity (168). Those atoms surviving this friction become representative of huge amounts of energy—but sound is also produced:

> La armonía vibratoria formada por proporciones numéricas, que resulta de este acomodo tanto como de la estructura poliédrica de los átomos, es el prototipo de las vibraciones armónicas que llamamos música, y que explica a la vez la "música de las esferas" de Pitágoras y el poder constructor de la lira de Amphion; pues siendo el sonido fuerza primordial, es naturalmente fuerza creadora. (168-69)

The creative potential of sound, which is manifest in a variety of creation myths across different cultures, is later also described as "una fuerza primordial [...] la que ordena los átomos en series armónicas" (189).

It would be more tempting to dismiss Lugones's literary re-valuation of sound as mere occultism were it not for the fact that many theorists of late have also been suggesting that more attention be paid to sound. As a recent volume titled *Hearing Cultures: Essays on Sound, Listening and Modernity* (Ed. Veit Erlmann, Berg Press, 2004) suggests, the hegemonic idea that vision and visuality are of greater importance than sound proves to be quite insufficient (see particularly Kahn, Douglas. "Ether Ore: Mining Vibrations in American Modernist Music," 107-30). In one of the volume's essays titled "Hearing Modernity: Egypt, Islam and the Pious Ear," Charles Hirschkind notes "a growing recognition in anthropology that central to the historical configuration of what we call modernity is a vast reorganization of sensory experience" (131). Similarly, the essays in the volume *Sound States: Innovative Poetic and Acoustical Technologies* seek "to give the reader an earful," as the collection's editor puts it (Morris 3), exploring the rich textures of sonorous realities. More broadly speaking, as this chapter will explore, there is a renaissance of the importance of sound in both cultural geography and even neuroscience, as scholars dispense with the erroneous assumption that sound is no more than a mere surface disturbance draped across our solid material realities.

In what follows, I want to address the complex role of sound as it appears in two of the stories from Leopoldo Lugones's

Chapter 3 - AIR

Las fuerzas extrañas ("La metamúsica" and "La fuerza Omega"). There is no mistaking the fact that, in these stories, Lugones invokes the occult pseudo-scientific understanding of the power of sound. Sound provides a point of entry into the chaotic unity that underlies our experience. This reading will not be content merely to locate Lugones within this occult tradition, however. Instead, the present discussion will be informed by contemporary perspectives on sound and music drawn from a variety of disciplines. In this way, I hope to show that Lugones's stories are pertinent to a more current philosophical reconciliation of material and immaterial realities. This chapter thus builds upon the resonance of *Las fuerzas extrañas* with a Latin American stylized literary modernism. As famed Argentine author and critic Jorge Luis Borges put it so well in his monograph on Lugones (titled simply *Leopoldo Lugones*), "La historia de Leopoldo Lugones es inseparable de la historia del modernismo, aunque su obra, en conjunto, exceed los límites de esta escuela" (15). Exploring the role played by sound in two of Lugones's stories offers a way to evaluate Borges's apt statement. As works of literature, both "La metamúsica" and "La fuerza Omega" incorporate Modernist principles; as documents of a turn-of-the-century fascination with pseudo-science, their significance goes beyond their literary context to anticipate more contemporary theoretical understandings of sound.

Lugones as Occult Neuro-Musicologist

> "La identidad de la mente con las fuerzas directrices del cosmos—concluía en ocasiones, filosofando—es cada vez más clara [...] [E]l sonido es materia."
> —Lugones, "La fuerza Omega" (1906)

The distinguished critic Howard M. Fraser ends his captivating study titled *In the presence of Mystery: Modernist Fiction and the Occult* (1992) with a call for criticism to synthesize occultism and Modernist literature. Responding to this call, I propose going one step further—thus this chapter not only delves into the infusion of occultism into Modernist literature but also underscores the relevance of a few of its pseudo-scientific premises for today's scientific understanding of sonorous realities. Although sound plays an important role in other stories by the argentine (including the speaking ape and flowers of "Yzur" and "Viola Acherontia," respectively; the potent death-inducing word at the end of the story "La estatua de sal"), it is in two outstanding stories of the volume *Las fuerzas extrañas* (1906) by Leopoldo Lugones (titled "La metamúsica" and "La fuerza Omega") that the literary presentation of the mysterious power of sound squares quite well with a contemporary scientific tendency that expounds a close relationship between the brain, music and emotion (Sacks, Levitin, Damasio). Rooted also in the sonorous inflection that has influenced contemporary sociology and geography, this study proposes a similar recovery of the importance of sound, one that is now taking hold in the fertile fields of various academic disciplines (See B. Anderson, Morton & Revill, Connell & Gibson, Smith, Waterman; regarding sociology, see DeNora).

In the figure of Lugones, we see not merely an enchanting poet and author of prose—who possessed a "genio […] fundamentalmente verbal (Borges)—but also an astute scientist, although not necessarily of the first order, who nevertheless enjoys greater recognition in the realm of literature. Leopoldo Lugones, the son of the famous author discussed in this chapter, has rightly emphasized that his father had explicitly studied occultism and had even carried out a few experiments in that area. Even if it is not possible to establish with certitude that the elder Lugones was much more than a neophyte in the universe of science, it without a doubt is worth the trouble to consider his literary presentation of music/sound as faithful not merely to the pseudo-science of his day, but also to the precepts of a science that is today more accepted. In brief, this chapter seeks to sustain that Lugones was in fact a neuro-musicologist before his time.

It is well known that sound played a highly important role in Modernism, understood as a literary movement native to Latin America. One has only to flip through the most canonical works of modernism, for example: the onomatopoeia of the "aserrín, aserrán" of "Los maderos de San Juan," by José Asunción Silva; the consonant rhyme of the musically-titled poem "Sonatina," by Rubén Darío; and, finally, the privilege given to musical form within modernism itself, a movement that emphasized the artistic genre of poetry over (but not to the exclusion of) others such as the short story

Chapter 3 - AIR

and the novel. Some now classic studies, notably those of Raymond Skyrme and Cathy Login Jrade, have emphasized the importance of music for the movement, which undoubtedly came to constitute an expression of a principle of unity based in Pythagorean harmony. For example, Skyrme uses a study by Erika Lorenz as his point of departure for signaling the importance of music for Darío, coming to proclaim that "Darío's Pythagorean concept of an ordering or unifying principle at work in an animate universe, which, when it is not directly identified as 'música,' is alluded to in four closely related terms: 'armonía,' 'número,' 'ritmo,' and 'idea'" (Skyrme 2; see also particularly chapters 2 and 6: "The World as Music," 4-21; "The Music of Poetry," 88-104). Although Jrade's volume spans a much broader critical perspective, it too underscores the role of music, highlighting its expressive power throughout the work and even speaking of the "musical pulse of the universe" (57, 60) and the "musical perfection of the macrocosm" (54). Nevertheless, understood in this way, sound belies modernism's incorporation of musicality as a structuring formal element, as a symbol or as a path to universal reconciliation—and strange as it may seem, stops short of delving into sound as a meaning in itself, as a referent, as content, as a topic in its own right.

The truth is that sound in Latin American literature—as a thing in and of itself, and not merely as a testament to the inheritance of the stylistic ornamentation of the Baroque—has never been studied in depth, and much less in relation to the role of sound in Theosophy, despite the fact that numerous key figures of Modernism read Theosophical treatises with interest.[1] Effectively, sound exists, and comes to constitute an aspect of a world that is not limited to being perceived through hearing. As a few highly readable critical texts on the topic written by Oliver Sacks (*Musicophilia*) and Daniel Levitin (*This Is Your Brain on Music*) and published in recent years signal, it requires neither metaphysics nor occultism-mysticism to suggest that sound in itself possesses a clue to life's mysteries. In this light, this chapter drives toward a doubled investigation. First, it constitutes a consideration of the topic of sound in two of Lugones's stories starting from their connection with the pseudo-mystical Theosophy of Madame Blavatsky. And simultaneously, it is an exploration of the close relationship between sound and the totality of a much more complex world—which comes to be a revindication of the very premises that Lugones explored in his experiments and his fantastic stories.

The influence that the infamous Madame Blavatsky had exercised over Lugones can be indisputably seen in the thematic composition of his fantastic stories, although few studies have explored this connection at length. For example, Jensen briefly mentions Blavatsky without going any further (note 15). As Hewitt and Abraham Hall note, the infrequent forays into this aspect of the work of Lugones are constituted by Speck, Pío del Corro and Marín. H. Fraser mentions Blavatsky in his book *In the Presence*, and he analyzes *Las fuerzas extrañas* in both *In the Presence* and "Apocalyptic Vision...". Monet-Viera admirably delves into Blavatsky and the Theosophical Society concluding that "Hence we see that Lugones's *Las fuerzas extrañas* essentially functions as a space of occult initiation" (130). As the two critical studies to deal most extensively with this connection, H. Fraser offers a glimpse of how, in *Las fuerzas extrañas*, Lugones blends vitalism and spiritualism with the scientific backgrounds of Blavatsky and Pythagoras, and Hewitt and Abraham Hall explore how, in a study the Argentine titles "Ensayo de una cosmogonía en diez lecciones" (included in the aforementioned collection of 1906), it is likely that the author has even plagiarized the work of Blavatsky. While I will shortly delve into the sonorous-esoteric contribution of the stories themselves, I want to first attempt to elucidate this connection between Lugones and Blavatsky, particularly as it relates to sound in and of itself. This primacy of sound is a significant aspect of the Argentine's works that criticism in general has not highlighted, even when it has managed to privilege occult science. Ultimately, the present work intends to go one step further by highlighting the occult power of sound and its resonance with current science and disciplinary shifts.

Who was the enigmatic Blavatsky? As Kurt Vonnegut Jr. began a brief description published in *McCall's* magazine: "Madame Helena Petrovna Blavatsky (1831-91) was a mannish, aggressively celibate Russian noblewoman who became a United States citizen at the age of forty-seven [...] in order to make her theories about occult matters more acceptable in America" (142). She was (along with Coronel Henry S. Olcott) founder of the *Theosophical Society*, which

Chapter 3 - AIR

attracted such distinguished members as Thomas A. Edison, W. B. Yeats and the painter Piet Mondrian, among others. Blavatsky wrote many books, directing them always to the general public (consider her short publication titled *Practical Occultism*) and dedicating herself to the effort as if she had no other goal in life other than that the spread of her theosophy might manage to conquer the entire world. Maybe one of the most extravagant affirmations perpetuated by the great lady of spiritualism is that she would receive the information she published in her numerous works via an ethereal connection with wise men in India. The image of Blavatsky suggested by the biography written by Marion Meade, for example, leaves the impression that she was a controlling but astute woman who, allowed adequate preparation, could and managed to manipulate the perceptions of a carefully selected public—even making them believe in spiritism.

Sound figures strongly in *The Secret Doctrine* (1888), the classic work of Blavatsky. Certainly sound was, through both its presence and absence, a great part of the creation myths in which her work was rooted: "Where was silence? Where the ears to sense it? No there was neither silence nor sound; naught save ceaseless eternal breath, which knows itself not" (1: 28). In her appropriation of a Hindu cosmology, sound enjoys a fundamental power that triumphs even over the other elemental forces of the universe: "'Sound is the characteristic of Akâsa (Ether): it generates air, the property of which is Touch; which (by friction) becomes productive of Colour and Light.'......(Vishnu Purâna.)" (1: 205; see also 2: 107). Sound has such power that Blavatsky makes an effort to wax poetic on the topic in the following way:

> We may say that SOUND, for one thing, is a tremendous Occult power; that it is a stupendous force, of which the electricity generated by a million of Niagaras could never counteract the smallest potentiality when directed with *occult knowledge*. Sound may be produced of such a nature that, the pyramid of Cheops would be raised in the air, or that a dying man, nay, one at his last breath, would be revived and filled with new energy and vigour.
>
> For Sound generates, or rather attracts together, the elements that produce an *ozone*, the fabrication

of which is beyond chemistry, but within the limits of Alchemy. It may even *resurrect* a man or an animal whose astral "vital body" has not been irreparably separated from the physical body by the severance of the magnetic or odic chord. *As one saved thrice from death* by that power, the writer ought to be credited with knowing personally something about it. (1: 555 original emphasis)

The personal testimony that Blavatsky includes in this description shows the enchanting and still deliberate, if not apparently truthful, tone through which she was able to galvanize the interests of a public that spanned the globe. But what is even more significant is the suggestion that the power of sound lies within reach of humankind. Although sound cannot be conquered through chemistry, she says, through alchemy it indeed can.

Certainly Blavatsky's influence on Lugones was not an isolated incident. As Douglas Kahn notes in his essay "Ether Ore: Mining Vibrations in American Modernist Music," the theosophist-appropriated notion of ether appealed more broadly to a range of (pseudo)scientists:

> During the late nineteenth century, theosophy and science often met on a common ground of the ethers. [...] As an unknown entity, the ethers provided a place where physics and metaphysics could meet, where the minute mechanical vibrations of musical acoustics could interact with the atomic vibrations of physics, and where a Pythagorean cosmological inheritance might find a home. (110-11)

It happens that alchemy—as Modernist criticism has sustained—is key for the understanding of this artistic movement. Among numerous others who have discussed the topic at length, the academic legacy of H. Fraser, developed across publications that focus on Modernism[2] shows the importance of the pseudo- or pre-scientific tradition of alchemists and its consequences for the literature of the time period. It is indeed true that, in many cases, alchemy can be read as a mere metaphor for the beauty of the poetic process itself, which Modernists saw as an inherently creative process. In this light, H. Fraser hits the bull's-eye when he points to "the relationship [for Darío] between the Occult and artistic inspiration" as encompassing

> the Unity of all artistic production; the magic inherent in the artistic enterprise; the pursuit of perfection as artistic Truth; and the spiritual essence that underlies art and which provides energy for the magnum opus in the creation of something eternal. (*In the Presence...* 27; see also Jrade)

Without a doubt, alchemy played a fundamental role for Modernists with respect to the movement's stylistic questions. Equally important is its key role at the level of literary content, in that authors gave complementary expression to these questions of style by means of a world populated by "princesas tristes," subterranean gnomes, rubies and other precious gems and metals. This fantastic world, constituted also a rebellion against the accumulative processes of a globalizing capitalism that, for Modernists, required and in turn instituted an overly-rational mindset in the modern human collectivity. As H. Fraser puts it, "the purpose of the *modernistas*' liberalism was freedom from the oppression exercised by excessive devotion to rationalism, materialism, and the slavishly destructive cultivation of the capitalist ethic" (*In the Presence...* 12). The use of alchemy was, for them, thus, doubly significant—relevant, first, to style, in order to better square with their valuation of art as a creative and elemental process; and second, to content, as an expression of a critical assessment of capitalism.

 For Blavatsky, on the other hand—or at least for the image of herself that H. P. B. sold to her public—alchemy was neither metaphor nor symbol but rather a reality, one more proof of the hidden world that surrounded her and that she herself had managed to dominate in the interests of humanity. In *The Secret Doctrine*, the author mentions one John Worrell Keely of Philadelphia who has performed various experiments that have revolved around an "*etheric* Force," of which he is the 'discoverer'—Blavatsky's word (1: 555-66). In *The Secret Doctrine*, just as in the pages of the series of the

Theosophical Publication Society (no. 9), the mother of Theosophy relates that Keely dreamed of dominating, or at least making use of the vibrations of the universe. Even given the limitations of his experiments, which were not wholly successful, Blavatsky sees what she dignifies as a triumph for scientific occultism (560), applauding such investigations into "molecular vibration"—the field of investigation explored by Keely using generators, and structures of electrical wire among other things (561). Both Keely and Blavatsky believed that, through experimentation, investigators of the occult would be able to access a supra-sensible but nevertheless real world.

Moreover, it appears that for the Modernists themselves— or at least for those key figures of the movement like Darío and Lugones, who, as Carilla points out based on the former's *Autobiography*, maintained a friendship based at least partially on Blavatsky's Theosophy (130-31)—Modernism also had an occult and even mystical function (H. Fraser *In the Presence*... 25). Given the conflict between this occult-mysticism and the stylistic, symbolic and thematic importance of alchemy to movement, it should not be surprising that a strain of Modernism might develop along an experimental path. This strain comes to be incarnated in the figure of Leopoldo Lugones more than in any other representative of Latin American Modernism. In the first footnote of the story "La fuerza Omega," el Lugones-hijo, now the editor of his father's work, writes that:

> El autor [Lugones-padre] sabía mucho de ciencias ocultas. En Córdoba, antes de cumplir sus veinte años, había tomado contacto con ellas y hasta realizó algunos experimentos, esotéricos como todos ellos. Ya en Buenos Aires, a fines del siglo pasado, estudió teosofía, basado en obras sencillamente extraordinarias, como *Isis sin velo*, cuya autora, Elena Petrova Hahn Blavatsky [sic]—tal su nombre completo— fue, precisamente, la fundadora, en 1873, de la 'Theosophical Society', con sede en Madrás, en la India. Madame Blavatsky compuso libros notables y voluminosos, como el antes mencionado, y *La doctrina secreta*, que es una síntesis de ciencia, religión y filosofía. En éstos y en otros, adquirió Lugones una pasmosa erudición en la materia. (195-96)

Chapter 3 - AIR

Similarly, Arturo Capdevila points out the direct influence of Blavatsky upon Lugones, noting that he "Leyó y anotó la *Isis sin Velo*, y con mayor entusiasmo aún *La Doctrina Secreta*, en cuyas *Estancias de Dzyan* se hallan los orígenes del más profundo y vasto de los libros de Lugones: *Prometeo o un proscripto del Sol*" (179).

It is necessary in this case that we understand the fantastic writings of the elder Lugones not merely as literature—a mere *reflection* or, to use a more sophisticated but still insufficient model, an *expression* of a social world—but instead as an integral part of an interdisciplinary conversation. In this way, we approach his work making *implicit* use of the method used in the field of cultural studies. I understand this field—one that cannot be too precisely defined without betraying its very goal, method and even its very contribution—as Raymond Williams understood it: as a refusal to give priority either to the art or to society (152); privileging both at once and reconciling intra- and extra-literary worlds.

As documents in the context of a literary modernism, Lugones's fantastic tales—especially those included in *Las fuerzas extrañas*—are easily labeled anti-positivists, and with great reason. With mechanical tools and rational theories, the scientist protagonists portrayed throughout their pages attempt to search for something that lies beyond quotidian human perception and end up either disfigured or even dead due to the mysterious power of the universe, the 'strange forces'—to return to the title of the collection—that subtend and make this universe possible. The scientists investigating the beyond find it difficult to control these forces. Within this realm, ratiocination and intellect, so applauded by these scientists in general, only scratch the surface of a dark and complex whole—a fragile membrane that, subjected to probing, becomes a portal to a world of unknown horrors. But, upon being limited to that characterization of anti-positivist, to put it that way, analysis loses the truly scientific value of these stories. Particularly in "La metamúsica" and "La fuerza Omega," the elder Lugones shows not merely a "genio [...] fundamentalmente verbal," as has been commented, but also a methodologically scientific attitude. The exploration of this attitude requires the following discussion about the relevance of sound for today's sciences and social sciences.

The story "La metamúsica" narrates the obsession of Juan,

an investigator working in the tradition of Keely, which centers around music. After two months of solitude, Juan, a pianist and musical scholar, introduces his unnamed friend (who is also the story's narrator) to a machine that works on the connection that has been constructed between his modified piano and the vibratory properties of ether. The machine consists of:

> una caja como de dos metros de largo, enteramente parecida a un féretro. Por uno de sus extremos sobresalía el pabellón parabaloide de una especie de clarín. En la tapa, cerca de la otra extremidad, resaltaba un trozo de cristal que me pareció la faceta de un prisma. Una pantalla blanca coronaba el misterioso cajón, sobre un soporte de metal colocado hacia la mitad de la tapa. (86)

Intercalating discussions about the mathematic base of the universe that touch on the theories of Pythagoras, Plato, Timaeus, Kepler, the musical theoretician Hanslick, and scholars of emotion such as Gozzi, Goethe, Schiller and J. Polti, Juan explains to him the operation of his musical apparatus, which is made possible only because "la onda aérea provoca vibraciones etéreas, puesto que al propagarse conmueve el éter intermedio entre molécula y molécula de aire" (84-85). A pavilion, says its constructor, brings soundwaves together:

> Este pabellón toca al extremo de un tubo de vidrio negro, de dobles paredes, en el cual se ha llevado el vacío a una millonésima de atmósfera. La doble pared del tubo está destinada a contener una capa de agua. El sonido muere en él y en el denso almohadillado que lo rodea. Queda sólo la onda luminosa cuya expansión debo reducir para que no alcance la amplitud suprasensible. El vidrio negro lo consigue; y ayudado por la refracción del agua tiene por objeto absorber el calor que resulta. (86)

The result, upon starting up the machine that Saturday night in the inventor's apartment, is horrifying—due to the unfortunate error that "habíasenos olvidado apagar la lámpara" (91). A "llama deslumbradora" jumps from the screen toward Juan and lights his eyes

Chapter 3 - AIR

on fire, which "acababan de evaporarse como dos gotas de agua bajo aquel haz de dardos flamígeros," during which time Juan was screaming "¡La octava del sol, muchacho, la octava del sol!" (91).

"La fuerza Omega," for its part, presents the reader with three friends, one of whom is "el descubridor de la espantosa fuerza que, sin embargo del secreto, preocupaba ya a la gente" (25)—yet another possible incarnation of Keely, if not Lugones himself. As this story constitutes the first narration of the Collection (at least in the Edition of 1966), it is not without significance that the narrator affirms in the first few pages—of the story and subsequently also of the book—that the discoverer is meddling in the "ciencias ocultas" (25) in order to elucidate "una fuerza tremenda [...] [d]e esas fuerzas interetéreas que acaban de modificar los más sólidos conceptos de la ciencia, y que justificando las afirmaciones de la sabiduría oculta, dependen cada vez más del intelecto humano" (26). In light of the elder Lugones's fondness for Theosophy, here it is necessary to understand that the author is pointing to not merely occultism in its general, common, superstitious forms, to put it one way, but rather to the systematic and pseudo-scientific occultism of Blavatsky. Thus the references to the "axiomas de filosofía oculta" (26) and the narrator's affirmation "que mi amigo no se limitaba a teorizar el ocultismo, y que su régimen alimenticio, tanto como su severa continencia, implicaban un entrenamiento" (27).

But if the investigator seeks to establish a "comunicación directa" (27) between humankind and "las fuerzas directrices del cosmos (26, epigraph above), he seeks to establish it—as many pages of *The Secret Doctrine* appear to suggest—precisely through what the discoverer terms "la potencia mecánica del sonido" (27). The result of his experiments, thus,

> no se trata de nada sobrenatural. Es un gran hallazgo, ciertamente, pero no superior a la onda hertziana o al rayo Roentgen. A propósito—yo he puesto también un nombre a mi fuerza. Y como ella es la última en la síntesis vibratoria cuyos otros componentes son el calor, la luz y la electricidad, la he llamado la fuerza Omega. (28)

The idea that forms the "base de todo el invento" is that "la vibración sonora se vuelve fuerza mecánica y por esto deja de ser sonido" (28-29). He continues to expound his hipótesis: "Una vez rota la relación entre la ondulaciones y su propagación, el éter sonoro no se difunde en la masa del cuerpo, sino que la perfora, ya completamente, ya hasta cierta profundidad" (32). Upon seeing the machine that the investigator thinks to use, the narrador and his friend are left disappointed: "Aquella caja redonda, con un botón saliente en su borde, parecía cualquier cosa menos un generador de éter vibratorio" (33). But nevertheless, on another visit, the two friends find the scientist already dead, "con la cabeza recostada en el respaldo de su silla" (36) and his cerebral substance smeared on the wall nearby.

From these most brief summaries it should already be quite clear that, more than offering a presentation of the fantastic that squares with that of other proponents of Modernism and even preparing the way for Borges, the two stories by Lugones also testify to a highly Theosophic vision. This vision celebrates the experimentation that comes to characterize the occult science of investigators of ether like Keely and at the same time makes use of the intimate connection between the world of the here and now and the world beyond—a connection sustained by Blavatsky in her writings. But it remains that the stories are also significant in that they underscore the importance of a few ideas regarding sound that have been confirmed with the recent publication of the books by Sacks and Levitin.

It is evident, given the warning with which *Las fuerzas extrañas* begins (the second edition of 1926, twenty years after the first edition of 1906), that Lugones possessed a strong self-awareness regarding the close link between his work and the extraliterary world of science.

>Algunas ocurrencias de este libro, editado veinte años ha, aunque varios de sus capítulos corresponden a una época más atrasada todavía, son corrientes ahora en el campo de la ciencia. Pido, pues, a la bondad del lector, la consideración de dicha circunstancia, desventajosa para el interés de las mencionadas narraciones. (Lugones 23)

If it is difficult for the reader to imagine the relevance of the events described in the book for the science of 1906, just as for the science of 1926, it should require no effort to see such relevance today given that the books of Sacks and Levitin, two respected authorities on the subject, have been published.

First, more than a simple document of scientific occultism, "La metamúsica" simultaneously documents the scientific reality of the phenomenon of synesthesia (of the visual-sonorous type).[3] The machine constructed by the inventor Juan has as its goal to allow him to see "los colores de la música," or in the narrator's words, "un fenómeno de adición coloreada" (81). As Sacks explains in the chapter of his bewitching book titled "The Key of Clear Green: Synesthesia and Music," over the course of centuries a link between music and color has been sought (among those seeking such a connection is none other than Isaac Newton). But only in 1883—a date curiously similar to the "época más atrasada todavía" of which Lugones wrote (above)—there appeared a systematic treatise on the subject in the form of *Inquiries into Human Faculty and Its Development* by Francis Galton. As Sacks himself admits, supported by his own experiences as a professional neurologist, synesthesia, as common as it may be, "is not something that brings patients to neurologists" (167), and that he thus was slow in realizing that synesthesia is a physiological phenomenon, dependent upon the cortical connections of the brain. Intriguing the reader of Lugones's stories are Juan's affirmations that "en todo sonido hay luz, calor, electricidad latentes" and that

> El 1 de do, está representado por las vibraciones de 369 millonésimas de milímetro, que engendran el violado, y el 2 de la octava por el duplo; es decir, por las de 738 que producen el rojo. Las demás notas, corresponden cada una a un color. (84)

Sacks's chapter suggests that Juan is correct, only that each synesthete (a person living with systematic synesthesia) experiences his or her own color correspondences (172). As Sacks relates with numerous examples and anecdotes, and basing himself on quite fascinating studies as that published by V. S. Ramachandran and E. M. Hubbard in the *Journal of Consciousness Studies* (2001), it appears that—in contrast with the state of scientific acceptance of synesthesia 100 years ago—today "there is little room for doubt, anymore, as to the physiological as well as the psychological reality of synesthesia" (180).

But "La fuerza Omega" develops a more fundamental connection between sound and the brain, no longer as a variation suffered (or enjoyed) by a small percentage of the global population as is synesthesia, but now as a fact relevant to the base of humankind's cognitive properties. As both Levitin (251-52) and Sacks (x) mention in their works on music and the brain, Darwin himself signaled the importance of music for evolutionary processes. Levitin maintains that many of the important emotional activities lead to motor movements (183), and from there to the cerebellum—what is also known as "the reptilian brain" (174):

> The cerebellum is the part of the brain that is involved closely with timing and with coordinating movements of the body. The word *cerebellum* derives from the Latin for 'little brain,' and in fact, it looks like a small brain hanging down underneath your cerebrum (the larger, main part of the brain), right at the back of your neck. The cerebellum has two sides, like the cerebrum, and each is divided into subregions. From phylogenetic studies—studies of the brains of different animals up and down the genetic ladder—we've learned that the cerebellum is one of the older parts of the brain, evolutionarily speaking. In popular language, it has sometimes been referred to as the reptilian brain. Although it weighs only 10 percent as much as the rest of the brain, it contains 50 to 80 percent of the total number of neurons. The function of this oldest part of the brain is something that is crucial to music: timing" (174).

Continuing in this vein, Levitin notes that "The cerebellum is central to something about emotion—startle, fear, rage, calm, gregariousness. It was now implicated in auditory processing" (187). Speaking in evolutionary terms, it is interesting that not all the connections between the inner ear and the brain lead to the auditory cortex—some penetrate directly into the cerebellum (184), suggesting an interesting and close link between emotion, sound and motor function

Chapter 3 - AIR

and activity.

Sound is not only closely linked to emotion, but moreover, as Antonio Damasio has affirmed in his book *Looking for Spinoza: Joy, Sorrow, and the Feeling Brain* (2003), to thought itself considered more broadly. Within cognitive science there has surged a debate that centers on the priority extended to music within evolution. Darwin placed music as prior to language (Levitin; Sacks), but the guru of popular cognitive science, the author Steven Pinker, for example, has completely negated this possibility, and has even said of music that it is "useless," an opinion unfortunately shared by the cosmologist John Barrow and the psychologist Dan Sperber (see Pinker, *The Language Instinct*; also Levitin 249). Nonetheless, as Levitin explores while citing authors on both sides of the debate, this opinion seems to be short sighted. In fact, music and language are similar with respect to the functioning of neurons in the brain (and Pinker also agrees with this).

> Music appears to mimic some of the features of language and to convey some of the same emotions that vocal communication does, but in a nonreferential, and nonspecific way. It also invokes some of the same neural regions that language does, but far more than language, music taps into primitive brain structures involved with motivation, reward, and emotion. (Levitin 191)

Moreover, writes Levitin, "[T]he arguments against music as an adaptation consider music only as disembodied sound, and, moreover, as performed by an expert class for an audience," a relatively recent development in evolutionary terms (257). Music, of course, is best understood as sound experienced by a body, and in this sense as action.

More than one essay included in a volume published after a conference on the cognitive neuroscience of music sponsored by the New York Academy of Science during May 2000 corroborates this perspective on the evolutionary importance of music. In "Music, Cognition, Culture and Evolution," Ian Cross argues "that 'music,' like speech, is a product of both our biologies and our social interactions" as well as that it "may have played a central role in the evolution of the modern human mind" (42). In David Huron's contribution titled "Is Music an Evolutionary Adaptation?," the author concludes "that there is indeed merit in pursuing possible evolutionary accounts" (57), an argument upon which Levitin and Sacks have implicitly based their claims.

Even though the experiment tragically carried out by the inventor of "La fuerza Omega" in his laboratory may perhaps not be possible today, the base of the story—understood as a recuperation of the powerful role of sound—the philosophical premise that inspires it continues to be vindicated by scientific contributions in recent years. The aforementioned works accentuate the fundamental power of sound in terms of both evolution and the everyday. Sound is no longer the mere surface of human life, but rather the raw matter for scientific investigations. It is necessary to understand how, in the same way that Lugones and his fictitious discoverer attempted to reconcile sound with the other forces that structured human life—that is to say, rescue it from a metaphysical (in the classic sense of the word) separation, critics from various disciplines in the humanities and social sciences also make an effort to incorporate sound into their respective disciplines, in order to retrieve it as an elemental consideration in their investigations, whatever they may be.

To give a significant example, various recent studies have emphasized emotion through what have been called 'emotional geographies'[4] at the same time that there has been much more attention given to the connection between music and geography.[5] As one critic has recently observed, "music and its relation to place has been a rather neglected topic in human geography" (Hudson 626; see also Zelinksy; Nash). More than anyone, Susan Smith has reconciled these two strains of thought (emotion-geography with music-geography), coming to pose a question that would have fascinated Lugones: "What would happen to the way we think, to the things we know, to the relationships we enter, to our experience of time and space, if we fully took on board the idea that the world is for hearing rather than beholding, for listening to, rather than for looking at?" ("Performing…" 90).

And as curious as it may seem, even in the study of music itself only recently has there surged a wave of criticism demanding a more profound consideration of music as sound in and of itself.

Chapter 3 - AIR

Simon Frith, for example, denounces the practice of ignoring the sonorous characteristics of sound. According to him, it is more common that the investigators analyze the structural and formal aspects of a piece of music in lieu of considering the "qualities of immediacy, emotion, sweat [which are] suspect terms in both the library and the classroom" (cited in Smith, "Performing..." 108). For his part, Sacks also notes that the affective aspects of music have not been sufficiently studied in the field of neuroscience.

> There is a tendency in philosophy to separate the mind, the intellectual operations, from the passions, the emotions. This tendency moves into psychology, and thence into neuroscience. The neuroscience of music, in particular, has concentrated almost exclusively on the neural mechanisms by which we perceive pitch, tonal intervals, melody, rhythm, and so on, and until recently, has paid little attention to the affective aspects of appreciating music. (Sacks 285)

Although it is certainly possible to doubt that Lugones as an investigator (and similarly his two literary pseudo-scientists) might have achieved an astounding experimental success, it is nevertheless necessary to give him credit for his intuition—that sound deserves to be privileged much more in experimental investigations. It is not even necessary to negate the point of view offered by Blavatsky and other Theosophists regarding sound. In every case, the idea that buttresses a vindication of sound is that "el sonido es materia" (Lugones, "La fuerza Omega" 32). Sound in and of itself indeed enjoys a direct connection with the universe, just as was suggested by Lugones through his stories and by Blavatsky through Theosophy. Although the dimensions of this sonorous connection may not be precisely those articulated by the Argentine, sound nevertheless is implicit in the forces of human evolution and makes possible the interweaving—by way of the cerebellum—of emotion, music and thought.

Lugones's stories deftly combined occult science (popularized by Blavatsky) with the aesthetic of the Modernist movement in order to inspire in their readers a lack of confidence in relation to the great narratives of the day. A reading of the works by Sacks and

Levitin achieves a similar effect, inducing the reader to tremble once faced with that which we still do not understand about an infinite universe that rationalism has not yet managed to entirely explain. Today's science, just as the science of one century ago, continues to push the horizon further and further... and the consequences of our investigations continue to be equally unclear.

The purpose of this section has been to argue that it is necessary to regard Leopoldo Lugones as a neuro-musicologist before his time. This goal has been carried out by delving into two of his stories, now understood not merely as works of fiction but also as documents of the praxis of an occult science with roots in the Theosophy of Madame Blavatsky. On the heels of other splendid studies on this connection, the present reconciliation between Lugones-the writer and Lugones-the practicing occultist has produced the possibility of gauging to what point the Argentine's pseudo-science squares with current and popular ideas (ideas that are becoming popularized) on the subject being advanced by contemporary neuro-musicologists. In light of what Sacks and Levitin suggest, we may no longer consider it so easy to completely negate the theses surrounding the properties of sound explored by Lugones through his stories.[6]

Toward Sonorous Geographies

The previous discussion of the role of sound in the stories of Leopoldo Lugones has been, simultaneously, an attempt to speak more broadly to the importance of reconciling material and immaterial realities. Returning to the song by The Pixies that served as the epigraph for this chapter, Lugones sought to emphasize that we necessarily live on a "Planet of Sound." The idea is that sound is not merely some peripheral element to our human experience but rather an integral and often-ignored aspect of it. Although the Argentine literary modernist (and practicing pseudo-scientist) accomplished this in his own way—in the form of fantastic stories—a similar revolution is occurring among contemporary cultural geographers who emphasize that we are all living on a planet of sound. Sound— whether music or speech—deserves to be privileged as an important

Chapter 3 - AIR

point of entry into the production of realities that are at once material and immaterial. Whereas I have already mentioned the return to sound by specialists in music, emotion and cognitive science in the previous section of this chapter, here I want to write more broadly of the other ways in which this return to sound is currently taking place. Specifically, I want to highlight some of the ways in which theorists have called/are calling for cultural, human and even urban geography to reconcile itself with the exploration of 'sonorous geographies.'

A recent article published in the *Journal of Social and Cultural Geography* provides a quite direct point of transition from the stories of Lugones. Geographer Deborah P. Dixon (2007) writes in her "I Hear Dead People: Science Technology and a Resonant Universe" on the phenomenon known as EVP (electronic voice phenomena) —a twentieth-century practice that has arguably has its roots in nineteenth-century occultism or pseudo-scientific practice. A notable example of this phenomenon is provided by the experiments of Latvian psychologist Konstantin Raudive, who in 1968 published a book ('The Inaudible becomes Audible') suggesting that electromagnetic tape, when played back, produced voices which were not heard by individuals present during the recording session. Raudive concluded the following:

> It certainly sounds fantastic to assert that we have made contact with spirit-beings, i.e. the dead, through tape recordings. Today, however, when more or less adequate technical devices are at our disposal, it is possible to test the facts by experiment and to lift them out of the realm of the fantastic. Taperecorder, radio and microphone give us facts in an entirely impersonal way and their objectivity cannot be challenged. (Raudive 1968, qtd. in Dixon 720)

Importantly, Dixon sees the body of thought and practice surrounding this phenomenon "not as a symptom of some underlying anxiety but rather as a destabilizing intervention" (720).[7] The author carefully explains that during the nineteenth century this need "to map the inner, psychological world and the outer, physical universe, as well as the relations between them" (720) was in no way limited to pseudo-science, but rather cut more broadly across engineering, poetry and physics, as well as spiritualism. What is at stake, as Dixon's engaging article makes clear, is a series of assumptions about knowledge; where it comes from, how it is constituted, and how it is limited and reduced by individual and social preconceptions. As her final words drive home, EVP offers "an insistence of something beyond perception and beyond imagining, the contemplation of which unsettles our sense of what it is to be human" (731), something which is also offered, as her article notes, by the revolutions within more privileged forms of science such as physics.

Undoubtedly Dixon's essay may be one of a mere handful that take-on pseudo-scientific practices within geography. Yet her article's implication that hearing may provide a path into relationships that are as of yet unknown (in my view the works of Sacks and Levitin are equally a step in this direction) is one that is supported by theorists whose work is more central to the field. For example, as one of the most well-known and influential geographers of the twentieth century, it is significant that Henri Lefebvre advocated a method that moved beyond traditional analytical geography to acknowledge the power and meaning of sound. In his aptly-titled (and posthumously published) work *Rhythmanalysis*, he explores an approach to the investigation of spaces that is sensitive to those areas of experience that are traditionally ignored–perhaps most intriguingly sound.

Lefebvre's rhythmanalytical project developed steadily over time and stemmed from his long-standing disenchantment with traditional forms of analysis, particularly with an analytical and bourgeois mode of thought whose operating principle was the fragmentation of reality. As he wrote in chapter five of his watershed text *The Right to the City*,

> During the course of the nineteenth century, the sciences of social reality are constituted against philosophy which strives to grasp the global (by enclosing a real totality into a rational systematization). These sciences fragment reality in order to analyse it, each having their method or methods, their sector or domain. (94)

His multi-volume *Critique of Everyday Life* (v. 1, 1947; v. 2, 1961; v. 3;

Chapter 3 - AIR

1981) was an attempt to recover the primary totality of life, everyday life as it eluded fragmentary knowledge and traditional analysis. As Stuart Elden highlights in the introduction to the writings published as *Rhythmanalysis*, Lefebvre borrowed the term from Gaston Bachelard, who borrowed it from the Portuguese writer Lucio Alberto Pinheiro (*Rhythmanalysis* xiii, also 9). Although Lefebvre most directly addresses the idea in these later writings, he broaches the topic much earlier in both the second and third volumes of his *Critique of Everyday Life* (vol. 2 1961, vol. 3 1981). Rhythmanalysis (*Critique of Everyday Life* v. 3, 1981, 130) is alluded to in *The Production of Space* (1974, 117)[8] and spelled out in his *Critique* as a "new science" that "is multi- or interdisciplinary in character" and situated "at the juxtaposition of the physical, the physiological and the social, at the heart of daily life" (130).

Nevertheless, it is the rhythmanalyst's method that sets him apart from more traditional researchers. While the traditional researcher approaches a mobile and fluid reality only from static poses or intellectual fragmentations of experience, the rhythmanalyst goes beyond the simplistic approach of pure intellection or ratiocination toward a more intuitive and inclusive relationship with the subject of his research. As Lefebvre explains, this is a science that is notably temporal and not merely spatial:

> For him [the rhythmanalyst] nothing is immobile. He hears the wind, the rain, storms, but if he considers a stone, a wall, a trunk, he understands their slowness, their interminable rhythm. This *object* is not inert; time is not set aside for the *subject*. It is only slow in relation to our time, to our body, the measure of rhythms. An apparently immobile *object*, the forest, moves in multiple ways: the combined movements of the soil, the earth, the sun. Or the movements of the molecules and atoms that compose it (the object, the forest). [...] He thinks with his body, not in the abstract, but in lived temporality. (1992: 20–21, original emphasis)

Thinking not in the abstract, but with the body, presents challenges for traditional analysis, which must now open itself up to alternative ways of knowing. The paradigm of traditional intellection strove for a pure and even disembodied knowledge, through prioritizing visual knowledge, that which can be observed from a distance. Rhythmanalysis, although it does not completely lack a visual component, downplays it. Lefebvre subverts the hegemony of the visual field, embracing the tactile, embracing sensations and especially sound, the act of listening ("He hears the wind," above).

Recognizing the significance of sound is a particularly important way for the researcher to plunge into the mysteries of time, and Lefebvre's text returns time and time again to the act of listening. As he elaborates, "The object resists a thousand aggressions but breaks up in humidity or conditions of vitality, the profusions of miniscule life. To the attentive ear, it makes a noise like a seashell" (1992: 20); and also "He will come to listen to a house, a street, a town, as an audience listens to a symphony" (22). Rhythmanalysis constitutes an attempt to reach the corporeal and the sensible,[9] both the tactile and more importantly given the present attempt, also the sonorous.

Sound is in no way peripheral to geographer and philosopher Lefebvre's new science, as he underscores in a chapter of *Rhythmanalysis* titled "Music and Rhythms" (57-66). But his fundamental incorporation of the sonorous occurs significantly in the book's first chapter. Therein, the philosopher fond of emphasizing relational triads (Hegel's 'thesis-antithesis-synthesis,' Marx's economic-social-political,' 1992: 12) suggests an appropriate triad for this new science: "melody-harmony-rhythm" (12). The importance given to this relational triad underlies his discussion of such concepts as measures (8), harmonics (60), musical time (64), of arrhythmia, isorhythmia, polyrhythmia, eurhythmia (16, 31, 67) and more generally of rhythm throughout the volume. This attempt to treat sound with more precision and more weight should be seen as part of Lefebvre's wider interest in the dialectical reconciliation of materialities and immaterialities.

Lefebvre undoubtedly has this reconciliation in mind when he writes—in a passage that resonates with the thoughts of Lugones's envelope-pushing pseudo-scientific investigators—that "Sound occupies a space, and the instruments of *existence*" (1992: 60; remember the assertion that "El sonido es materia" from "La

Chapter 3 - AIR

fuerza Omega," above). There is a most curious parallelism in the French philosopher's attempt to widen the aperture of theoretical knowledge, in part through a focus on sound, and Lugones's attempt to do the same both as the author of fantastic short stories and as practicing occultist. For Lefebvre, "The everyday is situated at the boundary between the controlled sector (i.e. the sector controlled by knowledge) and the uncontrolled sector" (*Critique of Everyday Life*, v. 2, 335). Returning to what he calls 'the everyday' through a rhythmanalytical method and an emphasis on embodied knowledge is concomitantly a critique of the limitations of disembodied knowledge that squares with Lugones's insistence that there are "strange forces" (*Las fuerzas extrañas*) beyond the codification of our scientific systems.

It is quite significant that recent years have seen the proliferation of numerous studies in cultural geography that implicitly or even explicitly invoke Lefebvre's rhythmanalytical project. For example: Reena Tiwari's "Being a Rhythm Analyst in the City of Varanasi" uses Lefebvre's method to construct what she calls "experiential maps" of the city (289); and Fraser Sturt even applies it to the maritime archaeology of prehistory. Tim Edensor and Julian Holloway's "Rhythmanalysing the Coach Tour: The Ring of Kerry, Ireland" looks at the multiple rhythms (some institutionalized) of tourist experience, highlighting the audio narratives of the coach drivers (491-93). Other articles have taken advantage of the concept of rhythmanalysis to look at such topics as street performance and street life in London (Simpson, Highmore), sidewalk talk on Calle Ocho in Miami (Price), the rhythms of breakfast in a city café (Laurier) and sound and the television-viewing experience (Obert). More importantly, critics have engaged the relevance of sound more generally, noting not merely the role of music per se (see my two article-length publications dealing with the jarring music of Basque Band Lisabö in the *Journal of Spanish Cultural Studies* 10.2 [2009] and in *Emotion, Space and Society* 4 [2011]), but also the sonorous realities of city life considered more broadly (Rihacek "What Does a City Sound Like?"; Fortuna "Soundscapes: The Sounding City and Urban Social Life" and "Images of the City: Sonorities and the Urban Social Environment").

There is a growing recognition that the meanings operative

across places are constituted, threatened, reinforced, and negotiated through the production of sounds. As Baldomero Lillo's volume *Sub terra* also testifies, one aspect of the rich textures of human experience and everyday life is comprised by a complex sonorous realm. This realm, as many critics have noted, is certainly worth paying attention to since it is an aspect that persists even when underground.

> Un rumor sordo, como de rompientes lejanas, desembocaba por aquellos huecos en oleadas cortas e intermitentes: chirridos de ruedas, voces humanas confusas, chasquidos secos y un redoble lento, imposible de localizar, llenaba la maciza bóveda de aquella honda caverna donde las tinieblas limitaban el círculo de luz a un pequeñísimo radio tras el cual sus masas compactas estaban siempre en acecho, prontas a avanzar o retroceder. ("El grisú" 29)

This is not to discount, either, the power of sound as manifest in spoken words—a power that Lillo drives home in the same story ("Aquellas palabras vibraron en sus oídos, repercutiendo en lo más hondo de sus almas como el toque apocalíptico de las trompetas del juicio final," 33). In Lugones's stories, however, the intrepid researchers' focus on sound goes far beyond the power of mere words as they struggle to go beyond the immediate and the tangible in order to listen to the deep structure of the cosmos. Similarly, researchers such as Susan Smith seek to go "Beyond Geography's Visible Worlds" to an aural world that is more often than not ignored. Her main point, that "human geography [...] has remained steeped in visual ideology" (524), is echoed in the work of others like Rowland Atkinson, who cautions *a la* Lefebvre that "we perhaps remain peculiarly detached or desensitized to the auditory life and possibilities of the city" (page 1915).

Whether or not we acknowledge it—and Lugones certainly has—we live on a planet of sound, something that is confirmed also in the short stories of Lillo. Tuning into the sonorous qualities of the Chilean's stories, one confronts the fact that perhaps one of the most powerful sounds in the underground world of the mines must have been that of enormous waves of water, rushing through tunnels to obliterate what had been and pave the way for a new world. In the following and last chapter of this book, I want to tune into the way both Lillo and Lugones harness the elemental power of water to tap into the turn-of-the-century idea of modernity as fluid—an ever-changing sequence of rapidly shifting and chaotic events.

4

WATER: A LIQUID MODERNITY (LUGONES/LILLO)

> Los antiguos decían, como se recordará, que el estado líquido, el cuarto estado de la material para ellos, corresponde a la primera posibilidad de nuestra vida orgánica. Por ello, los vehículos de esta vida son todos líquidos: el agua, la sangre, la leche, la savia, el semen. […] En mis *Fuerzas Extrañas*, he desarrollado esta idea. (*El origen del Diluvio*, y *Ensayo de una cosmogonía*, lección 7ª).
> —Leopoldo Lugones, *Prometeo* (1910)

> Was not modernity a process of 'liquefaction' from the start? Was not 'melting the solids' its major pastime and prime accomplishment all along? In other words, has modernity not been 'fluid' since its inception?
> —Zygmunt Bauman. *Liquid Modernity* (2000)

Argentine writer Leopoldo Lugones (1874-1938) was not only a significant figure of Latin American literary Modernism, he was also, an avid reader of Madame Blavatsky's Theosophy and even a practicing occultist (chapter three, this volume). Rooted in an understanding of the Modernist movement as a whole—which maintained a noteworthy connection with the occult, this section explores three selections from his collection titled *Las fuerzas extrañas* [*Strange Forces*] (1906) in order to assert the key importance of liquid for Lugones's occult science. Reconciling the occult power of fluids with their contribution to the history of nineteenth-century city planning (Haussmann, Sennett) and to current theories of urban life (Lefebvre, Castells, Delgado Ruiz, Harvey, Bauman) reveals the shared drive for unity underlying both pseudo-science and recent critiques of capitalist modernity.

Liquid Modernity/Modernist Liquidity

Figures associated with the literary movement known as Latin American Modernism (approx. 1880-1920) did not merely dabble in the occult—they waded through it, and almost drowned. The late-nineteenth/early-twentieth century was a great time for occultism; in particular, for Theosophy—the name that accompanying the work of Russian-born medium Madame Blavatsky (1831-1891), who became a U.S. citizen at the age of forty-seven. Helena Petrovna Blavatsky, or H. P. B. as she was known, published her epic 2 volume tome *The Secret Doctrine* in 1888, the same year that the Nicaraguan Modernist figurehead Rubén Darío published his *Azul* [*Blue*], a book widely considered to be the movement's most important canonical work. As numerous critics have pointed out, Modernism's connection with the occult was by no means casual. In fact, the movement was completely obsessed with magic, witchcraft, alchemy, precious gems and metals, the subterranean world of gnomes, the fantastic worlds of princesses... (Fraser 1992, Lodato 1999).

This obsession was, in part, metaphor. For the *modernistas*, who turned to poetry more than to any other genre, the craft of alchemy complemented the creative act of artistic expression. For Darío, as one critic notes, this connection underscored "the Unity of all artistic production; the magic inherent in the artistic enterprise; the pursuit of perfection as artistic Truth; and the spiritual essence that underlies art and which provides energy for the magnum opus in the creation of something eternal" (H. Fraser 1992, 27; see also Jrade 1983). Nevertheless, the escape to a fantastic world driven by unseen forces also served another purpose. This same critic notes

Chapter 4 - WATER

that the power of the occult resonated with the desire for "freedom from the oppression exercised by excessive devotion to rationalism, materialism, and the slavishly destructive cultivation of the capitalist ethic" (H. Fraser 1992, 12). After all, during this period (and still today), Latin America as a whole was caught in a postcolonial quagmire. By the 1820s, independence movements in the region had largely succeeded, but with that initial and not unproblematic success, new forms of economic dependence were forged between Latin American nations and the US and Europe. In was in this context that the Modernist movement embraced the occult both as an integral part of the movement's call for the creation of new economic and social relations and at the same time as a metaphor for the expressive nature of their art.

Yet, it bears repeating, this two-pronged obsession with the occult was metaphor only in part. Both Darío and Argentine Modernist author Leopoldo Lugones (1874-1938) wholeheartedly plunged into both Blavatsky's work and her pseudo-scientific world. Blavatsky's Theosophy even came to form the wellspring of their friendship (noted by Carilla 1967, 130-31, who references Darío's autobiography). Lugones, in particular, seemed to take Theosophical occult science seriously. His most famous collection of short stories, revealingly titled *Las fuerzas extrañas* (1906; recently made available in English translation by Gilbert Alter-Gilbert as *Strange Forces*, 2001), demonstrated the principles of occult science through tales of fictional alchemical and pseudo-scientific investigators who set out to harness the unseen powerful occult forces of the universe. In *Las fuerzas extrañas*, many of these investigators are killed or seriously injured in the process of unleashing forces beyond their control: as discussed in chapter three of this book, for example, in "La metamúsica," Juan burns out his eyes; and in "La fuerza Omega," the unnamed researcher ends up with his brain matter splashed against the wall of his laboratory—but nevertheless with his skull intact. To read such fantastic stories merely as entertaining literary tales, however, is to take a narrow view.

The best reason to steer clear of this view is that Lugones was himself, in fact, a practicing occultist. In his foreword to the English translation of the Argentine's work, Gilbert Alter-Gilbert (2001) reminds us that "for Lugones, his notions of supernatural operations and secret forces were not merely framing devices or dramatic pretexts on which to hang his stories, but actual verities; confirmed truths to which he wholeheartedly subscribed" (17). Upon encountering a footnote appearing in the Spanish re-print edited by Lugones's son, also named Leopoldo, (this and other footnotes have not been translated by Alter-Gilbert), the reader may be equally surprised to find it written that

> El autor [Lugones-padre] sabía mucho de ciencias ocultas. En Córdoba, antes de cumplir sus veinte años, había tomado contacto con ellas y hasta realizó algunos experimentos, esotéricos como todos ellos. Ya en Buenos Aires, a fines del siglo pasado, estudió teosofía, basado en obras sencillamente extraordinarias, como *Isis sin velo*, cuya autora, Elena Petrova Hahn Blavatsky [sic]—tal su nombre completo—fue, precisamente, la fundadora, en 1873, de la 'Theosophical Society', con sede en Madrás, en la India. Madame Blavatsky compuso libros notables y voluminosos, como el antes mencionado, y *La doctrina secreta*, que es una síntesis de ciencia, religión y filosofía. En éstos y en otros, adquirió Lugones una pasmosa erudición en la materia. (195-96)

The fantastic stories contained in *Las fuerzas extrañas*, then, are best understood simultaneously as both captivating fictions and also documents of an experimental occult science. Their power lies in the literary inflection Lugones gives to specific aspects of the occult understanding of the universe—for example, bi-location (see Barcía 1982), the power of sound, shadows, etc.,—all of which dovetail with the fundamental occult objective of "the complete spiritualization of man and the cosmos, and the attainment of a condition of unity" (Galbreath 1971, 728).

One of the most important aspects of Theosophical occultism probed by Lugones in his stories, as the epigraph at the start of this chapter underscores, concerns the potency of liquid. Specifically, through his stories "El origen del diluvio," "El psychon," and the seventh lesson from his "Ensayo de una Cosmogonía," Lugones uses the power of liquid to underscore the unity at the base of the occultist understanding of the universe. What is so intriguing from

Chapter 4 - WATER

today's perspective, for both occultists and non-occultists alike, is that a very similar notion of liquidity has come to characterize attempts to restore the unity of modern urban life. Theorist Zygmunt Bauman's recent work *Liquid Modernity* (2000), for example, is merely the most explicit articulation of a trend that has sought to employ a liquid metaphor in a critique of modern urban life. This trend resonates uncomfortably with the capitalist development schemes of the twentieth-century that employ a fragmentary approach to city-space, which themselves have their roots in the surgical metaphor that drove mid-nineteenth-century city planning. In the methodological tradition of occult science, which itself needs to be understood as a reconciliation of seemingly disparate worlds, this section similarly seeks to reconcile the pseudo-science of Lugones's time with contemporary debates on the fluid nature of modernity.

If asked to name a famous Argentine author, most English-language readers would surely point to Jorge Luis Borges rather than Lugones, whose name in all likelihood they would not even recognize. Nevertheless, Borges himself rightly saw fit to dedicate an entire book to a man who was, in many ways, his precursor (*Leopoldo Lugones*, 1965). In the judgment of the better-known Argentine author, "La historia de Leopoldo Lugones, es inseparable de la historia del modernismo, aunque su obra, en conjunto, excede los límites de esta escuela" (15). In this work, Borges treats Lugones as one of the masters of Argentina's literary landscape, but he does not do justice to his connection with occultism—one which, as I have attempted to sketch out in the above introduction, was significant. The conscious resonance of Lugones's stories with Theosophical ideas becomes quite overpowering, particularly when informed by the claim, compellingly made by Sandra Hewitt and Nancy Abraham Hall (1984), that the Argentine may even have plagiarized Blavatsky's work in writing his "Ensayo de una cosmogonía" (contained in *Las fuerzas extrañas*).

Liquid, for other Theosophical occultists just as for Lugones, was both a symbol of unity and the literal basis of life. The high priestess of Theosophy, Madame Blavatsky, herself affirms, in *The Secret Doctrine*, that "In all cosmogonies 'water' plays the same important part. It is the base and source of material existence" (1888, vol. I, 64), and it is not surprising that she returns again and again to give priority to "the 'water of life'" and speak even of "Astral Fluid" (1888, vol. I, 81). As Lugones himself mentions as the author of the "Ensayo" (included in the collection *Las fuerzas extrañas* but unfortunately not appearing in Alter-Gilbert's English-translation), the seventh lesson contained therein approaches the liquid element as the very origin of life (epigraph, *Prometeo*, 1910, 865). The seven concise paragraphs that make-up this seventh lesson constitute a relatively straight-forward presentation of the importance of the elements (gas, solid, liquid)—and of liquid in particular. In this cosmogony, liquid is the source of life, closest to the pure ether the Akâsa that was of key importance for Theosophists ("Lo líquido es, pues, dado nuestro punto de vista, más vivo, es decir más próximo al estado de energía pura o éter, y por esto el agua es la fuente de la vida orgánica," 172). The liquid even comes to generate the solid ("Esto bastará, según creemos, para demostrar que el estado líquido no es un estado amorfo, y que el sólido ha podido perfectamente deriver de él," 173). It is this primacy of the liquid, pertinent to occult science, upon which the stories in the volume (two in particular) draw in order to achieve their chilling effects.

In the first such story, "El origen del diluvio," Lugones produces a striking image in his mythological evocation of a liquid habitat (93-94) and his description of the "esbozos de hombres" (94) whose bodies move more like liquids than solids. These men "tenían la facilidad de reabsorberse en esfera de gelatina o la de expandirse como fantasmas hasta volverse casi una niebla" (94). The story foregrounds a quite literal melting of solids:

> Cierto día el vapor acuoso se precipitó en la atmósfera terrestre, y ésta vio aumentado su peso en varios miles de millones de toneladas. A tal fenómeno, unióse la acción catalítica del vapor, y entonces fue cuando empezaron a disgregarse los sólidos terrestres. (97)

Afterward, he writes, "Réstame decir que los primeros seres humanos fueron organismos del agua: monstrous hermosos, mitad pez, mitad mujer, llamados después sirenas en las mitologías. Ellos dominaban el sereto de la armonía original y trajeron al planeta las melodías de la luna que encerraban el secreto de la muerte" (98). The

Chapter 4 - WATER

story itself turns out to be the discourse of a medium (99), from whose left side a globule grows and detaches, dropping to the floor with tentacles moving in the shadows until the fearful medium's call for light prompts the creature's disappearance. "El origen del diluvio" ends with Lugones's characteristic unsettling twist—while cleaning up, one of those present at the medium's discourse finds a little dead siren amidst the mess. "En el fondo de la palangana, yacía no más grande que un ratón, pero acabada de formas y de hermosura, irradiando mortalmente su blancor, una pequeña sirena muerta" (100). In light of Lugones's significant connection with occult science, the tale is not merely entertaining—instead, in its emphasis on the mythological role of water, this story undoubtedly functions as a complement to Blavatsky's tract *The Secret Doctrine* while also managing to assert and support the significance of the figure of the Theosophical medium.

The story "El psychon" perhaps most forcefully expresses the elemental importance attributed to liquid by occult science. The scientist in this case is Dr. Paulin, a distinguished physicist dedicated to the liquefaction of gases and the accomplished inventor of the 'telectroscope,' the 'electrolide,' and the 'negative mirror' (a footnote in the Spanish version informs us that "Los descubrimientos que el auto atribuye a su personaje son de ficción."). As the narrator —an assistant in his experiments—puts it, Paulin "adolecía de un defecto grave"—"Era espiritualista" (136). Marginalized from mainstream academics (118), he settles in Buenos Aires to continue his investigations and, one day, speaks to his assistant of the "las exhalaciones fluídicas del hombre" seen by sensitives "en forma de resplandores, rojos los que emergen del lado derecho, azulados los que se desprenden del izquierdo" (137). Elaborate experiments follow, with human subjects and a clairvoyant named Antonia, and the researcher narrates his procedures referring also to the discovery of "tres elementos nuevos en el aire: el *krypton*, el *neón* y el *metargón*" (140). The doctor believes to have obtained, as a result of experiments of increasing complexity, a previously unknown substance, proclaiming that—"ese cuerpo bien podría ser pensamiento volatilizado" (142). By way of an explanation he tells his assistant that "El cerebro irradia pensamiento en forma de fuerza mecánica, habiendo grandes probabilidades de que lo haga también en forma fluídica"

(142). During the story's finale, the experimentally collected and now material thought is released from its container, and a great tumult ensues—furniture is thrown across the room, and strange and even criminal thoughts invade the minds of the doctor, the assistant and even the laboratory cat—"pues el pensamiento puro que habíamos absorbido, era seguramente el elixir de la locura" (145). Fittingly, given how Lugones's other stories end, the doctor is next seen in an asylum in Germany.

In Lugones's "Ensayo de una cosmogonía" and his two stories—all from *Las fuerzas extrañas*—liquid is thus consistently used to reference the fundamental unity at the base of Theosophy and occult science more generally. This unity is at once literary and pseudo-scientific, both mythological and literal. Through liquid, Lugones is able to reconcile the states of matter with one another ("Ensayo"), humankind's mythological past with its mysterious present ("El origen del diluvio") and, as "El psychon" shows, even the supposed immateriality of thought with the materiality of our seemingly simple physical world. The stories function as documents of a pseudo-science that did not negate more legitimized scientific inquiry, but rather built upon it, piggy-backing on the liquefaction of Lavoisier[1] and the discovery of neon, for example.

Whereas it may be easy for some to dismiss the individual experiments that underscored this pseudo-science, it is more difficult to do away with the Theosophical drive to recognize the fundamental unity of experience itself. This drive toward unity can currently be seen in the ongoing debates uniting quantum physics and consciousness studies (e.g. quantum physicist David Bohm's assertion that "thought is a material process," 1980, 53; also the conversations between Vedantic scholar Jiddu Krishnamurti and Bohm 1985, 1999), and arguably also constitutes the motor force of the interdisciplinary academic work today, which seeks a philosophical and methodological reconciliation of the sciences, social sciences and the humanities.

In the spirit of just such a reconciliation, in the next section, I want to underscore the primary role of fluids in both the development of the modern city and also the contestation of overly static forms of the production of city-space. While this is, effectively, to pass from the realm of occult science to an area that has not overtly

Chapter 4 - WATER

addressed any connection with occultism or pseudo-science, I want to assert that the recourse to metaphors of liquidity on the part of contemporary urban theorists serves the same reconciliatory function that liquid exercised in Lugones's literary work. In both cases, it is a matter of drawing attention back to a fluid, moving reality that is insufficiently explained by overly-rational theories. In essence, modern urban life enjoys, at its base, the property of variegated unity and interconnection that so enthralled occult science. As key theorists have pointed out, this unity is discarded by fragmentary approaches to the urban that seek to structure human relationships to the point of systematization.

If, for occult science, liquid was the basis of all life—it is nonetheless true that modern urban life itself owes a great debt to fluid. From the birth of modern city-planning, in which fluids—bodily fluids, specifically— played a significant role, to the theoretical accounts of contemporary urban life, the elemental force of liquids has been expressed through powerful conceptual metaphors. Baron Georges Haussmann (1809-1891) famously conceived his reconstruction of Paris in the terms of an explicit metaphor highlighting the motion of blood, consciously envisioning its streets as arteries in the model of a "general circulation system" (Choay 1969: 18). As such, the application of biological metaphors to city life was absolutely foundational in the birth of modern city planning (Choay 27), which today still owes much to Haussmann's mid-nineteenth-century legacy. Even before Haussmann, of course, as Richard Sennett notes in his most recent work, *The Craftsman* (2008), "The scalpel had permitted anatomists to study the circulation of the blood: that knowledge, applied to the circulation of movement in streets, suggested that streets worked like arteries and veins; this was thus the era in which planners began to incorporate one-way streets in their designs" (204).[2]

Nevertheless, the bodily metaphor that was consciously applied to cities during the nineteenth century (itself stemming from an earlier discovery of the circulation of blood), was to give rise to a surgical approach to the production of city-space that was far from expressing the occultist notion of the unity of all things. Urban theorist Henri Lefebvre famously stated that capitalism had survived throughout the twentieth century "by occupying space, by producing a space" (1973, 21; also *The Production of Space* 1974). As I have explored in more depth elsewhere (B. Fraser 2008, 2007a), this project —tied as it was to capital accumulation and intercity competition— did not intend to reconcile, but rather to partition and spatialize a fluid reality in the interests of improving the turnover time of investments. In opposition to this wholesale partitioning of city-space, theorists critical of this practice have turned to emphasize the fluid nature of the modern life that underlies the strict structures of urban design.

I will briefly cite just two notable examples of this trend. First, there is the Spanish-born critic Manuel Castells, who is best known for popularizing the phrase "the network society" in the title of his book *The Rise of the Network Society* (1996). In a portion of the latter work titled "The Space of Flows" (1996), he articulates the idea that a "new spatial form" in our society is "constructed around flows: flows of capital, flows of information, flows of technology, flows of organizational interaction, flows of images, sounds and symbols" (344). The second is the University of Barcelona's anti-urbanist critic Manuel Delgado Ruiz. Delgado—explicitly taking up the Lefebvrian tradition (B. Fraser 2007b)—opposes the "conceived city" to the "practiced city" and thus the strict top-down designs of planners to the unpredictable, 'mobile' and 'fluid' nature of city-life that escapes or subverts these designs (*Sociedades movedizas*, 2007).[3]

The recent series of books by sociologist Zygmunt Bauman on what he calls *Liquid Modernity* (2000; also *Liquid Love* 2003, *Liquid Life* 2005, *Liquid Fear* 2006, *Liquid Times* 2007) constitutes the most concerted attempt to incorporate the metaphor of fluidity into a theoretical account of modern urban life. Like numerous other theorists (Rosa Luxemburg, Guy Debord, Henri Lefebvre, David Harvey, etc.) he has noted that the twentieth century saw a shift from the earlier strategies of capital accumulation critiqued by Marx (the phrase 'melting of solids' appearing in Bauman's epigraph above is taken from *The Communist Manifesto*). Yet, he has worked harder than any other theorist to consistently frame this shift in terms of a liquid metaphor. Most recently, Bauman has written passionately of

> the passage from the 'solid' to a 'liquid' phase of modernity: that is, into a condition in which social forms (struc-

Chapter 4 - WATER

tures that limit individual choices, institutions that guard repetitions of routines, patterns of acceptable behavior) can no longer (and are not expected) to keep their shape for long, because they decompose and melt faster than the time it takes to cast them, and once they are case for them to set. Forms, whether already present or only adumbrated, are unlikely to be given enough time to solidify, and cannot serve as frames of reference for human actions and long-term life strategies because of their short life expectation: indeed, a life expectation shorter than the time it takes to develop a cohesive and consistent strategy, and still shorter than the fulfillment of an individual 'life project' requires. (2007, 1; also 2005, 1; 2000)

It might be argued, as Larry Ray (2007) has done, that a single such metaphor cannot be sufficient to explain the complexity of our modern world. Yet, putting aside, for a moment, the truth there undoubtedly is in Ray's statement, we might consider that this metaphor does not so much reveal something intrinsic about our complex reality in itself as it does about the dialectical relationship between capitalists and urban designers on the one hand, and the built environment on the other.

The recent move of 'liquidizing' power from the macro the micro levels (a complement to Lefebvre [1961] and Debord's [1967] 'colonization' of everyday life) that comes to characterize the postwar era in the advanced capitalist countries has been facilitated, or course, by very real and tangible processes of power, processes which are beyond the control of those people on the street. If the 'liquid modern' (Bauman 2005, 1) is a society in which the conditions and context changes faster than individuals can respond to those changes, there are still, as Bauman's refusal to abandon Marxism testifies, specific activities and persons responsible for those conditions and contexts. After all, the liquefying "social disintegration" of which Bauman speaks is, as he himself reminds us, both the *outcome of* and the *condition for* a drastic change in modernity (2000, 14).

Although, in essence, Bauman inverts the liquid metaphor as it appears in Lugones's stories (and in Manuel Delgado Ruiz's theory as well), there is still room for comparison. Whereas, for the

Argentine occultist, liquid was the basis and the very source of life whose enduring if not eternal force could not be channeled without risking injury or death; for the Polish sociologist, the liquid metaphor expresses the individual's chaotic immersion in relatively recent strange forces of modernity that lie beyond his control. In each case the problem of seeking unity is paramount—a frustrating search in which the individual must attempt to go beyond himself to reach something larger. While Lugones's researchers challenge themselves to discover this unity at any cost, Bauman's work poses a challenge to the reader—the challenge of working to overcome the dissolution of communitarian institutions and values that many contemporary theorists have also approached, each in their own way (e.g. Harvey 2006 on capitalism's contrived individualism).

The gap that separates Lugones and Bauman is certainly substantial, and yet the passage from the early twentieth-century author's fantastic stories to contemporary debates on urban life illustrates something more important than merely the elemental power that liquid metaphors manage to hold over us, occultists or not. Although the treatment of this metaphor may differ, in both cases, the respective search for unity must be approached through its connection with the developments characteristic of twentieth-century capitalism. At the turn of the century, the Latin American Modernists (1880-1920) faced a world of static spatial structures and overly-rational processes which left room for neither imagination nor autonomy. For many twenty-first-century theorists of urban life, on the other hand, capitalism has accelerated, coming to so thoroughly dominate space through time that its capacity to restructure human relationships is best approached as a liquid or flow. The spiritualist-occultism of one hundred years ago sought to combat the disintegration of social unity through metaphysical experiments. Perhaps what we need today is a materialist-occultism that can construct solid inter-personal relationships, coming to fjord the rivers of an alienating capitalism in which Lugones's investigators metaphorically drowned.

Given the importance attributed to liquid by occultism, it is interesting that metaphors of fluidity were instrumental in the development of the nineteenth-century modern urban form. Even more significant, recent theorists of modern urban life have returned to the fluid nature of experience in condemnation of the overly-rational processes of city-planning, which have partitioned city-space on their path to capital accumulation. Thus, whereas we have every right to be skeptical regarding the specific experiments performed by practicing occultists such as Lugones, it would be a grave mistake, indeed, to neglect the intuition of unity that subtended their investigation, as we are reminded by re-reading Waldo Tobler's aptly named First Law of Geography, "everything is related to everything else, but near things are more related than distant things."[4]

Argentine Leopoldo Lugones—both as occult scientist and as singular literary phenomenon—explored the potency of liquid in his Modernist short stories. For the Theosophist writer, adapting the insights of Madame Blavatsky into his works of fiction, liquid was the mythological and even literal basis of life. Liquid functioned not merely to underscore the symbolic connection of all things, but to underscore the occult premise of a foundational unity underlying the experience of humankind. Through their pseudo-scientific investigation, his fictional researchers managed to momentarily puncture the thin veneer of rationality to gain insight into the interconnectedness of all things—often with tragic consequences. On the other hand, liquid in the work of Lillo, as might be expected, takes on more of a social character as it is used to portray the complex tension between individualism and community identity as well as point to the contradictory meanings of emancipation and destruction.

Reconciling the 'Ballena'/'Barrena' Dichotomy

As critic José Zamudio has pointed out, Lillo has all too often been pigeon-holed as the writer of 'cuadros mineros,' a categorization that was unfortunately played up even by the Chilean himself.[5] This myopic perspective has prevented critics from seeing beyond his depictions of mining life to regard other aspects of his literary production. As Zamudio states in the prologue to the posthumous collection of tales he titled *El hallazgo y otros cuentos del mar*, "Por ejemplo, casi nadie se ha detenido en el formidable narrador de escenas marinas. Sus cuadros de la caza de la ballena, como el descrito en 'La Ballena', de *Relatos Populares*, o en 'El hallazgo', que contiene el presente volumen, son magníficos exponentes de este matiz de Baldomero Lillo" (13). Along with their emphasis on the harsh realities of mining life, Baldomero Lillo's stories also turned to the elemental power of water to evoke the chaos the modern experience over a number of volumes, and not just in the two stories singled out by Zamudio. In several stories from his book *Sub sole* (1907), water is seen as representative of change itself ("Las nievas eternas"), as the chaotic ground of modernity in which humankind is often lost ("El ahogado," "El remolque"). Lillo also turns to water to suggest the world of dreams ("El rapto del sol"), and the fluid nature of memories ("El ahogado"). As will be discussed in this chapter, "La ballena" and "El hallazgo" delve into the realities of whaling off the Araucan Gulf coast. But water, too, figures into the stories of *Sub terra*, most significantly in the previously discussed "Juan Fariña" and "La barrena" (see chapter two).[6] This section will first explore the undeniably modernist power of water in Lillo's non-mining stories, before returning to this pair of captivating tales that draws upon the destructive power of water to point to a sea-change wrought by modernity. This exploration of this elemental force will ultimately bring us full circle, from Lillo's water tales back to his mining tales, from 'ballena' to 'barrena' as it were, as the Chilean consistently paints the picture of modernity as a clash of the elemental forces of water and earth.

In a number of Lillo's stories—just as forcefully as it does in Lugones's stories—liquid announces an impending fundamental shift in reality, as in the story which begins the original 1907 publication of the volume *Sub sole*. In the tale, titled "El rapto del sol," a powerful king has a portentous dream which sets in motion a series of events that threaten his power and involve him in a rebirth that transcends his own ego.

> Soñó que se encontraba al borde de un estanque profundísimo en cuyas aguas, de una diafanidad imponderable, vió un estraordinario pez que parecía de oro. En derredor de él i bañados por el májico fulgor que irradiaban sus áureas escamas, pululaban una infinidad de seres: peces rojos que parecían teñidos de púrpura, crustáceos de todas formas i colores, rarísimas algas e imperceptibles átomos vivientes.

Chapter 4 - WATER

De pronto, oyó una gran voz que decía: ¡Apoderaos del
radiante pez, i todo en torno suyo perecerá! (5-6)

Here Lillo directly engages the modernist tradition of short fiction pioneered by Darío, calling upon the fable-like narration of fairy-tale worlds of kings as an expression of the upheaval represented by modernity. In the story, a bloodbath ensues as the king eventually decides to capture the hearts of those standing between himself and ultimate power. What is remarkable is that the fairy-tale ending, whereby the kind and others are drawn upwards to form a new sun shining upon a new humanity, is the liquid character of the description of this final event. "Sintió, entónces, que penetraba en él un fluido misterioso [...] y [...] a través de las manos entrelazadas, pasó un estremecimiento, una cálida vibración que abrazó todos los pechos anegando las almas en un océano de luz" (18). The old regime is washed away as a new "comunión de almas" creates "una nueva humanidad" (18). In "El rapto del sol," Lillo successfully articulates the chaotic nature of the modern experience—a modern world where "all that is solid melts into air" and where the only continuity is offered by "the transient, the fleeting, the contingent" (Marx, Baudelaire)—in a characteristically modernist aesthetic by escaping to a world of fairytales, kings and dreams.

Lillo builds upon this successful modernist rendering of the fluid nature of contemporary times in another story titled "Las nieves eternas." The tale, which in Fernando Alegría's estimation directly influenced Augusto D'Halmar's "A rodar tierras" (xxii), Lillo's storytelling is at its most modernist. The narration focuses on the life and ultimately the death of a snowflake who melts into a drop of water, traveling from the peak of a high mountain to a stream, evaporating up into the clouds and finding itself once again on a high mountain peak at the narration's close. There is a simple fairy-tale quality to the story, which recalls the work of quintessential modernists such as Rubén Darío. Yet the story, as Alegría notes briefly, "without doubt one of Lillo's masterpieces, differs from the poetic legends of Darío in the marvelous simplicity of the language and the really profound philosophy of the central idea" (xxii). Alegría's succinct interpretation correctly notes the story's allegorical relevance to the cycles of human life wherein "man acquiesces [...] in the critical moments of love, in suffering, pity, pride, ambition and egotism (xxii). Yet more important, still, in my view, is that Lillo makes a philosophical point regarding the permanence of change and the ephemeral illusion of stability, an intuition at the heart of the experience of a chaotic and contradictory modern experience. Moreover, in delivering sentient consciousness to an otherwise inanimate object, the Chilean approximates the Modernist idea (adapted from Pythagoras) that all the world is alive.

The story seeks to posit the modernist notion that mobility—and not the stability offered by solid transcendent forms—is the basis for existence. Implicitly elaborating on the animist principle of universal sentience favored by a number of more canonical modernist writers, Lillo's plot advances the story of one "Blanca plumilla de nieve," a snowflake who wakes up in a solid state clinging to the side of a mountain rock. As if herself a foil for the modern subject, adrift in a liquid reality changing too fast to cling to, she has no knowledge of her past (the story begins by establishing that "Sus recuerdos anteriores eran mui vagos," 61), and is bored by being trapped in an immobile and frozen state: "Allí aprisionada, pasó muchas e interminables horas. Su forzada inmovilidad aburríala estraordinariamente" (61). Driven to envy by the change symbolized by the passing of clouds and the flight of birds, she implores the sun to free her from prison, to return her freedom to her. The sun obliges, heating her up and returning her to her watery state, and she is immediately thrust into movement.

> El sol, compadecido, la tocó una mañana con uno de sus rayos al contacto del cual vibraron sus moléculas, i penetrada de un calor dulcísimo perdió su rijidez e inmovilidad, i como una diminuta esfera de diamante, rodó por la pendiente hasta un pequeño arroyuelo, cuyas aguas turbias la envolvieron i arrastraron en su caída vertijinosa por los flancos de la montaña. Rodó así de cascada en cascada, cayendo siempre, hasta que, de pronto, el arroyo, hundiéndose en una grieta, se detuvo brusca i repentinamente. (62)

Suspended on a stalactite, she gains an aerial view of a beautiful grotto, which Lillo describes in the same lyrical tone he used to paint the exterior landscape of one of his mining stories (above, chap-

Chapter 4 - WATER

ter one "Earth"). Touched by light which shines through her as if through a prism, she ponders her own beauty, comparing herself to the precious gems that were invoked by the modernists as a synecdoche for the mystical non-rational world that evaded the grasp of the capitalists above ground ("Ora semejaba un brillante de purísimas aguas, ora un ópalo, una turquesa, un rubí ó un pálido zafiro," 62-63; see Fraser 1992, Lodato 1999). Nevertheless, her stillness is ephemeral, and swelling with pride (63) she drops once again into the water.

She watches as her fellow drops of water offer themselves to a thirsty band of swallows "que las absorbieron unas tras otras, con un *glu glu* musical i rítmico," their leader announcing that they will soon cross the sea (63). Wondering what this 'sea' is, but fearful of being absorbed by the swallows, she escapes. The current brings her down the mountain, passing the beautiful flowers "Violetas i lirios, juncos i azucenas" (64) also favored by the Modernists. The stream goes underground and later bursts upward into sunlight once again. This time, the presence of one of the swallows she saw earlier connotes that she is at the sea amongst the waves. The swallow sadly dies from thirst which might have been quenched by the freshwater she carries. The sun's heat soon causes her to evaporate upwards where she can again see the valleys, hills and mountains (67). Now in a cloud, she manages to avoid condensation for a period of time, but is soon delivered by a sudden gust to the top of a mountain where she is rendered a snowflake once again.

> Pero cuando mas embelesada estaba contmeplando el vasto horizonte, un viento impetuoso, venido del mar, la arrastró hasta la Nevada cima de una altísima montaña, i antes de que se diera cuenta de lo que pasaba se encontró bruscamente convertida en una leve plumilla de nieve que descendió sobre la cumbre, donde se solidificó instantáneamente. (68)

Finding herself in a predicament similar to that in which she found herself at the beginning of the narrative, she grows angry and appeals to the sun once more to liberate her and deliver her to the stream of continuity and change that for her is the base of existence—but no to avail. The sun takes no pity on her this time, and merely responds, "—Nada puedo contra las nieves eternas" (69). The story's central philosophical idea is pointed to by what is likely another snowflake at her side once she is again atop the frigid mountainside at the close of the story's action. The voice, unaware, celebrates her stoic ability to remain unchanged by the world:

> —¡He aquí que retorna una de las elejidas! Ni en pólen, ni en rocío, ni en perfume despilfarró una sola de sus moléculas. Digna es, pues, de ocupar este sitial excelso. Odiamos las groseras trasformaciones i, como símbolo de la belleza suprema, nuestra visión es permanecer inmutables e inaccesibles en el espacio i en el tiempo. (69)

Yet the snowflake cannot ultimately take pride in what the voice sees as her triumph. Certainly, her desire throughout has been, as the voice makes clear, to remain unchanged, observing a static reality. This is emphasized throughout the story's narration of a repeated pattern of events—on the stalactite gazing down below where she dwells selfishly on her own beauty, as the swallows drink up her peers ("¡Cómo pueden ser así [...] Morir para que esos feos pajarracos apaguen la sed! Qué necias son!"), as the stream rushes her down the mountain ("Arroyo [...] Deteneos un instante para recibir la ofrenda de tus predilectas," 64), when she denies a plant's request to quench her thirst ("Tú me darás la vida, piadosa gotita," 65), when she once again denies the swallow a drink ("Tu petición es absurda i ridícula en demasía," 67) and later when she refuses to rain down from a cloud to give sustenance to the thirsty vegetation below ("Yo no he nacido para eso," 68). At the end, however, as at the beginning, what the snowflake longs for is to be immersed in change itself— itself an awareness of the sea-change wrought of the fluidity of modern experience.

Here is the story's contradictory essence and its distilled philosophical contribution, and most importantly one that recovers the modernist sensibility. Although we may desire stability it is change itself that is fundamental, change itself that provides the shifting foundation from which static patterns may be observed. The snowflake is trapped in the modern experience, one where, as Marx noted "All that is solid melts into air," one where change is the unchanging. In "Las nieves eternas," Lillo's storytelling most clearly resonates with the well-crafted tales of other modernists who used stylized fairytale narrations to assert the reality of time (Nájera's "Rip-rip el aparecido," itself modeled on Washington Irving's "Rip Van Winkle," for example; see Fraser 1992). Yet from another perspective, the process evoked in "Las nieves eternas" can be read also in terms of the decidedly modern struggle of individuation. Zygmunt Bauman writes that:

> Casting members as individuals is the trade mark of modern society. That casting, however, was not a one-off act: it is an activity re-enacted daily. Modern society exists in its incessant activity of 'individualizing' as much as the activities of individuals consist in the daily reshaping and renegotiation of the network of mutual entanglements called 'society'. Neither of the two partners stays put for very long. […] 'Individualization' now means something very different from what it meant a hundred years ago and what it conveyed at the early times of the modern era—the times of the extolled 'emancipation' of man from the tightly knit tissue of communal dependency, surveillance and enforcement. (31)

Thus we see the snowflake engaged in that behavior Bauman describes, attempting to define herself as an individual, many times explicitly by turning her back on others as the story makes clear. The processual, even circular, narrative makes clear that this is not accomplished in a day by starting and ending the story atop a mighty mountain peak. Each day consists of opportunities for the story's protagonist to join in a larger community or to individuate herself. Notably, of course, she chooses the latter option. As Bauman makes clear, in this quotation and throughout his work, there is a difference between the 'individualization' of one hundred years ago and the individualization of late-twentieth-century capitalism. David Harvey's *A Brief History of Neoliberalism* (2006), for example, goes further into this debate than does Bauman's *Liquid Modernity*, focusing on the particular understanding of individual subjectivity harnessed by advanced capitalist countries in the late-twentieth century. Yet importantly, Bauman's 'one hundred years ago' places us precisely at the time of Lillo's short fiction—a time when the upheaval described earlier by Marx ("All that is solid..."; his point was precisely the following one) was in full swing, undermining the social, religious and communitarian bonds and giving priority to a newly woven economic (but not solely economic) fabric that was shaping the modern experience (Bauman: "The melting of solids led to the progressive untying of economy from its traditional political, ethical and cultural entanglements" 4). In its protagonist snowflake's struggle to differentiate herself and her final, if only momentary, pull back into the crowd, "Las nieves eternas" expresses a more balanced tension (even if evolving toward the imbalance noted by Bauman, Harvey and others) between the pull of individual autonomy and social compromise as it likely existed at the turn of the twentieth-century. In this context, the frozen mountain peaks not only emphasize the fundamental role of change, the tension between solid and liquid, grounded heavy-capitalism and an incipient fluid modernity, but also the persistence of the 'tightly knit tissues' at the turn of the early twentieth century whose unraveling has been for one hundred and fifty years at the center of debates surrounding modernity from Marx to Lefebvre, to Harvey and Bauman and beyond.

In addition to these two stories where liquidity plays a key role—pointing to the fluid nature of the modern experience—Lillo also penned a number of tales that take place on or near the sea in the Araucan Gulf of south central Chile. While these stories can be seen as a counterpart to his mining stories, where a stylized naturalism is clearly evident as Lillo depicts the life and customs of the Chilean region's indigenous poor, it is possible that the watery environments that he depicts themselves encourage a kind of literary flourish that goes beyond the simplistic realism assessed by many critics. In "El ahogado," for example, another story from *Sub sole*, Lillo perhaps chooses the waters of the gulf as the perfect backdrop for a tale of madness. The story opens with a character named Sebastián using an oar to push away from the land on a skiff. The narration describes him as having "una mirada vaga, inespresiva como si soñase despierto" (21), however, he is not really sleepwalking ("Mas aquella inconsciencia era sólo aparente"), but rather reliving the past: "En su cerebro las ideas fulguraban como relámpagos. La vision del pasado surjía en su espíritu luminosa, clara i precisa" (21). Catching a glimpse of a woman standing outside of an impressive house ("una rústica casita cuya techumbre de zinc i muros de ladrillos rojos acusaban en sus poseedores cierto bienestar," 22), he frowns and pushes on toward the south, flying across "la bruñida sábana líquida" (22). While physical water is described in terms of a flattened two-dimensionality as a sheet at the story's beginning, as Sebastián delves deeper into his memories, the distance between himself and the shore grows considerably. Dwelling on the sight of the woman on the shore, he plunges deep into his own past: "Sebastián, recogijo en sí mismo, fijaba en aquellos parajes, para él tan familiares, una mirada de intensa melancolía. I de pronto la vieja historia de sus amores surjió en su espíritu vívida i palpitante, como si datara solo de ayer" (23). He begins to revisit the story of his youthful love for Magdalena, like him, the child of a fisherman of modest means.

As his recollections inform the reader, when Magdalena's mother abruptly receives an inheritance, everything changes as if overnight ("El ajuar de Magdalena se trasformó completamente" 24). Her mother tells Sebastián that he must make someone of himself if he is to wed her daughter. Soon enough, a sailor arrives and begins to court Magdalena (25). Although, on one instance, protesting rough treatment by the newcomer she calls out to Sebastián, who indeed saves her, the tide begins to turn. Sebastián is slow in improving his situation, falls out of favor with Magdalena's mother, and soon his rival, away on a whaling vessel that has proved to be a lucrative journey, sends a note asking for Magdalena's hand in marriage. "Sus intenciones eran establecerse en la Ensenada e inverter su capital en grandes empresas de pesca, a las cuales asociaría a su futuro suegro" (27).

Importantly, the narration stitches together Sebastián's immediate visions with the memories of his past. Initially, catching a glimpse of the woman at the house's door leads him to dwell on his past (22); later, the distant scene of "los buques anclados en el puerto" provides an impetus to continue the memory, recalling the arrival of his rival (24). Again, he returns to the familiar realm of his memories: "Un suspiro se escapó del pecho del pescador. Entornó los ojos, i un episodio grabado profundamente en su memoria, se presentó a su imaginación" (25). This cross-cutting narration—quite prominent in the story—has the events of Sebastián's memories parallel the current state of the sea, as when his rival sets out on a whaling vessel and Sebastián's sight of a slight cloud announces that "Ahora venía una época de relative calma" (26). But when his regret at having fallen out with Magdalena's mother surfaces, "un relámpago pareció animar las apagadas pupilas del pescador" (26). By constructing a pattern intimately linking what Sebastián sees in his mind's eye and what he experiences in the present while adrift at sea, Lillo prepares the reader for the meaning inherent in the story's final scene.

Magdalena, of course, eventually sides with her mother and father: "había ido poco a poco cediendo a las instancias maternales y a la sazón, aunque no mostraba gran entusiasmo por el nuevo i ventajoso partido que se le proporcionaba, su repugnancia se había debilitado en gran parte." (27). Sebastián sees his failure in material terms as caused by a lack of money, and he dreams of a sudden change of luck: "Pensó en los tesoros que guardaba avaro en su seno el mar. En las leyendas fantásticas de cofres llenos de corales i de perlas, flotando a merced de las olas i que el jenio de las aguas ponía al alcance de un humilde pescador" (28). Taking a swig of a bottle of alcohol he has stored under the prow, and rounding a reef he is shocked to see a human head floating in the water—a nude submerged child is floating vertically in the water, aided by a life-ring bearing the name "Fany." Sebastián notes this is the name of the frigate which departed last night, still visible on the horizon. The child appears to be alive, although speechless from fatigue and the cold water:

> viendo que las azules pupilas del naúfrago se clavaban en las suyas suplicantes, le dirijió algunas palabras en esa jerga tan común a la jente del mar. Pero de aquella boca, cuyos labios recojidos mostraban los blancos dientes, no brotó ningún sonido. La vida del grumete parecía haberse refujiado toda entera en sus inquietos i móviles ojos, cuya imploración muda hizo por un instante olvidar a Sebastián sus propios pesares. (29-30)

When Sebastián finds a purse filled with gold coins on the boy, he

Chapter 4 - WATER

begins to consider what it could do for him, almost as if a wish-fulfillment dream. Taking yet another swig off the bottle stowed in the prow, he envisions himself the owner of a large fishing boat with eight oars—sure to impress Magdalena's mother—and even the day of his wedding to the girl (30, 31).

Caught up in his dream and tempted by the promise of these gold coins, the floating boy seems to Sebastián be more of an inconvenience. When the "Fany" in the distance begins to turn around, as if in search of the money stolen by its young deserter (31), it seems that Sebastián's decision is made for him—he sinks the boy. "El salvavidas se desinfló instantáneamente; la rubia cabeza se hundió en el agua, i Sebastián vió durante un segundo los ojos azules del náufrago crecer, aumentar, salirse casi de las órbitas, sin que pudiera apartar sus ojos de la terrible vision" (32). As the boy is pulled down, drowning, the moneypurse is pulled over into the sea.

Abruptly the narration undergoes a temporal cut and it is now six days later. After waking up in a ditch in front of the local tavern, Sebastián heads out to sea once again on his skiff (33), his mind empty and his eyes captivated by hallucinations.

> En su cerebro hai un enorme vacío, i ve las mas estrañas i raras figuras desfilar por delante de sus ojos. Todo lo que mira se transforma el punto en algo estravagante. El dorso de un arrecife es un disforme monstruo que le acecha a la distancia, i la extremidad del remo se convierte en un diablillo que le hace burlescos visajes. Por todas partes seres estraños, con vestimentas azules o escarlatas, bailan infernales zarabandas. (33)

Finding himself in the area of his encounter with the boy he drowned, he becomes frightened (33-34), and staring into the waters he sees the boy's body "El cuerpo está acostado de espaldas, con las piernas entreabiertas i los brazos en cruz" (34). Unable to turn his gaze away from the body, he sees the boy's cadaver rising from the deep: "Y, el muerto, sube. Abandona suavemente su lecho de conchas i asciende en línea recta a la superficie sin cambiar de postura" (35). Shaking like an epileptic now (35), he witnesses the body's accelerated rise to the surface: "Y, el ahogado, sube, sube cada vez mas aprisa. Ya está a diez brazas, ya está a cinco, luego a dos" (35). As the dead boy's arms reach out toward him in "a deathly embrace" (35), Sebastián leaps onto the surface of a reef, and running from one to another he attempts to flee from his frightful vision. Everywhere he goes and looks, the apparition follows him ("Es que él está ahí y lo persigue," 35). Finally, he becomes trapped on an isolated reef where the rising tide threatens to drown him. As the water advances, and as the apparition redoubles his efforts, a strong wave throws Sebastián into the water, presumably to his own watery death (36).

In contrast with many of his mining stories, Lillo's evocation of the water environment in one of his earliest stories, "El ahogado," heightens the isolation of the modern individual. Certainly this theme is not unique to the Chilean. In the context of American 20th-century literature one need only point to the memorable works of Hemmingway and Cheever, to cite only two examples. Similarly, for Lillo, the sea is a place where men lose themselves, where they become alienated from one another, and ultimately go mad and even drown in the chaotic waters of modernity. Zygmunt Bauman has pointed out that this isolation has been seen to characterize modernity in both its early and more recent periods: "Let there be no mistake: now, as before—in the fluid and light as much as in the solid and heavy stage of modernity—individualization is a fate, not a choice" (34). In Lillo's story, Sebastián's isolation is portrayed as the result of events over which he has little or no control. Although this may be representative more broadly of the author's engagement with a naturalist aesthetic, it also works to paint the picture of a modern world in which individualization is the norm, and connections with others are difficult to maintain if not largely absent—(as they are for the urban protagonist of Lugones's "La lluvia de fuego").

Whereas "El ahogado" takes advantage of a calm sea to narrate the turbulent inner state of its protagonist, "El remolque" heightens the effect of a horrifying and chaotic event at sea by placing it in the context of a storm. The story's narrator is an experienced sailor telling the tale of a tragedy he was involved in while still a lad aboard a towing vessel named the "San Jorje," based out of the port of Lota. By all accounts, the captain was an exemplary man who cared for his crew ("¡I qué hombre era nuestro capitán! ¡Cómo le queríamos todos! Mas que cariño, era idolatría la que sentíamos

Chapter 4 - WATER

por él!" 122). The five-man crew was one of the most united of any at the time ("Nunca hubo en barco alguno una tripulación mas unida que la de ese querido <<San Jorje>>" 122).

The story develops slowly. The crew sets out toward "Santa María" to find another boat and tow it back to port. Curiously, the "lancha de maderas" is carrying "pieles de lobo marino" (123) destined to be shipped off on a transatlantic ship the following day. The other boat's owner is none other than the captain's son, Marcos "su querido Marcos." The narrator's description of him rivals the praise earlier directed at his father. Due to who knows what reason, the cargo is not delivered to the lancha until late in the day, and the calm weather conditions have changed. After they are only at sea for a short while, rain and hail begin to assault the vessels:

> Todo marchó bien al principio mientras estuvimos al abrigo de los acantilados de la isla; pero cambió completamente en cuanto enfilamos el canal para internarnos en el golfo. Una racha de lluvia i granizo nos azotó por la proa i se llevó la lona del toldo que pasó rozándome por encima de la cabeza como las alas de un juganteco petrel, el pájaro mensajero de la tempestad. (125)

As the storm grows, the narrator gives a very detailed account of the pervasive "sombras cada vez mas densas de la media noche" (127). Wave after wave assaults the towing vessel, and it is suddenly headed quickly and dangerously toward "los bajíos de la Punta de Lavapié."

It is at this turning point—of both the vessel's trajectory and the story's plot—that the narrator states: "No sé qué pensarían mis compañeros, pero yo asaltado por una idea repentina dije en voz baja, temerosamente: El remolque es nuestra perdicion" (127). It is in fact, as the narrator says, the boat they are towing that has been changing their course for the worse, directing them toward a dangerous outcropping and impeding their progress forward—"no solo disminuía la marcha del remolcador sino que tambien llegaba hasta anularla por completa. Desde que salimos del canal no habíamos avanzado gran cosa siendo arrastrados por la corriente hacia el banco que creíamos a algunas millas de distancia" (128). As the narrator sees it, the captain is faced with a terrible dilemma "o perecíamos

167

todos o salvaba su buque enviando su hijo a una desastrosa muerte" (128). As the storm grows, however, the captain does nothing, and the San Jorje comes dangerously close to destruction (129). As the machinist shouts a warning ("¡Capitán, nos vamos sobre el banco!," 130), still the captain does nothing to change their course. The narrator witnesses the machinist pleading with the captain to save the lives of his crew, but apparently to no avail. It is then that the narrator professes to hear the voice of Marcos calling out through the darkness saying "¡Padre, cortad el cable, pronto, pronto!" (131). Now crying himself because of the difficult task with which he believes he has been charged, the narrator hears the machinist also shout to him to grab the axe and cut the cable ("¡Antonio, un hachazo a ese cable, vivo vivo!" 132).

The fight between the maquinista and the captain continues as each tries to influence the young deckhand who is also the story's protagonist ("Escuché un furioso clamoreo: ¡Cortan el cable, cortan el cable! Asesinos! Malditos! No, no!..." 132). Ultimately, the young boy cuts the cable, severing the towline and surely sentencing Marcos and his crew to a watery grave. In a brief subsequent struggle between the injured captain and the protagonist, the captain is pushed overboard by a wave. The remaining crew presumably make it to shore sometime after this, but the details are elided as the narration somewhat abruptly cuts back to the frame story where the narrator sums up the story for the crew of his own ship, concluding that: "—Lo demás de la historia carece de interés. El <<San Jorje>> se salvó i yo, al día siguiente, me embarcaba como grumete a bordo de el <<Delfín>>. Han pasado ya quince años... Ahora soi su capitán" (134).

It should be pointed out that, although we cannot be certain this was his intention, Lillo interestingly gives us reason to question the reliability of the framed tale as related by the narrator-protagonist. As opposed to the vast majority of the Chilean's other tales, which are narrated from a third-person perspective in which the act of storytelling is rendered imperceptible (squaring of course, with the naturalist aim of giving a faithful picture of a harsh reality), here we have perhaps the only instance of a first-person narration in which the act of storytelling is emphasized through a frame story. Following this hypothesis, Lillo's use of an unreliable narrator em-

Chapter 4 - WATER

phasizes the sea—as it doubtless was and still is—as a realm vastly subject to opportunism. In this context, the details of the horrific if necessary murder of Marcos are themselves suspect, as it is all too convenient that Marcos and his crew as well as his father, the captain of the narrator's vessel, are all killed at sea. It seems reasonable that the captain, although certainly beloved if we believe the narrator, may not have been able to garner the respect required for the tough sea-faring life, and may have been seen as weak due to his not being able to dole out tasks:

> Siempre tomaba [el capitán] para sí la tarea más pesada, ayudando a cada cual en la propia con un buen humor que nada podia enturbar. ¡Cuántas veces viendo que mis múltiples faenas teníanme rendido, reventado casi vino hácia mí diciéndome alegre i cariñosamente: <<Vamos, muchacho, descansa ahora un ratito mientras yo estiro un poco los nervios>>. (122)

Although the narrator, at least on one level, intends this remark as praise, on another, it functions to effectively question his powers of leadership. Regarding the possibility that the captain was not respected by his crew, it is significant that the narrator mentions that the captain has the eyes of a child "sus ojos azules de mirada tan franca como la de un niño" (122), perhaps implying once again a lack of the commanding presence required by one who leads a crew of seamen.

Moreover there is an element of hyperbole and convenience to the narrator's description of the crew's love for the captain himself. The description of the captain as overly helpful (122) is either a convenient lie or it serves as a contrast with the sublimated opportunism exercised by the narrator. The possible contempt felt by the crew toward the captain would have applied equally toward his son, as every effort is made by the narrator to point out that they had the same temperament. The similarity between the captain and his son Marcos, as described by the narrator Antonio, is of note: "Marcos hijo único del capitán, era también un amigo nuestro, un alegre i simpatico camarada. Nunca el proverbio <<de tal palo tal astilla>> había tenido en aquellos dos seres tan completa confirmación. Semejantes en lo físico y en lo moral era aquel hijo el retrato de su padres, contando el mozo dos años mas que yo que tenía en ese entonces veintiuno cumplidos" (123). At the very least, the crew would have been deeply upset over captain's inability to take decisive action while in a storm. It is also possible that there was a tangible benefit yielded by the costly cargo picked up on the island (animal pelts, which we never hear of again). From this perspective, the hesitance with which the narrator begins the tale may have been feigned ("...Créanme Uds. Que me cuesta trabajo referir estas cosas. A pesar de los años, su recuerdo me es todavía mui penoso," 121). One must remember also, that the story is narrated by the current captain of a ship, the Delfín, to his crew in a moment of rest, which would certainly raise doubt in the minds of his men and testify to his own reputation for decisive action from a young age—a quality that would be undoubtedly an asset as a sea-captain consistently trying to maintain order over a crew.

Whether or not the reader accepts this argument, however, it is doubtless significant that here Lillo plays up the power of the sea as a chaotic environment, characterized by sharp and violent changes similar to those attributed by nineteenth-century thinkers to modernity itself. Oportunism or not, the main thrust of the story "El remolque" pits man against the elements—the harshness of the sea—in a struggle that not everyone can win. In both stories, the social nature of the events—while still clearly evident in the class distinction at the heart of Sebastián's jealousy-induced madness in "El ahogado" and the opportunism arguably described in "El romolque"—is rivaled by the fluid texture of the sea-faring life. While in many of Lillo's mining stories, the hard walls of the pit invite literary critics to view them in terms of the social restrictions of cultural norms and the psychological determinism characteristic of naturalist approaches, in his sea-stories, the openness of being at sea encourages change and unpredictability itself to be taken as the ground of experience.

This unpredictability is also the central core of the story titled "Sub-sole" and published in the later collection *Relatos populares* (1942). In Lillo's tale, a fisherwoman named Cipriana carries her young child down to the beach in order to gather mollusks on the rough shoreline. Yet this quotidian event ends badly, with each

Chapter 4 - WATER

been consigned to a watery grave. The sea is undoubtedly both the background and the motor force of the story, and is, given its multiple roles, appropriately multidimensional. At first, it appears flat and unthreatening as the narrator refers to "la líquida llanura del mar" (11) evoking the peace and tranquility of the Platonic ideals beyond day-to-day experience: "las aguas, en las que se reflejaba la celeste bóveda, eran de un azul profundo. La tranquilidad del aire y la quietud de la bajamar daban al océano la apriencia de un vasto estanque diáfano e inmóvil" (11). Lillo emphasizes this immobile quality of the sea throughout the early part of the story where he writes of "las dormidas aguas" (12) and "la calma del océano" (14), which even seems to have the stillness of water trapped in a lake: "El océano asemejábase a una vasta laguna de turquesa líquida" (15). Nevertheless, this stillness is only illusory, as while Cipriana collects food in her basket, the morning tide subtly begins to builds in strength. "Aunque hacía ya tiempo que la hora de la bajamar había pasado, la marea subía con tanta lentitud que sólo un ojo ejercitado podía percibir cómo la parte visible de la roca disminuía insensiblemente. Las aguas escurrían cada vez con más fuerza y en mayor volumen a lo largo de las cortaduras" (15).

In order to gain access to the precarious holes below where her young child would only encumber her needlessly, she lays the child on a platform where she believes he will be safe. As Lillo builds the tension through references to the water's slow rise, the woman tragically becomes stuck. Trying to extract a snail from a small hole, and finally grasping it, her fist will not pass up through the hole (17). The water continues to creep higher and higher, almost reaching the level of the platform upon which she has placed her child (19). It is then that the ocean reveals its nuanced character, changing suddenly for the worse:

> El océano, hasta entonces tranquilo, empezaba a hinchar su torso y espasmódicas sacudidaas estremecían sus espaldas relucientes. Curvas ligeras, leves ondulaciones interrumpían por todas partes la azul y tersa superficie. Un oleaje suave, con acariciador y rítmico susurro, comenzó a azotar los flancos de la roca y a depositar en la arena albos copos de espuma que bajo los ardientes rayos del sol, tom-

aban los tonos cambiantes del nácar y del arco iris. (19)

As she is irrevocably stuck, the water up to her neck, she pleads with God to release her to help her child or to take her own life instead of his. Ultimately, her prayers go unanswered, and both mother and child perish in the shifting tide of the ocean (23). Like a wetnurse ("una nodriza cariñosa," 23) the sea lulls the child to sleep—i.e. to sudden death by drowning in a watery grave.[7]

Finally, a pair of stories, "La ballena" from *Relatos populares* and "El hallazgo" from *El hallazgo y otros cuentos del mar* (both posthumously published, 1942 and 1956, respectively) center on the dangerous hunt for and ultimate recovery of a whale off the Central Chilean coast. The stories can be interpreted together as narrating the same whale's capture in two parts, first from the perspective of the whaling party, who harpoons the creature but eventually loses sight of the beast and is forced to follow the trail of its blood in the sea, and second from that of a fisherman of modest means who risks his life and that of his stepdaughter to recover the motionless cadaver and bring it in to land before it disappears with the tide never to be seen again.

"La ballena" opens in the waters of a cove with the signal given by a young man to eager boaters: "ballena a la vista" (181). Numerous happy onlookers soon show up to watch as the cove is transformed into the arena for a spectacle of sorts—the introductory paragraph chronicles "las exclamaciones de la alegre turba de muchachos y muchachas que ascendían los ásperos flancos del monte para presenciar, desde la altura, los incidentes de la liza" (181). As elsewhere, here Lillo describes the sea in poetic terms, as when a whale crests "sobre la bruñida y esmeraldina superficie del mar" (182). His description of the view from the young vigía's elevated vantage point is equally poetic: "Desde aquel elevado observatorio descubríase un inmenso panorama, iluminado por el fulgurante sol de octubre, suspendido en el cénit del cielo azulino y diáfano" (182). Before returning to the plot, Lillo pursues an extended atmospheric description of this watery habitat. The apogee of this description features an implied contrast between the story's landed onlookers who, as Lillo explicitly paints the vigía, are likely caught up in being "inmóvil" (182), and the rushing qualities of the water moving in

Chapter 4 - WATER

their devouring gaze.

A la izquierda de la barra, como una prolongación de la granítica base del Tope, surge próximo a la ribera el desnudo islote del Guape. En su derredor las aguas se agitan, saltan y rebullen aspumosas, presas de una rabia frenética. Las rocas negruzcas, pulimentadas y brillantes por el latir ciclópeo y eterno de las olas, muestran sus punteagudas aristas y sus bruñidos flancos através de los blancos vapores que, a cada embate de la masa líquida, levántanse y caen sobre el arrecife, cual torbellinos de nieve pulverizada. (183)

While the immobile onlookers gaze out into the cove toward the whale, their eyes "fixed" (183) on the small boats approaching the animal, the whale moves, accelerates and circles back (183).

The whale of this story of Lillo's is not merely a catch but instead, as the careful narration reveals, a spectacle. The cove is a "liza"; the onlookers, inmóvil," their eyes "fijos," "devorando con la vista" the event unfolding in the water, "contemplan ávidos los movimientos de la ballena" (184). The discovery that there is not merely one whale but instead two, a mother and a child (184), is followed in the narration by attempts to calculate the exchange value of the beast. One onlooker suggests that "hay para un par de barricas de aceite. ¡Tiene una panza!" (184), while "los ojos juveniles y codiciosos que contemplan las dimensiones gigantescas de la madre, calculan mentalmente el espesor de la grasa y los barriles de aceite que una vez derretida producirá" (185). Another onlooker continues this commodification of a living creature, warning that "Lo primero es no echar las cuentas antes de tiempo [...] Los quinientos galones están nadando todavía" (185). It then becomes a race to see which crew will advance across "la tersa superficie marina" (185) most quickly. The idea is not merely to catch the whale in the easiest manner, but also to entertain the crowd: "Un doble motivo los impulsa: acorralar la ballena en la caleta, lo que hará más fácil y menos pelirosa su captura, y que los de la tierra sean a la vez testigos de su destreza y de su arrojo" (186).

Lillo creates a captivating tale by cross cutting between the boats and the land, evoking pathos through sympathetic discussions of the plight of the mother and child ("Está mamando debajo de la aleta")—a focus that foregrounds the greedy character of the hunters in a way that the story of a single whale might not have been able to do. Certainly there is an attempt in this story, as in others by Lillo, to deliver a faithful picture of the customs of boating, and in this spirit the narration devotes multiple paragraphs to careful descriptions of the harpoons and the mechanisms used to capture whales, the duties and composition of a whaling crew, and even the pressure on the harpooner and the social consequences of failure such as having to deal with the "vengativa hostilidad" (188) of the public should he fail. We are told by the story's narrator that a whale whose child is killed will not flee but will instead attack the boats, which is precisely what happens here. First, the child is harpooned: "A Ricardo le bastó un Segundo para apuntar y lanzar el arpón, y el animal herido mortalmente después de agitarse un instante tiñendo de rojo el mar, se hundió en él a plomo para flotar un rato después con el hierro clavado hasta el mango, inmóvil, rígido" (191). Subsequently, the mother whale does indeed attack. First the boat called the "Gaviota," which although not smashed to pieces, is flooded with the water from a resulting wave: "Esta vez no salió tan bien librada la 'Gaviota', porque si logró evitar el coletazo que la hubiera reducido a fragmentos, no pudo esquivar la montaña de agua que el formidable apéndice del gigante alzó de pronto y que la abordó por el costado" (192). The mother whale then attempts to carry her child off under her fin ("la madre quiere alejar del peligro a su cría. Tal vez cree que no está muerta," 193), but is ultimately unsuccessful. As the lines still connected to the harpoons sunk in the flesh of both whales are subsequently tugged by this movement, the "Delfín" also takes on "una gran cantidad del salobre líquido" (194). As the boats are pulled toward each other, the lines are cut to avoid distaster (195). The story ends abruptly with the whalers following the trail left by the mother and cub in the water: "Minutos después ambas seguían a todo remo en persecución del detáceo que se dirigía hacia el norte, dejando señalada su ruta con una estela sanguinolenta (195).

Perhaps the most entrancing—and certainly the most lengthy—of Lillo's water tales is titled "El hallazgo" from *El hallazgo y otros cuentos del mar* 1956.[8] In a sense, the story picks up where "La

Chapter 4 - WATER

ballena" leaves off; it begins as Miguel Ramos looks from his carpentry workshop toward the mine to the south and then toward the seaboard of the north, uniting in this glance the two cohabiting socio-economic aspects of Chile's modern environment detailed in Lillo's stories: "Por el sur, a la orilla del mar, en una elevación del terreno, las construcciones de la mina destacaban a la distancia sus negras siluetas y, por el norte, siguiendo la línea de la costa, se distinguía vagamente a través de la bruma la faja gris del litoral" (17). Ramos is known for his pleasant mood and his jokes, a carpenter of modest means who enjoys hunting and fishing in his free time (18), accompanied by his step-daughter Rosalía—a valuable helper due to her sharp vision as well as her intrepid nature and maritime skills (19). His wife Juana envies the hold the sea has on her husband: "Juana se mostraba orgullosa de la sobriedad de su marido y su felicidad hubiera sido completa si la passion de él por el mar fuse menos absorbente" (20). Lillo's descriptive narration soon turns to action as a messenger (speaking in an idiolect rendered through the text's omission of certain instances of the letter 'd') comes to tell Ramos that there's something in the water beyond la Piedra de los Lobos: "On Panta ice que a él le parece una chalupa daa vuelta" (21). Having always wanted a chalupa of his own, he and Rosalía soon head out with some oars for the boat bearing the name "*El Pejerrey*" [peje – fish / rey – king] (22), ultimately to discover that "lo que flotaba allí pesadamente [...] era el cadaver de una ballena" (24). The only issue, of course, is that, as testified to by the harpoon in the animal's side engraved with the initials C.B.S.M., the whale is undoubtedly the catch of the Compañía Ballenera Santa María (25). The catch, Ramos surmises, has "aceite bastante para llenar algunas decenas de barriles, lo que constituía, dado el alto precio del producto, una verdadera fortuna" (26). Although the mine would certainly pay for the work necessary to extract the precious substances in the cadaver, what is less apparent is how he might tow the beast to shore.

Ramos assesses the complex situation before him, taking into account the changing tide and winds, the risks of the whale being pulled out to sea, and decides on a plan. He must keep guard over the whale until favorable conditions permit him to bring it back into the cove. Lillo describes in detail his meditations on these and other problems relevant to the situation, ultimately leading to Ramos's decision to wait and keep Rosalía on the boat with him for a possibly dangerous night at sea (28). Finding the line still attached to the harpoon, which is itself stuck in the dead whale, he secures it around the prow of his boat and attempts to tow the dead beast. Initially he does not even advance, and in fact moves further out to sea (30), but at least he is slowing the drift to some degree. Lillo describes the gradual fall of night: "A medida que las sombras aumentaban y en lo alto aparecían las estrellas, íbanse borrando los contornos y detalles de los objetos" (30-31). The narration continues to splendidly chronicle the experience, the waves eventually getting rougher, and the wind changing direction (32). As Rosalía is told to bail out the boat, the waves come forcefully and small, threatening to fill the boat and ultimately to sink it" Al chocar en su flanco embarcaban cierta cantidad de agua por encima de la borda. Muy pronto este lastre líquido comenzó a inquietar seriamente al carpintero. ¿Podría la pequeña aligerar al zarandeado esquife con la rapidez necesaria para mantenerla a flote? (34). The struggle continues, as the narration chronicles the shifting situation of the sea as well as the vacillating thoughts of *El Pejerrey*'s captain. Sooner than Miguel has calculated, in fact, the tide shifts and conditions become favorable for bringing the whale in to land (36).

As the boat and the whale get closer to shore, Lillo uses the vocabulary of the sea to describe the positive emotions of Ramos: "viendo que la amenaza había pasado y que sus pronósticos resultaban exactos, *una ola de orgullo* dilató su pecho" (38, emphasis added). After twelve hours of rowing (38), in the morning light Miguel notices a large crowd of onlookers on the beach who, he thinks, will be able to help him pull the whale in by the 300-meter tow line, but also, however, a whaling vessel with numerous oars advancing, evidently having tracked the whale. He sees

> los captores del cetáceo, que, por un accidente cualquiera, fue a morir lejos de sus enemigos, en las proximidades de esta parte de la costa. Pero los tenaces perseguidores no abandonaron la magnífica presa, sino que, al contrario, siguieron pacientes la huella de la fugitiva a través de los invisibles caminos del mar. (41)

Chapter 4 - WATER

This event, a clear tie-in with the conclusion of the story "La ballena" discussed above, leaves Miguel disheartened. As he watches the arrival of not one, but two whaling boats, the passing minutes are "crueles y angustiosos para Miguel," and his heart drops when he realizes that the four letters painted on both boats are the same ones he has seen engraved on the harpoon stuck in the side of the dead whale (42).

Lillo's narration cuts to the competing crew members remembering the original chase of the whale and the moment in which the order was given to cut the harpoon line by which the whaling vessel had become tethered with potentially disastrous results. The crowd of crewmembers only pays attention to Miguel and his step-daughter in order to make fun of him, tease him for towing a whale in such a small craft that would be more appropriate for towing sardines ("Oiga, amigo, ¿no le parece que para un pejerrey una ballena es demasiado lastre? Una sardinita le cuadraría mejor. Mire, aquí y en este sandwich hay una. Alléguese para acá y si tiene hile de volantín se la amarramos para que la remolque," 47). After being subjected to this harsh treatment, Miguel at first laughs along with the crowd and then seizes the opportunity to stake his claim to the beast he has towed in to shore, "puesto que con riesgo de su vida logró apartarlo del abismo donde iba a desaparecer para siempre"—a declaration that is only met with more laughter (47). But when Miguel asserts that without his help, they would never have found the whale, soon the crew members begin a discussion and ultimately agree to pay him 10 pesos. Miguel replies that he would rather receive nothing.

Together, unpremeditated, Rosalía and Miguel manage to create what is in effect a lie, that the expensive harpoon line was cut while they were at sea when it is in effect still in their possession ("llegaría a tierra con algo que serviría para atentuar, siquiera en parte, la pérdida que las chalupas le habían tan intempestivamente irrogado," 52). This allows them to sell it later to the mine where Miguel works for a modest sum of 100 pesos. Whereas the brutal mercantilist competition of the whalers triumphs over doing what is right ("una vez más veía confirmarse el humano principio de que cuando asoma el interés la equidad y la justicia desaparecen," 50), Miguel's moral character is upheld ("Hacer el mal por el mal era algo que repugnaba al character honrado del carpintero," 50). Taking both of these stories together reveals a tough competitive modern world in which the fruits of one's labor may be just as easily claimed by another. It is this world of shifting economic relations that Lillo points to through the liquid qualities of the ocean in his many water-stories.

Just as Lillo is more than just a chronicler of the realities of mining life, his story "La ballena" is more than "a mood story [...] with no outcome" (Alegría xxv); his water stories taken as a whole can directly engage the emphasis on the fluidity/liquidity of modern life. In the case of the twin stories "La ballena" and "El hallazgo," Lillo documents the dissolution of community life as a direct result of changes signaling the upheaval of modernity. The contrast between the landed community where Ramos and his step-daughter live and the men aboard the large-scale whaling vessels is at the heart of the story and gives the finale is dramatic character. In a sense, this contrast points to the incipient shift of modernity where being place-bound, as are Ramos and his family to a certain degree, is more and more becoming a liability. Bauman writes:

> Throughout the solid stage of the modern era, nomadic habits remained out of favour. Citizenship went hand in hand with settlement, and the absence of 'fixed address' and 'statelessness' meant exclusion from the law-abiding and law-protected community and more often than not brought upon the culprits legal discrimination, if not active prosecution. [...] the era of unconditional superiority of sedentarism over nomadism and the domination of the settled over the mobile is on the whole grinding fast to a halt. We are witnessing the revenge of nomadism over the principle of territoriality and settlement. In the fluid stage of modernity, the settled majority is ruled by the nomadic and exterritorial elite. (13)

The whaling vessels, which for the purposes of the story command a power that goes beyond the area where Ramos lives, are a nomadic force, sailing in at the end of "El hallazgo" and seizing the whale's cadaver—trumping all of Ramos's hard work. The story paints this

Chapter 4 - WATER

superiority through the scene in which they laugh at Ramos, showing that he has, in effect no power to command that he be listened to, even in his home-environment. The outsiders need not be and in fact are not sympathetic to his plight. If one turns to the difference between strategies and tactics outlined by Michel de Certeau (*The Practice of Everyday Life* 1988), strangely enough these nomads are the ones using strategies and the hard-rules of sea-faring vessels while Ramos must and does in fact turn to the more shifting discourse of tactics to guarantee compensation for his efforts.

Throughout Lillo's short fiction, water is always used to speak of sharp changes in the very fabric of the modern experience. But in no case is it used as effectively to represent the problematic and contradictory notions of both emancipation and destruction than in a few of the mining stories discussed earlier in the chapter on "Earth." Even in Lillo's depiction of working life underground, water plays the role of the unexpected shift that holds disastrous consequences. In "La compuerta número 12," for example, the narrator draws our attention to the somewhat unique geographical location of the mines in South central Chile, which have been dug many times under the Araucan Gulf itself: "Un ruido sordo y lejano, como si un martillo gigantesco golpease sobre sus cabezas la armadura del planeta, escuchábase a intervalos. Aquel rumor, cuyo origen Pablo no acertaba a explicarse, era el choque de las olas en las rompientes de la costa" (17). Also, as we have seen both "La barrena" and "Juan Fariña" end with the destruction of a mine through water. Foreshadowing the end of the story, "Juan Fariña" notably begins by accentuating the dualistic cohabitation of the Chilean mines with the neighboring sea: "allá abajo en las habitaciones escalonadas en la falda de la colina las voces de las mujeres y los alegres gritos de los niños se confundían con el ruido del mar en aquel sitio siempre inquieto y turbulento"; "Algunos años atrás ese paraje solitario era asiento de un poderoso establecimiento carbonífero y la vida y el movimiento animaban esas minas donde no se escucha hoy otro rumor que el de las olas, azotando los flancos de la montaña" (98). The cataclysmic final sentences to the story "La barrena" note that after the disaster causcd by an overzealous drilling competition, "sucedió lo que debía suceder, que el techo de la galería, apuntalado a la ligera, se derrumbó, dando paso al agua del mar. / Seis meses después, la famosa mina de Playa Negra era solo un pozo de agua salobre que la arena de las dunas iba rellenando lentamente" (134-35). These catastrophic events, of course, are necessarily influenced not only by the very real possibility of such an incident in the mines dug under the Araucan Gulf but also by their literary predecessor, Zola's *Germinal*, where the 'voracious' mine is similarly flooded. Likewise, the relatively recent film *The Matrix* (the third film in the series with Keanu Reeves) ends with the emancipatory flooding of underground tunnels, thus recalling the climactic scenes of all three aforementioned works.

Returning to Zygmunt Bauman's central thesis may help to explain why this image of a flooded mine is so powerful and enduring whether in Lillo's short fiction, Zola's novel or even the film series *The Matrix*. The theorist's writings on modernity are by and large centered around a core idea that modernity has consisted of two phases: a heavy/solid phase and a soft/liquid phase. Since the mining environment represents the stage of heavy capitalism, its being flooded announces a shift toward a liquid modernity. The solid structures of a nascent heavy capitalism are washed away as the infrastructure of the mine is destroyed.

> Solid modernity was, indeed, also the time of heavy capitalism—of the engagement between capital and labour fortified by the *mutuality of their dependency*. Workers depended on being hired for their livelihood; capital depended on hiring them for its reproduction and growth. Their meeting-place had a fixed address; neither of the two could easily move elsewhere—the massive factory walls enclosed and kept both partners in a shared prison. (original emphasis, 145)

In Lillo, in Zola and even in *The Matrix*, the destruction of this shared prison—the subterranean/mining environment and by extension the more fixed aspects of a solid/heavy twentieth-century capitalism—leads to an emancipation of sorts. There is, in the destruction of the mines, a momentary release from the oppressive structures that loom large over modern productive work. But this emancipation is also, through the ability and even the necessity of capitalism

Chapter 4 - WATER

to reinvent itself a re-enslavement of sorts. As Henri Lefebvre wrote in the first tome of a multi-volume work that sought to expand upon Marx's delineation of the concept and reality of alienation (*The Critique of Everyday Life*), history itself should be seen in terms of the dialectical movement between alienation and dis-alienation (vol. 1, 1947: "Alienation persists, or is even born again in new forms, along with its contradictory process, the process of 'disalienation,'" 63; "But man has developed only through alienation," 249).[9] It is not clear from the literary works mentioned above what lies beyond the destruction of the mines, beyond the disalienation from solid/heavy forms of capitalist production. Significantly, each author leaves the destruction of the mine for the work's climax or dramatic close. In no case are we given further direction as to what socio-economic changes, if any, will occur.

Yet the choice of water for the mines' destruction may provide an answer to this sort of speculation, returning us from the purely ideal pole of utopia to the possibilities as they have been revealed throughout history. The liquid destruction of heavy capitalism becomes a metonymical sign pointing to a more fluid form of capitalism more appropriately (perniciously) adapted to a liquid modernity. The simplistic notion that equates with water the emancipatory dream of freedom is insufficient and to a large degree escapist. The challenge to heavy capitalist mining enterprise presented by Zola and Lillo is, in each case, ephemeral. Yet the effect is different. There is a great distance between Zola's heavy/solid depiction of mining strife involving a 'voracious' giant and the cumbersome body of a large quantity of poorly united workers function in rebellion as a lumbering machine and Lillo's short narratives, which paint a more persistent image of positive change in their layering of frequent upheavals, even despite his emphasis on the significance of the ongoing 'solid' working conditions. In this way, Lillo's descriptions of the flooded mines more fully speak to the contradictory shift wrought of the experience of modernity. This shift promises not an end to exploitation, but a qualitative change in how it is carried out.

CONCLUSION

The elemental forces of earth, fire, air and water harnessed by Baldomero Lillo and Leopoldo Lugones in their short fiction were in every case used to illustrate the qualities associated with a fundamental shift in the modern experience.

As we have seen, each writer saw this shift in his own terms. The Chilean immersed himself deeply in the material struggles that characterized his native region, chronicling the lives of men and women of modest means in fishing and mining communities where large-scale mining and whaling operations had been introduced. Lillo saw these changes as being, on the whole, for the worse. His stories charted how the drive for mining profits, fueled many times by greed, international connections, and lack of concern for local subterranean workers, led to poverty, life-long debt, injury and most of all death. Not merely adults, but also children and animals, perished beneath the surface of the earth as the direct result of unfair practices and unaddressed dangerous working conditions. Modernity, in Lillo's *Sub terra, Sub-sole, Relatos populares* and *El hallazgo y otros cuentos del mar*, pitted the individual against a rigidly defined system that cared only for the bottom line.

The Argentine, for his part, approached modernity in less material terms. For Lugones, the modern experience was governed by strange forces beyond our control and many times beyond our prediction or even our perception. His *Las fuerzas extrañas* depicted pseudo-scientists working at the frontiers of knowledge and suffering disastrous but unforeseeable consequences. Although he also approached modernity as a sea-change in experience, Lugones grappled with the degree to which this change was almost literally unthinkable. As his protagonists proved, modernity had the power to disfigure and even to kill.

For the Argentine as for the Chilean, modernity was built on unequal terms and even on contradiction. In the spirit of this contradictory, complex and uneven understanding of modernity, a hallmark of such thinkers as Marx, Lefebvre, Bauman, and a host of others, this book has attempted to advance a similarly complex understanding. This reading has expanded upon the characterization of Lillo as merely the author of mining stories, delving into his water stories and complementing a view of the Chilean as purely a naturalist with an understanding of the modernist aspects of his works. Similarly, it has widened the relevance of the more questionable occult claims made by Lugones through his protagonists. Most significantly it has seen Lillo and Lugones each as one-half of the modernity's contradiction between the seemingly discrete terms of materiality and immaterialty.

And yet, this book has been written to address first and foremost the mistaken idea that Lillo and Lugones are relegated to literature's past. Instead, I have attempted in each chapter to breathe life into the work of these two authors whose work has often been either underappreciated or misunderstood by tying their stories to contemporary theoretical debates. Their stories are not merely examples of fascinating Southern Cone literature of the early twentieth-century, but are also intriguing points of departure for discussing some of today's key interdisciplinary questions from cultural geography: from the study of landscape as a cultural process to an awareness of alienation, from the connection between music and the brain and finally to a liquid understanding of modernity.

Although some readers grounded within traditional disciplinary boundaries may find this volume lacking from the perspective of either literary criticism or geographical theory, my task has been neither to stick exclusively to a close-reading of primary texts nor to fully pursue a decontextualized and abstract theoretical debate. In this way, I hope to have placed disciplinary reconciliation itself at the center of this project. Both literary criticism and cultural geography must open outward toward one another if we are to understand the complex immaterially material world in which we live,

CONCLUSION

write and think.

NOTES

Introduction

1   Julio Ramos's *Divergent Modernities* (2001) contains only two cursory references to Lugones, and broadly-defined volumes without a single substantial reference to one of modernism's greatest authors include: Gerard Aching's *The Politics of Spanish American Modernismo* (1997), Garfield and Schulman's *Las entrañas del vacío. ensayos sobre la modernidad hispanoamericana* (1984).

2   It should be noted that Fraser upholds the categorization of Lillo as a naturalist in his volume as a point of contrast for the more modernist stories of Darío, for example (25).

3   "Modernity was an issue of particular urgency in regard to culture and politics, and it emerged in a variety of designations which still leave the term ill-defined and somewhat misleading. The modern cannot simply be equated with any specific method or country, though one must agree that it was inseparable from progress, from technology, and (at the end of the eighteenth century) from industrialization. This process was determined by what I have called in earlier work an *industrial imaginary* [...] the industrial imaginary conveys an optimism for the mode of production which leaves its mark in symbolization, thus giving rise to themes, ideologies, and social meaning which introduce a modern semiotic practice by calling into question restrictions on teleological universals: the texts question not only tradition, heritages, religion, and the promise of civilization but also what was addressed as an opposition between barbarism and nature" (Zavala 28).

4   Rafael Gutiérrez Girardot's *Modernismo: supuestos históricos y culturales* (1988) is fairly typical of this strain of criticism. Although the quintessential Latin American modernist Rubén Darío relocated to Europe, living in both Spain and France, there remains much debate surrounding the nature and appropriateness of this comparative approach.

5	I was fortunate enough to take a number of classes with Shaw while an undergraduate Spanish major at the University of Virginia.
6	See for example "The Ayacucho Address," delivered in 1924, included in English translation in Eds. Weisman and Kirkpatrick's recent *Leopoldo Lugones, Selected Writings* 2008).
7	As do other critics, Canedo sees a trip made by the author to Europe as influential in this shift. "En 1897 Leopoldo Lugones militaba en una fracción del socialismo de avanzada. Su lucha política estaba dirigida a demostrar que la incipiente burguesía argentina tendía a reprimir la libertad de los hombres. Combatía con tenacidad al Estado burgués en nombre del principio anarquista por el cual los hombres deben hacer uso libremente de los medios de producción como paso primero para construir la sociedad socialista (10). After his trip to Europe, however, continues Canedo, "Es evidente que la ideología de fuerza y orden de las derechas europeas habría de influir en el pensamiento político de Leopoldo Lugones. [...] Lugones regresa a Buenos Aires persuadido de que el anarquismo el sindicalismo y el comunismo son doctrinas incompletas (11).
8	Significantly, Lugones published a book titled *Emilio Zola* (1902, Buenos Aires), see Irazusta 122.
9	Roland, as above, presents an unorthodox image of Lugones in this regard: "Todo nos induce a pensar que Lugones "adoptó" el modernismo simplemente como recurso literario, sin que esas formas arraigaran en él espiritualmente" (28).
10	Irazusta lists 45 books authored by Leopoldo Lugones (122).

1. *Earth*

1	In highlighting the relation between landscape and human work, Mitchell makes reference to Marx's idea of "dead labor," to David Harvey's (1982) return to this idea noting that dead labor can affect "living labor"(94), to the idea of Carl Sauer (1925: 343) that landscape is "fashioned from a natural landscape by a culture group" (102), and to that of Alexander Wilson (1991) that landscape is "an activity" (102) or a relationship between people and

NOTES

place.

2   "He ahí un elemento ausente de las asociaciones que suscita Lota. No ha contribuído, por su parte, a divulgarlo nuestra literatura, que, siguiendo la pendiente, suele preferir otros efectos. Basta, en esa esfera, mencionar los relatos, ciertamente admirables, de Baldomero Lillo, para advertir el tono que los autores nacionales han impreso al vocablo" (16).

3   As related by Baldomero's brother Samuel (see Alegría 1959, 251-52).

4   The zone was also arguably important for another great Chilean writer- José Donoso. A visit there supposedly prompted his last novel *El mocho*.

5   As Román-Lagunas (1991: 145) points out, these are: "—Bryan, Leonard. 'The Ontological and Existentialist-Theological Symbolic Form of BL's *Sub-Sole*' (University of Arizona, 1969), 388 páginas. —Sedgwick, Ruth. 'BL, Chilean Short Story Writer.' (Tale University, 1936), 194 páginas. —Smith, Elena Piskuriew. "La cuentística de BL" (Texas Technological University, 1981)." The Masters thesis is "—McQuaig, Neil M. 'BL, a Chilean Short Story Writer' (Tesis de Maestría, University of North Carolina at Chapel Hill, 1924)."

6   Gayatri Spivak in her *Death of a Discipline* (2003) points to this sort of disciplinary reconciliation as an important part of the emerging paradigm of contemporary comparative studies.

7   In *Rhythmanalysis*, Lefebvre writes that "The brave people [...] not only move alongside the monster [that is capital] but are inside it; they live off it" (54-55).

8   One of the now classic debates over Modernism questions whether it is a school or an epoch (see Davison 1966). As Davison notes, Ricardo Gullón and Juan Ramón Jiménez opted for the latter. Davison's chapter 2 titled "The Consensus" gives an excellent critical overview of the sources and influences that came to constitute Modernism.

9   For many, the influence of French Symbolists and Parnassianists on Modernists was decisive. Darío Herrera noted in 1894 that Modernism was "Spanish writing sifted through the filter of good French prose and verse" (related by Ureña and quoted by Davison 13).

10   To cite one notable example of such interest in prose by Modernists, Washington Irving's important dreamer character as narrated in the story "Rip Van Winkle" was imitated by the Mexican Manuel Gutiérrez Nájera in his story "Rip-rip el aparecido" (1890).

11   "El joven autor chilena continua en el sendero abierto por el más prestigioso novelista francés de sus días, agregándose a ello la provocative significación política que el naturalismo proyectaba en la América Latina" (74).

12   Curiously also, the dream sequence was cut from the second edition of *Sub Terra* in 1917 (see Oelker 1988). The English translation of 1959, "Pay Day," reflects this previous cut. Nevertheless, in the 13th version of *Sub Terra* (Santiago, Nascimiento, 1966), which I have used in preparing this chapter, the dream sequence has been reinstated. Oelker argues that this cut, and others made in various stories contained in *Sub Terra*, had the effect of intensifying the naturalism of the stories. It may not be so strange, if Oelker is right, to see the dream sequence brought back during or after a time in which the pre-Boom prose of Jalisco, Mexico's Juan Rulfo (esp. *Pedro Páramo*, 1955) or the less-realist stories of Boom authors from Latin America (José Donoso, Gabriel García Márquez, etc.) had already changed the literary landscape drastically since Lillo's time.

13   "It would mean the instant demise of that squat and sated deity, that monstrous idol hidden away in the depths of its temple, in that secret far-away place where it fed on the flesh of poor wretches who never even set eyes upon it." (532)

14   "Yes, labour was going to call capital to account and confront this anonymous god that the worker never met, the god that squatted somewhere in its mysterious inner sanctuary and sucked the blood of the poor devils that kept it alive! They would go there themselves and they would finally see its face by the light of the coming conflagration; and then they would drown the filthy swine in its own blood, they would destroy this monstrous idol that had gorged on human flesh" (291); and also "he came to believe that a third month of resistance would finish the monster off, that weary, sated beast squatting like an idol in its far-away temple" (384).

15   Toward a similar end, the novelist references water

NOTES

throughout the novel. A subsequent chapter of this book discusses these instances.

16   The story "El pago," also in *Sub Terra* similarly includes a reference to "el portero de ocho años" (53).

17   Durán Luzio (1988) points to this similarity (67-68), although I have attempted to do so above more extensively.

18   Durán Luzio (1988) appears to be the first to draw attention to this correspondence (73).

19   Pilar V. Rotella (2004) points out that Lillo diverges from "the basic tenets of rules of naturalism" (206) in that his narrators often break out of the expectation of impersonality to launch a direct critique of exploitative social practices, as in "El Chiflón del Diablo" (207).

20   As when Zola writes that "In due course Etienne also began to suffer less from the humidity and airlessness at the coal-face. The chimney now seemed an ideal way up, as though he himself had somehow become molten and could pass through chinks in the rock where once he wouldn't even have ventured his hand" (138).

21   For an enlightening forum on Tobler's First Law of Geography, the reader may wish to consult the *Annals of the Association of American Geographers* Volume 94, June 2004 Number 2 for a series of seven authors' comments including a reply by Tobler himself.

22   In his edition of Lillo's *Obras completas*, Raúl Silva Castro also points out that it was difficult for Lillo, as for others, to avoid the influence of Darío at the time (Lillo 1968, 16). Rotella (2004) also draws attention to the poetic description of landscape in Lillo's stories (207).

23   The 2005 reprint includes a short literary biography of Lillo (pp. 263-68) republished from *La compuerta número 12 y otros cuentos* (Serie del Nuevo Mundo, Editorial Universitaria de Buenos Aires, 1964).

24   Cousiño's role is compared explicitly to that of B. O'Higgins in the struggle for Chile's independence (109).

25   "Otra de las dificultades que en los primero tiempos tuvo que vencer don Matías Cousiño fue la de formar mineros en una zona donde todos los brazos eran campesinos y pescadores.

Pero los interesó con buenos salarios y otras conquistas, tales como habitaciones y mejores condiciones de trabajo, logrando convertir rápidamente en minera una población que era esencialmente agrícola" (109).

26   Moreover, as Marx and later Lefebvre so clearly point out through their critiques of ideology and alienation (Lefebvre 1947, 249), one of the key problems of capitalism is that, through ideology, the true function of the beast of capital is hidden from those who suffer most under it. Marxist philosopher Lefebvre's four volume *Critique of Everyday Life* (1947, 1961, 1981, 1992) in effect updates Marx's critique of capital for the post-war years, and even for the post 1973-sea change in flexible accumulation in describing how "daily life has been colonized" (1961).

27   Although a decade after the publication of *Sub Terra*, Mills's continued description of a modern Lota is illuminating, "The great underground (and undersea) galleries are lit by electric light and served by electric tramways, and are well formed and organised in every detail" (Mills 1914, 155).

2. FIRE

1   www.offroaders.com/album/centralia/centralia.htm.

2   Also: "Yes, labour was going to call capital to account and confront this anonymous god that the worker never met, the god that squatted somewhere in its mysterious inner sanctuary and sucked the blood of the poor devils that kept it alive! They would go there themselves and they would finally see its face by the light of the coming conflagration; and then they would drown the filthy swine in its own blood, they would destroy this monstrous idol that had gorged on human flesh" (291).

3   As in "La compuerta," "El grisú" also bemoans the harsh conditions faced by child-laborerd in the mines, as in the following passage describing the engineer's cruel treatment of a young boy as a beast of burden: "Dos muchachos, sin más traje que el pantalon de tela, conducían el singular vehículo: el uno empujaba de atrás y el otro, enganchado como un caballo, tiraba de delante. Este

NOTES

último daba grandes muestras de cansancio; el cuerpo inundado de sudor y la expresión angustiosa de su semblante, revelaban la fatiga de un esfuerzo muscular excesivo. Su pecho henchíase y deprimíase como un fuelle a impulso de su agitada respiración que se escapaba por la boca entreabierta apresurada y anhelante. Una especie de arnés de cuero oprimía su busto desnudo y de la faja que rodeaba su cintura, partían dos cuerdas que se enganchaban a la parte delantera de la vagoneta" ("El grisú," 25).

    4   "Economism has long represented itself as Marxist, even though it is a debasement of Marxism. Marx never affirmed absolute causality or determinism" (Lefebvre, *The Explosion* 20). Again on p. 35: "It cannot be sufficiently emphasized that it is impossible to reduce Marxist thought to economism."

    5   Similarly, in "Cañuela y Petaca," not included in the original edition of *Sub Terra*, two young boys, the cousins Petaca and Cañuela, steal gunpowder to go on a hunting expedition and fear explosion at any moment: "Durante los días que precedieron al señalado, Cañuela no cesó de pensar en la posibilidad de un estallido que, volcando la olla de la merienda, única consecuencia grave que se le ocurría, dejase a él y a sus abuelos sin cenar" (172).

    6   In his "Ensayo de una cosmogonía del universo en diez lecciones" included in *Las fuerzas extrañas* (1906), Lugones again refers to this phenomenon: "Sabe todo el mundo que la actividad cerebral produce fenómenos eléctricos; y los sensitivos y lúcidos de de [sic] Rochas, dicen que durante dicho trabajo ven a las células cerebrales relumbrar como estrellas" (179-80).

    7   Note, in this regard, Lefebvre's insistence upon treating certain psychic phenomena as material "For our present purposes, we need to consider and elaborate upon a number of relationships usually treated as 'psychic' (i.e. relating to the psyche). We shall treat them, however, as *material*, because they arise in connection with the (material) body/subject and the (material) mirror/object" *The Production of Space* 186).

3. Air

    1   Certainly, there are numerous meritorious feminist studies of sound underscoring the power of the voice, that feminine

protagonists are in one way or another silenced or hidden—but even when a 'literal' loss of voice is discussed, such criticism still relies on a metaphor, given that the audible voice in this case is nothing other than the representation of a process of social actualization that can be carried out by way of the voice either through writing or through the mere physical presence and systemic incorporation of the feminine in some of the economic-cultural operation from which she has been marginalized. Neither do we do well in ignoring the social struggle of the deaf, and the culturally Deaf, not necessarily the same thing (see B. Fraser 2007), who do not have the same access to that which we refer to as the sounds of the world, of which some are at the same time vibrations that can be felt with the entire body.

    2   H. Fraser explores Modernism in the following Publications: "Apocalyptic Vision…"; "Decadentism…"; "*La edad de oro* and José Martí…"; *In the Presence*…; "La magia"; "Magic and Alchemy…"; "The Uses of Enchantment…".

    3   Speck notes that "para Lugones, la sinestesia es más que un recurso poético, es una teoría cosmogónica y una fuente de argumentos fantásticos" (420).

    4   See B. Anderson; K. Anderson & Smith; Davidson & Milligan; Ettlinger; Tolia-Kelly; Wood & Smith. It should also be noted that a journal titled *Emotion, Space and Society* has been created. The journal's home page can be found on the web: www.elsevier.com/wps/locate/emospa [accessed 23 July 2008].

    5   See B. Anderson, Morton & Revill; Connell & Gibson; Smith; Waterman. On music and sociology see DeNora.

    6   Regarding Blavatsky's mysticism and the peculiarities of the experiments carried out by literary scientists now deceased, I have my doubts. But, in the end, if there is something that know to be true, it is that one can indeed dialogue with the dead—as this discussion has proved without a doubt (I dedicated the Spanish version of this analysis, published in *Hispania* 91.4 (2008) to the memory of my father Howard M. Fraser, 1943-1998).

    7   The phenomenon of EVP also appeared on the television show *Twin Peaks* created by David Lynch, a program that similarly sought to be a destabilizing intervention, uprooting the logical sequences of thought that reduce experience to what can be easily assimilated.

8   "Naturally, the history of space should not be distanced from in any way from the history of time (a history clearly distinct from all philosophical theories of time in general). The departure point for this history of space is not to be found in geographical descriptions of natural space, but rather in the study of natural rhythms, and of the modification of those rhythms and their inscription in space by means of human actions, especially work–related actions. It begins, then, with the spatio–temporal rhythms of nature as transformed by social practice" (*The Production of Space* 117).

9   One could reach, by a twisty road and paradoxically beginning with bodies, the (concrete) universal that the political and philosophical mainstream targeted but did not reach, let alone realize: if rhythm consolidates its theoretical status, if it reveals itself as a valid concept for thought and as a support in practice, is it not this concrete universal that philosophical systems have lacked, that political organizations have forgotten, but which is lived, tested, touched in the sensible and the corporeal? (Lefebvre 1992: 44-45; see also 67).

4. Water

1   An excellent essay on Antoine Lavoisier and Joseph Priestly appears as chapter two of Michael White's *Acid Tongues and Tranquil Dreamers. Eight Scientific Rivalries that Changed the World.* pp. 62-103. Lugones mentions Lavoisier explicitly in his story "El psychon," p. 118.

2   Interestingly enough, although it is William Harvey who is often cited as having discovered the circulation of blood in 1628, Benedictine Monk and Spanish scholar of the Enlightenment Benito Jerónimo Feijóo included this discovery along with that controversial Spanish novelty of "teaching the deaf to speak" in his laundry list of Spanish inventions appropriated by foreigners in a document from 1752: "And thus, this [teaching the deaf to speak] comes to be just like the case of the circulation of blood, discovered by a Spanish farrier-veterinary surgeon named Francisco de la Reina, where afterwards, authors of various nations have proceeded to rack their brains to find out whether the discoverer was Cisalpino, Aqua-

pendente, the servita Pedro Sarpi, Miguel Servet or Harve[y], without the faintest memory of our surgeon." My English translation.

3   Although they may appear to be similar, these two readings in fact diverge considerably when considered from the Lefebvrian point of view. Manuel Castells was in fact an outspoken critic of Lefebvre, who advised the former while he was writing his dissertation in Nanterre, France during the 1960s. Delgado's explicit return to Lefebvre's books and their concepts, on the other hand, is carried out wholly as a praise of the latter's work. Nevertheless, although my personal take is to side with Delgado in seeing the flow as the raw material of modern urban life which is subsequently shaped through spatialization, the fact is that these two —in many ways, contradictory— attempts at reading the modern city have started from the same metaphor of fluidity.

4   For an enlightening forum on Tobler's First Law of Geography—a series of seven authors' comments including a reply by Tobler himself—the reader may wish to consult the *Annals of the Association of American Geographers* Volume 94, June 2004 Number 2.

5   Zamudio writes that "estos 'cuadros mineros', como los denominó con énfasis su propio autor, no han permitido ver con la amplitud necesaria otros aspectos muy interesantes en la labor de Lillo" (12). Also consider: "Este aspecto de la contribución extraliteraria de Lillo, para despertar la conciencia de sus contemporáneos y para dar a conocer la dura labor en los establecimientos mineros de la zona del primer libro, ha sido, seguramente, el que ha servido para juzgar en bloque la obra narrativa del autor de *Sub sole*, dejando como en segundo plano las demás facetas del cuentista" (12).

6   The story titled "La barrena," appeared first in *Sub Sole*, and later was incorporated into subsequent publications of *Sub Terra* itself.

7   "Juguete de las olas, el niño lanzaba en la ribera vagidos cada vez más tardos y más débiles, que el océano, como una nodriza cariñosa, se esforzaba en acallar, redoblando sus abrazos, modulando sus más dulces canciones, poniéndolo ya boca abajo o boca arriba, y trasladándolo de un lado para otro, siempre solícito e infatigable. / Por último lo lloros cesaron: el pequeño había vuelto

NOTES

a dormirse y aunque su carita estaba amoratada, los ojos y la boca llenos de arena, su sueño era apacible; pero tan profundo que, cuando la marejada lo arrastró mar adentro y depositó en el fondo, no se despertó ya más" (23).

8 Fernando Alegría writes that the whale-hunt described in the middle of "El hallazgo" "is nothing less than a synthetic version of the story 'The Whale' ('La ballena') included in a previous volume" (xxvi).

9 As Lefebvre makes clear, alienation must always be understood as spanning not only the ideological, social, political, and economic aspects of life but also the philosophical (*Critique of Everyday Life*, v. 1, 249). Alienation is not a single unit or entity—in fact there are many alienations (1961; *Critique of Everyday Life*, v. 2, 207). It is always a matter of the process that involves seeing activities as things, conceiving relations as objects. For Lefebvre, alienation does not merely erupt abruptly onto the scene with the advent of postwar capitalism, or with the sea-change in understanding time and space he places around 1910, or for that matter the nineteenth-century rise of the bourgeoisie.

REFERENCES

Aching, Gerard. *The Politics of Spanish American Modernismo.* Cambridge: Cambridge University Press, 1997.
Alegría, Fernando. "Introducción a los cuentos de Baldomero Lillo." *Revista Iberoamericana* 24 (1959a): 247-63.
──────. "Introduction." *The Devil's Pit and Other Stories.* Trans. Esther S. Dillon and Angel Flores. Washington D.C.: Pan American Union, 1959b. i-xxx.
Alter-Gilbert, Gilbert. "Foreword." In *Strange Forces.* Trans. and ed. Gilbert Alter Gilbert. Pittsburgh: Latin American Literary Review Press, 2001. 11-20.
Anderson, Ben, Frances Morton & George Revill. "Editorial: Practices of Music and Sound." *Social & Cultural Geography* 6.5 (2005): 639-44.
Anderson Imbert, Enrique. *Spanish-American Literature: A History.* Trans. John V. Falconieri. Detroit: Wayne State University Press, 1963.
Ara, Guillermo. *Leopoldo Lugones: uno y multiple.* Prólogo Roberto F. Giusti. Buenos Aires: Maru, 1967.
Atkinson, Rowland. "Ecology of Sound: The Sonic Order of Urban Space." *Urban Studies* 44.10 (2007): 1905-17.
Aztorquiza, Octavio and Oscar Galleguillos V. *Cien años del carbón de Lota (1852-septiembre-1952).* 1952. Santiago: Orígenes, 2005.
Ball, Jr., Richard E. "The Contrast of Light and Shadow in Baldomero Lillo's Poetic Vision of Hell." *Revista Interamericana de Bibliografía / Review of Inter-American Bibliography* 39.3 (1989): 329-33.

Barcía, Pedro Luis. "Los cuentos desconocidos de Leopoldo Lugones." *Leopoldo Lugones: cuentos desconocidos.* Buenos Aires: Ediciones del 80, 1982. 7-52.
Baudelaire, Charles. "The Painter of Modern Life." 1863. *Selected Writings on Art & Artists.* Trans. P.E. Charvet. Cambridge: Cambridge UP, 1972.
Bauman, Zygmunt. *Liquid Modernity.* Cambridge: Polity Press, 2000.
___. *Liquid Love.* Cambridge: Polity Press, 2003.
___. *Liquid Life.* Cambridge: Polity Press, 2005.
___. *Liquid Fear.* Cambridge: Polity Press, 2006.
___. *Liquid Times.* Cambridge: Polity Press, 2007.
Berman, Marshall. *All that is Solid Melts into Air: The Experience of Modernity.* 1982. New York: Penguin, 1988.
Blavatsky, Helena Petrovna. *Practical Occultism and Occultism Versus the Occult Arts.* Adyar, Madras, India: The Theosophical Publishing House, 1967.
___. *The Secret Doctrine.* 2 vols. London: Theosophical Publishing Company, 1888 (Facsimile edition; Pasadena, CA: Theosophical Publishing Company, 1999).
Bocaz, Luis. "Sub Terra de Baldomero Lillo y la gestación de una conciencia alternativa." *Estudios Filológicos* 40 (2005): 7-27.
Bohm, David. *Wholeness and the Implicate Order.* London; Boston: Routledge & K. Paul, 1980.
Borges, Jorge Luis. *Leopoldo Lugones.* 2ª edición. Buenos Aires: Pleamar, 1965.
Brown, Donald F. "A Chilean Germinal: Zola and Baldomero Lillo." *Modern Language Notes* 65.1 (1950): 47-52.
Butland, Gilbert. *Chile: An Outline of Its Geography, Economics, and Politics.* 3rd edition. London: Royal Institute of International Affairs, 1956.
Canal-Feijóo, Bernardo. *Lugones, y el detino trágico. Erotismo, Teosofismo, Telurismo.* Buenos Aires: Plus Ultra, 1976.
Canedo, Alfredo. *Aspectos del pensamiento político de Leopoldo Lugones.* Buenos Aires: Marcos, 1974.
Capdevila, Arturo. *Lugones.* Buenos Aires: Aguilar, 1973.
Carilla, Emilio. *Una etapa decisiva de Darío: (Rubén Darío en la Argentina).* Madrid: Gredos, 1967.
Carvalho, Susan. *Modernisms and Modernities: Studies in Honor of Donald*

REFERENCES

L. Shaw. Newark, DE: Juan de la Cuesta, 2006.
Castells, Manuel. "The Space of Flows." *The Castells Reader on Cities and Social Theory*. Ed. Ida Susser. London: Blackwell, 2002. 314-66. (Originally in *The Rise of the Network Society*, volume I of the trilogy, *The Information Age: Economy, Society and Culture*. Oxford: Blackwell, 1996).
Chavarri, Jorge M. "El significado social en la obra literaria de Balomero Lillo." *Kentucky Foregin Language Quarterly* 13 (1966): 5-13.
Choay, Françoise. *The Modern City: Planning in the 19th Century*. Trans. Marguerite Hugo and George R. Collins. New York: George Braziller, 1969.
Connell, John and Chris Gibson. "World Music: Deterritorializing Place and Identity." *Progress in Human Geography* 28.3 (2004): 342-61.
Corvalan, Octavio. *Modernismo y vanguardia*. New York: Las Americas Publishing Co., 1967.
Cross, Ian. "Music, Cognition, Culture and Evolution." *The Cognitive Neuroscience of Music*. Ed. Isabelle Peretz, Robert Zatorre. Oxford: Oxford University Press, 2003. 42-56.
Damasio, Antonio. *Looking for Spinoza: Joy, Sorrow and the Feeling Brain*. Orlando: Harcourt, 2003.
Davison, Ned. *The Concept of Modernism in Hispanic Criticism*. Albuquerque: University of New Mexico Press, 1966.
Dear, Michael. *The Postmodern Urban Condition*. Oxford; Malden, Mass.: Blackwell, 2000.
Debord, Guy. *The Society of the Spectacle*. 1967. Detroit: Black and Red Books, 1977.
Delgado Ruiz, Manuel. *Sociedades movedizas: Pasos hacia una antropología de las calles*. Barcelona: Anagrama, 2007.
DeNora, Tia. "Music Sociology: Getting the Music into the Action." *British Journal of Music Education* 20.2 (2003): 165-77.
Díaz Rodríguez, Manuel. "El modernismo." Originally from *Camino de perfección*, 1908. Republished in Englekirk, John et al. *Anthology of Spanish American Literature*. 2nd ed. New York: Appleton-Century-Crofts, 1968. 434-35.
Dixon, Deborah P. "I Hear Dead People: Science, Technology and a Resonant Universe." *Social and Cultural Geography* 8.5 (2007):

719-33.

Durán Luzio, Juan. "Secuencias Paralelas en 'La compuerta número 12' de Baldomero Lillo. *Revista Chilena de Literatura* 31 (1988): 63-79.

———. "Entre el infierno y el cielo: Dos obras de la narrativa chilena en 1904." *Revista Iberoamericana* 60 (1994): 915-24.

Edensor, Tim and Julian Holloway. "Rhythmanalysing the Coach Tour: The Ring of Kerry, Ireland." *Transactions of the Institute of British Geographers* NS 33 (2008): 483-501.

Englekirk, John, et al. *Anthology of Spanish American Literature*. 2nd ed. New York: Appleton-Century-Crofts, 1968.

Feijóo y Montenegro, Benito Jerónimo. *Cartas eruditas y curiosas, en que (por la mayor parte) se continúa el designio del Theatro crítico universal, impugnando, o reduciendo a dudosas, varias opiniones comunes*. Vol. IV. Madrid: Imprenta del Supremo Consejo de la Inquisición, [1752] 1759.

Ferrari, Marcelo, dir. *Sub terra*. Perf.: Francisco Reyes, Paulina Gálvez, Héctor Noguera. Infinity Films S.L., 2003.

Fisk, Clarence. "El Chiflón del Diablo en Lota." gosouthamerica. about.com/od/chisursoncepcion/a/ChiflonDiablo.htm. Posted 2004. Accessed 1 April 2009.

Fortuna, Carlos. "Sundscapes: The Sounding City and Urban Social Life." *Space and Culture* 11-12 (2001): 70-86.

———. "Images of the City: Sonorities and the Urban Social Environment." *Revista Crítica de Ciencias Sociais* 51 (1998): 21-41.

Foucault, Michel. *Discipline and Punish*. 1975. New York: Penguin Books, 1978.

Fraser, Benjamin. *Henri Lefebvre and the Spanish Urban Experience: Reading the Mobile City*. Lewisburg: Bucknell UP, 2011.

———. *Encounters with Bergson(ism) in Spain: Reconciling Philosophy, Literature, Film and Urban Space*. Chapel Hill: U of North Carolina Press [NCSRLL #295], 2010.

———. "Re-scaling Emotional Approaches to Music: Basque Band Lisabö and the Soundscapes of Urban Alienation." *Emotion, Space and Society* 4 (2011): 8-16.

———. "The Bergsonian Link Between Emotion, Music and Place: From the 'Motion of Emotion' to the Sonic Immediacy of Basque Band 'Lisabö.'" *Journal of Spanish Cultural Studies* 10.2

REFERENCES

(2009): 241-62.
———. "Toward a Philosophy of the Urban: Henri Lefebvre's Uncomfortable Application of Bergsonism." *Environment and Planning D: Society and Space* 26.2 (2008): 338-58.
———. "The Publicly-Private Space of Madrid's Retiro Park & the Spatial Problems of Spatial Theory." *Social and Cultural Geography* 8.5 (2007a): 673-700.
———. "Manuel Delgado's Urban Anthropology: From Multidimensional Space to Interdisciplinary Spatial Theory." *Arizona Journal of Hispanic Cultural Studies* 11 (2007b): 57-75.
———. "Deaf Cultural Production in Twentieth-Century Madrid." *Sign Language Studies* 7.4 (2007c): 431-57.
Fraser, Howard. "Apocalyptic Vision and Modernism's Dismantling of Scientific Discourse: Lugones's 'Yzur.'" *Hispania* 79.1 (1996): 8-19.
———. "Decadentism, Darío and 'The Nightingale.'" *Romance Notes* 19 (1978): 206-11.
———. "*La edad de oro* and José Martí's Modernist Ideology for Children." *Revista Interamericana de Bibliografía / Inter-American Review of Bibliography* 42.2 (1992): 223-32.
———. *In the Presence of Mystery: Modernist Fiction and the Occult*. Chapel Hill: North Carolina Studies in the Romance Languages and Literatures, 1992.
———. "La magia y la alquimia en 'El rubí' de Rubén Darío." *La literatura iberoamericana del siglo XIX. Memoria del XV Congreso Internacional de Literatura Iberoamericana*. University of Arizona, Tucson, 21-24 enero 1971. Ed. Renato Rosaldo and Robert Anderson. Tucson: U of Arizona P, 1974. 237-43.
———. "Magic and Alchemy in Darío's 'El rubí.'" *Chasqui* 3.2 (1974): 17-22.
———. "The Uses of Enchantment in Modernist Fantasy Fiction." *Postscript* 1 (1983): 67-74.
Frith, Simon. "Music and Identity." *Questions of Cultural Identity*. Ed. S. Hall, P. DuGay. London: Sage, 1996. 100-27. 1996.
Galbreath, Robert. "The History of Modern Occultism: A Bibliographical Survey." *The Occult: Studies and Evaluations*. Ed. Robert Galbreath. Special Issue of the *Journal of Popular Culture* 5.3 (Winter 1971): doubled pagination 726/98-754/126.

Garfield, Evelyn Picon and Ivan A. Schulman. *Las entrañas del vacío: ensayos sobre la modernidad hispanoamericana*. Mexico: Ediciones Cuadernos Americanos, 1984.
González, Aníbal. *A Companion to Spanish American Modernismo*. Woodbridge, UK: Tamesis, 2007.
Green, Toby and Janak Jani. *Footprint Chile*. Footprint Travel Guides, 2003.
Grogin, R. C. *The Bergsonian Controversy in France 1900-1914*. Calgary: University of Calgary Press, 1988.
Gullón, Ricardo. "Pitagorismo y modernismo." *Estudios críticos sobre el modernismo*. Madrid: Gredos, 1968. 359-83.
Gutiérrez Girardot, Rafael. *Modernismo: supuestos históricos y culturales*. Mexico: Fondo de Cultura Económica, 1988.
Gutiérrez Nájera, Manuel. *Cuentos completos y otras narraciones*. Ed. E. K. Mapes. México: Fondo de Cultura Económica, 1958.
Harvey, David. *Justice, Nature and the Geography of Difference*. London: Blackwell, 1996.
_____. *Spaces of Hope*. Berkeley: California UP, 2000.
_____. "What's Green and Makes the Environment Go Round?" *The Cultures of Globalization*, Ed. Fredric Jameson and Masao Miyoshi. Duke: Duke UP, 1998. 327-55.
_____. *The Urban Experience*. Baltimore: Johns Hopkins UP, 1989.
_____. *The Condition of Postmodernity*. Cambridge, MA & Oxford, UK: Blackwell, 1990.
_____. *Spaces of Hope*. Berkeley: California UP, 2000.
_____. "Afterword." *The Production of Space*. Henri Lefebvre. Trans. Donald Nicholson-Smith. Oxford, OX, UK; Cambridge, Mass., USA: Blackwell, 1991. 425-34.
_____. *A Brief History of Neoliberalism*. Oxford: Oxford UP, 2006.
Hewitt, Sandra and Nancy Abraham Hall. "Leopoldo Lugones and H. P. Blavatsky: Theosophy in the 'Ensayo de una cosmogonía en diez lecciones.'" *Revista de Estudios Hispánicos* 18 (1984): 335-43.
Highmore, Ben. "Street Life in London: Towards a Rhythmanalysis of London in the Late Nineteenth Century." *New Formations* 47 (2002): 171-93.
Hirschkind, Charles. "Hearing Modernity: Egypt, Islam and the Pious Ear." *Hearing Cultures: Essays on Sound, Listening and Mo-*

REFERENCES

dernity. Ed. Veit Erlmann. Oxford; New York: Berg, 2004. 131-51.
Hudson, Ray. "Regions and Place: Music, Identity and Place." *Progress in Human Geography* 30.5 (2006): 626-34.
Huron, David. "Is Music an Evolutionary Adaptation?" *The Cognitive Neuroscience of Music*. Ed. Isabelle Peretz, Robert Zatorre. Oxford: Oxford UP, 2003. 57-75.
Irazusta, Julio. *Genio y figura de Leopoldo Lugones*. Buenos Aires: Editorial Universitaria de Buenos Aires, 1968.
Jensen, Theodore W. "El pitagorismo en *Las fuerzas extrañas* de Lugones." *Otros mundos, otros fuegos; fantasía y realismo mágico en Iberoamérica; memoria del XVI Congreso Internacional de Literatura Iberoamericana*. Lansing: Michigan State UP, 1975. 299-307.
Jessop, Bob. "Narrating the Future of the National Economy and the National State: Remarks on Remapping Regulation and Reinventing Governance." Ed. George Steinmetz. *State/Culture: State-Formation After the Cultural Turn*. Ithaca & London: Cornell UP, 1999. 378-405.
Jrade, Cathy Login. *Rubén Darío and the Romantic Search for Unity: The Modernist Recourse to Esoteric Tradition*. Austin: University of Texas Press, 1983.
———. *Modernismo, Modernity and the Development of Spanish American Literature*. Austin: University of Texas Press, 1998.
Kahn, Douglas. "Ether Ore: Mining Vibrations in American Modernist Music." *Hearing Cultures: Essays on Sound, Listening and Modernity*. Ed. Veit Erlmann. Oxford; New York: Berg, 2004. 107-30.
Kirkpatrick, Gwen. *The Dissonant Legacy of Modernismo: Lugones, Herrera y Reissig and the Voices of Modern Spanish American Poetry*. Berkeley: University of California Press, 1989.
Krishnamurti, Jiddu and David Bohm. *The Limits of Thought*. London; New York: Routledge, 1999.
———. *The Ending of Time*. San Francisco: Harper & Row, 1985.
Latham, Alan & Derek McCormack. "Moving Cities: Rethinking the Materialities of Urban Geographies." *Progress in Human Geography* 28.6 (2004): 701-24.
Laurier, Eric. "How Breakfast Happens in the Café." *Time & Society* 17.1 (2008): 119-34.

Lefebvre, Henri. *Rhythmanalysis*. Trans. Stuart Elden and Gerald Moore. London; New York: Continuum, 2006.
_____. *The Survival of Capitalism*. London: Allison & Busby, 1973.
_____. *The Explosion: Marxism and the French Upheaval*. 1968. Trans. Alfred Ehrenfeld. New York and London: Monthly Review Press, 2005.
_____. *The Right to the City*. Reprinted in *Writings on Cities*. Ed. and Trans. Eleonore Kofman and Elizabeth Lebas. Oxford: Blackwell, 1996. 63-184.
_____. *Critique of Everyday Life, v. 1*. 1947. Trans. J. Moore. London, New York: Verso, 1991.
_____. *Critique of Everyday Life, v. 2*. 1961. Trans. J. Moore. London, New York: Verso, 2002.
_____. *Critique of Everyday Life, v. 3*. 1981. Trans. G. Elliott. London, New York: Verso, 2005.
_____. *The Production of Space*. 1974. Trans. D. Nicholson–Smith. Oxford; Cambridge, Mass.: Blackwell, 1991.
Levitin, Daniel J. *This is Your Brain on Music: The Science of a Human Obsession*. New York: Plume, Penguin Group, 2006.
Lillo, Baldomero. *Sub Terra: cuadros mineros*. 1904. 13th ed. Santiago: Nascimento, 1966.
_____. *The Devil's Pit and Other Stories*. Trans. Esther S. Dillon and Angel Flores. Washington D.C.: Pan American Union, 1959.
_____. *Obras completas*. Ed. Raúl Silva Castro. Santiago: Nascimiento, 1968.
_____. *Sub-sole*. Santiago: Imprenta Universitaria, 1907.
_____. *Relatos populares*. Ed. González Vera. Santiago: Nascimento, 1942.
_____. *El hallazgo y otros cuentos del mar*. Ed. José Zamudio Z. Santiago: Ercilla, 1956.
Lindstrom, Naomi. *Twentieth-Century Spanish American Fiction*. Austin: University of Texas Press, 1994.
Lodato, Rosemary C. *Beyond the Glitter: The Language of Gems in Modernista Writers Rubén Darío, Ramón del Valle-Inclán and José Asunción Silva*. Lewisburg: Bucknell University Press, 1999.
Lorenz, Erika. *Rubén Darío: "bajo el divino imperio de la música."* Trans. Fidel Coloma González. Managua: Academia Nicaragüense de la Lengua, 1960.

REFERENCES

Lugones, Leopoldo. *Las fuerzas extrañas*. 1906. Buenos Aires: Editorial Huemul, 1966.
———. *Prometeo (Un proscripto del sol)*. 1910. *Obras en Prosa*. Ed. Leopoldo Lugones, Jr. Mexico: Aguilar, 1962. 770-1076.
———. *Las fuerzas extrañas*. 1906. Buenos Aires: Editorial Huemul, 1966.
———. *Strange Forces*. Trans. and ed. Gilbert Alter Gilbert. Pittsburgh: Latin American Literary Review Press, 2001.
———. *Leopoldo Lugones, Selected Writings*. Ed. Sergio Gabriel Weisman, Gwen Kirkpatrick. Oxford: Oxford University Press, 2008.
Madanipour, Ali. *Design of Urban Space: An Inquiry into a Socio-spatial Process*. Chichester: Wiley, 1996.
Marín, Gladys. "Leopoldo Lugones y el pensamiento simbólico." *Megafón* 1 (Dic. 1975): 171-76.
Marston, Sallie. "The Social Construction of Scale." *Progress in Human Geography* 24.2 (2000): 219-42.
———. "What's Culture Got to Do with It?: A Response to Jakobsen and Van Deusen." *Political Geography* 23.1 (2004): 35-39.
Martí, José. "Los pinos nuevos." Originally from a speech given at Tampa, Florida on November 27, 1891. Republished in Englekirk, John et al. *Anthology of Spanish American Literature*. 2nd ed. New York: Appleton-Century-Crofts, 1968. 373-76.
Martínez Estrada, Ezequiel. *Leopoldo Lugones, retrato sin tocar*. Buenos Aires: Emecé, 1968.
Marx, Karl. *Manifesto of the Communist Party*. 1848. London: Pluto, 2008.
Meade, Marion. *The Woman Behind the Myth*. New York: G. P. Putnam's Son's, 1980.
Millán, Rafael. "Introducción." *Baldomero Lillo: tres cuentos*. Ed., introd. y glosario por Rafael Millán. Philadelphia: The Center for Curriculum Development, 1972. 7-13.
Mills, George J. *Chile: Physical Features, Natural Resources, Means of Communication, Manufactures and Industrial Development*. Introd. W. H. Koebel. London:Putnam and Sons, 1914.
Mitchell, Don. *Cultural Geography: A Critical Introduction*. Oxford: Blackwell, 2000.
Mitchell, Tim. "Society, Economy, and the State Effect." *State/Cul-*

ture: State-Formation After the Cultural Turn. G. Steinmetz, Ed. Ithaca & London: Cornell UP, 1999. 76-97.

Monet-Viera, Molly. "Strange Forces: Occultism and the Inauguration of the Fantastic Genre in Latin America." *Romance Studies* 19.2 (2001): 123-34.

Moreau, Pierina Lidia. *Leopoldo Lugones y el simbolismo.* Buenos Aires: Ediciones "La Reja," 1972.

Morris, Adalaide. "Introduction." *Sound States: Innovative Poetic and Acoustical Technologies.* Ed. Adalaide Morris. Chapel Hill and London: The University of North Carolina Press, 1997. 1-14.

Nash, Peter H. Review of *The Sounds of People and Place: A Geography of American Folk and Popular Music. Annals of the Association of American Geographers* 86 (1996): 796-98.

Obert, Julia C. "Sound and Sentiment: A Rhythmanalysis of Television." *Continuum: Journal of Media & Cultural Studies* 22.3 (2008): 409-17.

Oelker, Dieter. "Baldomero Lillo, *Sub Terra*: variantes." *Acta Literaria* 13 (1988): 93-108.

de Onís, Federico. *España en América.* Madrid: Universidad de Puerto Rico, 1955.

Pedraza Jiménez, Felipe B., coordinator. *Manual de literatura hispanoamericana. III. Modernismo.* Pamplona: Cénlit, 1998.

Pinker, Steven. *The Language Instinct.* New York: W. Morrow and Co., 1994.

Pío del Corro, Gaspar. *El mundo fantástico de Lugones.* Córdoba, Argentina: Universidad Nacional, 1971.

Preble, Oralia M. "Contrapunto emotivo en 'El Chiflón del Diablo' de Baldomero Lillo." *Romance Notes* 17 (1976):103-07.

Price, Patricia. "Cohering Culture on *Calle Ocho*: The Pause and Flow of *Latinidad.*" *Globalizations* 4.1 (2007): 81-99.

Ramos, Jorge A. "Naturalismo romántico y modernista en los cuentos de Baldomero Lillo, Javier de Viana y Augusto D'Halmar." *Excavatio* XIV nos. 1-2 (2001): 334-43.

Ramos, Julio. *Divergent Modernities. Culture and Politics in Nineteenth-Century Latin America.* Trans. John D. Blanco. Durham and London: Duke University Press, 2001.

Raudive, Konstantin. *Breakthrough: An Amazing Experiment in Elec-*

REFERENCES

tronic Communication with the Dead. 1968. Trans. N. Fowler. Gerrards Cross, UK: Colin Smythe, 1971.

Ray, Larry. "From Postmodernity to Liquid Modernity: What's in a Metaphor?" *The Contemporary Bauman*. Ed. Anthony Elliott. London; New York: Routledge, 2007. 63-80.

Rebaudi Basavilbaso, Oscar. *Leopoldo Lugones*. Buenos Aires: Casa Pardo, 1974.

Rihacek, Tomas. "What Does a City Sound Like? The Urban Sonic Environment from Scoundscape Concept Perspective." *Socialni Studia* 2 (2006): 155-71.

Rodríguez Fernández, Mario. *El modernismo en Chile y en Hispanoamérica*. Santiago: Instituto de Literatura Chilena, 1967.

Roland, Alfredo E. *Leopoldo Lugones, poeta nacional*. Buenos Aires: Ediciones Culturales Argentinas, 1981.

Román-Lagunas, Jorge. "Bibliografía de y sobre Baldomero Lillo." *Revista Chilena de Literatura* 37 (1991): 141-56.

Rotella, Pilar V. "*Sub Terra*: Lives in/of Darkness." *Excavatio* XIX nos. 1-2 (2004): 200-12.

Sacks, Oliver. *Musicophilia: Tales of Music and the Brain*. New York/Toronto: Knopf, 2007.

Santos González Vera, José. "Baldomero Lillo." *La compuerta número 12 y otros cuentos*. Buenos Aires: Editorial Universitaria de Buenos Aires, 1964. Reprinted in Aztorquiza, Octavio and Oscar Galleguillos V. *Cien años del carbón de Lota (1852-septiembre-1952)*. 1952. Santiago: Orígenes, 2005. 263-68.

Sauer, Carl. "The Morphology of Landscape." *University of California Publications in Geography* 2 (1925): 19-54, cited in Don Mitchell.

Schulman, Ivan A., ed. *Nuevos asedios al modernismo*. Madrid: Taurus, 1987.

———. *Génesis del modernismo*. México: Washington University Press, 1966.

Sedgwick, Ruth. "Baldomero Lillo y Emile Zola." *Revista Iberoamericana* 7.14 (1944): 321-28.

Sennett, Richard. *The Craftsman*. New Haven: Yale UP, 2008.

Sharman, Adam. *Tradition and Modernity in Spanish American Literature: From Darío to Carpentier*. New York: Palgrave McMillan, 2006.

Simmel, Georg. "The Metropolis and Mental Life." 1903. *Readings in Social Theory: The Classic Tradition to Post-Modernism*. 3rd ed. Ed. James Farganis. New York: McGraw Hill, 2000. 149-57.

Simpson, Paul. "Chronic Everyday Life: Rhythmanalysing Street Performance." *Social and Cultural Geography* 9.7 (2008): 807-29.

Singer, Ellen. "Atmosphere in 'La compuerta número 12.'" *Romance Notes* 16 (1975): 526-29.

Skyrme, Raymond. *Rubén Darío and the Pythagorean Tradition*. Gainesville: University Presses of Florida, 1975.

Smith, J. Russell. "The Economic Geography of Chile." *Bulletin of the American Geographical Society* 36.1 (1904): 1-21.

Smith, Susan J. "Performing the (Sound)World." *Cultural Geography. Critical Concepts in the Social Sciences*. London and New York: Routledge, 2005. 90-119.

——. "Performing the (Sound)World." *Environment and Planning D: Society and Space* 18.5 (2000): 615-37.

——. "Beyond Geography's Visible Worlds: A Cultural Politics of Music." *Progress in Human Geography* 21.4 (1997): 502-29.

Soja, Edward W. *Thirdspace. Journeys to Los Angeles and Other Real-and-Imagined Places*. Oxford: Blackwell, 1996.

Speck, Paula. "*Las fuerzas extrañas*: Leopoldo Lugones y las Raíces de la Literatura Fantástica en el Río de la Plata." *Revista Iberoamericana* 42 (1976): 411-26.

Spivak, Gayatri. *Death of a Discipline*. New York: Columbia University Press, 2003.

Sturt, Fraser. "Local Knowledge is Required: A Rhythmanalytical Approach to the Late Mesolithic and Early Neolithic of the East Anglian Fenland, UK." *J Mari Arch* 1 (2006): 119-39.

Thorns, David. *The Transformation of Cities: Urban Theory and Urban Life*. Houndmills, Basingstoke, Hampshire: Palgrave, 2002.

Tilly, Charles. "Epilogue: Now Where?" *State/Culture: State-Formation After the Cultural Turn*. G. Steinmetz, Ed. Ithaca & London: Cornell UP, 1999. 407-419.

Tiwari, Reena. "Being a Rhythm Analyst in the City of Varanasi." *Urban Forum* 19 (2008): 289-306.

Tobler, Waldo. "A Computer Movie Simulating Urban Growth in the Detroit Region." *Economic Geography* 46 (1970): 234-40.

REFERENCES

Valenzuela, Víctor M. "Lillo and Modernism." *Hispania* 39.1 (1956): 89-91.

Virgillo, Carmelo. "Symbolic imagery in Baldomero Lillo's 'La compuerta número 12.'" *Revista Canadiense de Estudios Hispánicos* 2 (1978): 142-53.

Vonnugut, Kurt, Jr. "The Mysterious Madame Blavatsky." *McCalls* (March 1970): 142-44.

Waterman, Stanley. "Geography and Music: Some Introductory Remarks." *GeoJournal* 65 (2006): 1-2.

White, Michael. *Acid Tongues and Tranquil Dreamers. Eight Scientific Rivalries that Changed the World.* New York: Perennial, 2002.

Williams, Raymond. "The Future of Cultural Studies." 1986. In *Politics of Modernism: Against the New Conformists.* London: New York: 2007. 151-62.

Wilson, Alexander. *The Culture of Nature: From Disney to the Exxon Valdez.* Oxford: Blackwell, 1991.

Wrangham, Richard. *Catching Fire: How Cooking Made Us Human.* New York: Basic Books, 2009.

Zamudio Z., José. "Prólogo." *El hallazgo y otros cuentos del mar.* Ed. José Zamudio Z. Santiago: Ercilla, 1956. 7-16.

Zarate, Armando. *Literatura hispanoamericana de protesta social.* Lanham, Maryland: University Press of America, 1994.

Zavala, Iris M. *Colonialism and Culture: Hispanic Modernisms and the Social Imaginary.* Bloomington and Indianapolis: Indiana University Press, 1992.

Zelinsky, Wilbur. Review of *The Place of Music. Economic Geography* 75.4 (1999): 420-22.

Zola, Émile. *Germinal.* 1885. London: Penguin, 2004.

Made in the USA
Charleston, SC
06 September 2013